Madmen and Geniuses

Madmen and Geniuses

The Vice-Presidents of the United States

Sol Barzman

Follett Publishing Company
Chicago

Manufactured in the United States of America.
Library of Congress Catalog Card Number: 74-78583
ISBN: 0-695-80487-1

First Printing

1-16-75

For Anita Jo and Karen-edis

Madmen and Geniuses

Contents

	Author's Notes and Acknowledgments	ix
	Prologue	3
1	The Vice-Presidents	7
2	John Adams	15
3	Thomas Jefferson	21
4	Aaron Burr	27
5	George Clinton	35
6	Elbridge Gerry	41
7	Daniel D. Tompkins	47
8	John C. Calhoun	53
9	Martin Van Buren	61
10	Richard Mentor Johnson	67
11	John Tyler	73
12	George Mifflin Dallas	79
13	Millard Fillmore	85
14	William Rufus De Vane King	91
15	John Cabell Breckenridge	97
16	Hannibal Hamlin	103
17	Andrew Johnson	109
18	Schuyler Colfax	115
19	Henry Wilson	123
20	William Almon Wheeler	129
21	Chester Alan Arthur	135
22	Thomas Andrews Hendricks	141

23 Levi Parsons Morton   147
24 Adlai Ewing Stevenson   153
25 Garret Augustus Hobart   159
26 Theodore Roosevelt   165
27 Charles W. Fairbanks   175
28 James Schoolcraft Sherman   183
29 Thomas Riley Marshall   189
30 Calvin Coolidge   197
31 Charles G. Dawes   205
32 Charles Curtis   213
33 John Nance Garner   221
34 Henry A. Wallace   229
35 Harry S Truman   237
36 Alben W. Barkley   245
37 Richard M. Nixon   253
38 Lyndon Baines Johnson   263
39 Hubert H. Humphrey   273
40 Spiro T. Agnew   283
41 Gerald R. Ford   293
42 The Eagleton Affair   301
Epilogue   307
Bibliography   313
Index   327

Madmen and Geniuses

Author's Notes and Acknowledgments

Of the forty men who have so far served in our vice-presidency, less than half are familiar to the general public. The others are men of mystery and darkness, consigned to anonymity by silence or ridicule.

A similar ratio applies to our vice-presidential literature. Vice-presidents of the more recent twentieth century and those who succeeded to the presidency, whether on their own or through the death of a president, have had a rather largish body of material written about them. The rest have been woefully neglected, some to the point of oblivion.

This neglect, while distressing, is not surprising, for the American vice-presidency has been abused, maligned, and denigrated from its inception. As an office, it has been shabbily treated by politicians and historians alike; the men who occupied that office have fared no better.

In 1906, well over a century after the creation of the vice-presidency, Finley Peter Dunne's amiable yet sardonic spokesman, Mr. Dooley, made a few biting observations on the second chair, including this perceptive comment:

"At a convintion nearly all th' dillygates lave as soon as they've nommynated th' prisidint f'r fear wan iv thim will be nommynated f'r vice-prisidint."

Twenty-six years later there was no improvement. George S. Kaufman and Morrie Ryskind, writers of the book for *Of Thee I Sing*, Pulitzer Prize winning musical of 1932, created the most endearing yet surely the most incompetent of political characters in Alexander Throttlebottom.

After Throttlebottom had been nominated for the vice-presidency, he wandered into a hotel room occupied by the bosses of his party. They didn't recognize him, not even the man who had placed his name in nomination. When they finally learned who he was, one of them chidingly said to him:

"Say, look here a minute. You know, vice-presidents don't usually go around in public. They're not supposed to be seen."

Throttlebottom answered plaintively:

"But I'm not vice-president yet. Couldn't I go around a little longer?"

Such cynicism was no isolated exaggeration; it accurately reflected the attitudes of the professional politicos who were responsible for choosing the second in command, or at least pushing his candidacy. It is no accident, therefore, that almost nothing has been written about many of our vice-presidents, for they were thought of as nonentities and treated the same way. Some of them do have biographies, but these are to be regarded with skepticism, for most are hastily prepared campaign tracts that make little effort at critical examination. Page after page of laudatory and sometimes purple prose may give us vital statistics but in the end tell us nothing of the man.

Every vice-president has had some material written about him, if only a brief sketch in the *Dictionary of American Biography*. And newspapers of his day occasionally mentioned him, so that it is possible, with diligent and exhausting research, to construct a workable portrait. Some vice-presidents left papers and correspondence that are now in state, local, or private collections in various parts of the country. These collections, like the old newspapers, are often extremely difficult to study because of inaccessibility and distance.

One newspaper, *The New York Times,* I found especially useful because of its thorough index, which begins with the issues of September, 1851. Other newspapers can of course be helpful, but because they lack an index they require patience and time to research. The reader who may want to look at a local paper for reference to a specific vice-president is advised to examine newspaper encyclopedias for the existence and/or location of the particular issue he may be seeking, since many issues are no longer available. (See Bibliography—"General Sources" for these encyclopedias.)

During the course of my lengthy research, I consulted or read hundreds of books and dozens of newspapers and magazine articles. Many of them gave me almost no information on the man I was researching, although they did give me a feel of the times. In an attempt to simplify the reader's task (for those who may want to pursue further the study of the vice-presidency or of a particular vice-president) I have listed in my Bibliography, under "General" and "Specific Sources," those books that were the most helpful to me. Most of these volumes have an index, for quick and easy reference.

My "Specific Sources" have been arranged for groups of vice-presidents, beginning with Adams, Jefferson and Burr, and ending with Agnew and Ford. Such groupings will permit the reader to concentrate on a particular span of years and a particular phase in American history.

Library staffs, too, can be helpful. For their never-failing cooperation, I must express my thanks to the staffs of the New York Public Library, the New York Society Library, the New York Historical Society, the Boston Public Library, the American Antiquarian Society, and the Library of Congress.

As in the past, Professor S. D. Ehrenpreis of the Bronx Community College, City University of New York, spent long hours checking my manuscript for historical inaccuracies. I am most grateful for his corrections and suggestions.

Finally, my thanks go once again to my wife, Belle Barzman, who served as my painstaking research assistant and persevering critic.

Madmen and Geniuses

Madmen and Geniuses

Prologue

October, 1973 For President Richard M. Nixon the spring and summer of 1973 produced an agonizing time of accusation, ordeal, and erosion of confidence. Almost daily, another astonishing revelation of misdeed and dirty tricks plotted and executed by members of his administration was reported to a disbelieving nation. Each day, it seemed, excited newscasters announced still one more sensational development, and nationally syndicated columnists turned the words "unprecedented" and "historic" into journalistic clichés.

A battered President Nixon removed himself into brooding isolation. Only a few short months before, he and Vice-President Spiro T. Agnew had received one of the largest majorities ever recorded in a presidential election. The people had given them what appeared to be an unqualified and overwhelming mandate. Yet, within a brief time of that impressive triumph, President Nixon had crashed from the crest of popularity to the humiliation of discredit and doubt.

The Watergate scandals, at first treated like a minor aberration, exploded with megaton intensity. The White House was rocked by mushrooming charges; unbelievably, the President found himself fighting threats of impeachment and demands for resignation.

Throughout this time of turmoil for the President, Vice-President Agnew stood untouched by scandals swirling about the chief executive. Agnew calmly, although equivocally, announced his belief in the President's innocence, and quietly reveled in his unchallengeable detachment from the Watergate affair.

Agnew could well pride himself on being the "Mr. Clean" of the Nixon administration. He had had nothing whatever to do with the planning and execution of the Watergate break-in, the subsequent cover-up or any of the other dirty tricks attributed to members of the Nixon staff and cabinet. He became a symbol of purity; the White Knight of Maryland was uncorrupt and incorruptible, his virtue undimmed. The sinfulness of Watergate submerged others, but not him.

But suddenly, in the first week of August, the heavens fell in upon the White Knight, and the Mr. Clean of the Nixon administration was publicly accused of being not so clean after all. The Justice Department, it was announced, was investigating the possibility that Agnew had accepted bribes and kickbacks while serving as county executive and governor of Maryland during the 1960s.

An astounded nation now realized that "unprecedented" and "historic" applied with stunning impact to the situation facing the country in the late summer and early fall of 1973.

Never before had both the president and the vice-president of the United States stood accused at the same time of wrongdoing in separate matters.

Never before had both the president and the vice-president at the same time been forced to defend their individual innocence and to fight off demands for impeachment or resignation.

Even as Agnew heatedly denied all charges against him and labeled them "damned lies," the rumor pot continued to simmer ominously as one newspaper after another published additional accusations against him and foreign editorials took note of the tragic effect the Agnew affair had already had upon the United States.

". . . It is as though the last symbol of integrity and decency has been lost," sadly noted the London Daily Express.

The Times of India observed that "to nobody's surprise, except perhaps his own, nemesis has caught up with Mr. Agnew."

A few weeks later, so had justice and retribution. On October 10, 1973, a pale and chastened Spiro Agnew, his hands showing a slight tremor, appeared before United States District Judge Walter B. Hoffman in a Baltimore courtroom and pleaded no contest to a charge of tax evasion in 1967. Only a few minutes before, his resignation as vice-president of the United States had been handed to Secretary of State Henry Kissinger in Washington.

With these two developments, the most dramatic chapter in the checkered history of the vice-presidency reached an incredible climax. For the first time, the second most important man in the country had publicly admitted the commission of a crime. With his plea of "nolo contendere," or no contest, Agnew accepted the full weight of guilt in his admission of taking bribes and not reporting them as income. Judge Hoffman made it clear that the plea of no contest was "the full equivalent of a plea of guilty." Agnew said he understood. So he stood exposed now before the entire world as a "crook" (a word scathingly used by one of the government prosecutors) and as a convicted felon.

To a shocked nation, the disgrace of Spiro Agnew seemed almost too much to comprehend. People could only shake their heads in numbed disbelief and wonder how such a man, a self-confessed criminal, could have been a single heartbeat away from the presidency. If these same people had taken the time and trouble to examine the history of the vice-presidency, they might well have found some answers.

We have fostered a system that rewards inadequacy and resists change, particularly change that shatters time-honored institutions, even though they should never have been permitted to exist in the first place. We continue to choose our vice-presidents the way they have always been chosen, whether they deserve the office or not. Our bitter lessons of the past have taught us nothing, as we demonstrated in the choice of Agnew's successor, Congressman Gerald R. Ford of Michigan. In Ford's case, only the mechanics were different; the delusive formula of settling for mediocrity remained as it had for almost two hundred years. Never would we have knowingly voted for Ford to be president, yet we allowed him, with little dissent, to stand not only a heartbeat away from the executive chair, but an impeachment away.

October, 1973, will not be a proud month in our history. It was then that we learned, to our horror, that our second best man was far less than that, and it was then that we chose to succeed him an amiable, well-meaning congressman totally devoid of the decisive qualities that we must demand of our chief executive.

We have never known an occasion that can equal the immensity of Agnew's disgrace, but the vice-presidency has given us many other uncomfortable moments that we have chosen to forget.

Madmen and Geniuses

The Vice-Presidents

At thirty minutes past the hour of midnight, on Palm Sunday, April 4, the President of the United States died of pneumonia and fatigue. He had served exactly thirty-one days.

Even the weather seemed to be aware of the melancholy occasion, for it rained in the federal capital all that night and continued on into the following day.

John Quincy Adams noted the President's passing in his diary. The aging representative was filled with foreboding and gloom.

"The influence of this event upon the condition and history of the country can scarcely be seen," Adams wrote. "In upwards of half a century, this is the first instance of a Vice-President being called to act as President of the United States, and brings to the test that provision of the Constitution which places in the Executive chair a man never thought of for it by anybody."

What a remarkable statement for a former chief executive. John Quincy Adams had served his country for six decades. He had been secretary to a diplomatic mission at the age of fourteen, and president of the United States from 1825 to 1829; he had always been an acute and often acerbic observer of the American political scene. Now, as if for the first time, it occurred to him that "a man never thought of for it by anybody" was to succeed to the presidency. Even more astonishing is Adams's admission that no one else in the country had ever considered the Vice-President qualified for the top spot.

Yet the Vice-President's party had deliberately chosen him for what should have been the second most important office in the country, and a majority of the people had so voted for him. Thus it was, in an atmosphere of depression and uncertainty, that John Tyler of Virginia became the tenth president of the United States on April 6, 1841, when he took the oath of office at twelve noon in the Indian Queen Hotel, Washington, D.C.

In view of the reason for the vice-presidency (the office exists solely as a back-up to the presidency) it is regrettable that astute politicians should not have been aware of its importance. But the sad truth is they were not. Almost from the very beginning, the vice-presidency was treated like a step-child or an afterthought, nor has there been much improvement since.

Perhaps the voters are not aware that twelve of the thirty-six men who have so far served as our presidents were vice-presidents. Of these twelve, eight succeeded to the chair of the chief executive upon the death of the president, and four were former vice-presidents who later ran for the presidency and were elected on their own.

The vice-presidency, then, is not "the most insignificant office that ever the invention of man contrived or his imagination conceived," as John Adams described it. Perhaps many vice-presidents do no more than fill in time and try not to look bored as they preside over Senate sessions; but when one-third of our presidents have come from the ranks of the vice-presidents, choice of the second in command assumes an importance far beyond the whims or needs of political bosses.

As an illustration, we have the eight vice-presidents who became accidental presidents: John Tyler, Millard Fillmore, Andrew Johnson, Chester A. Arthur, Theodore Roosevelt, Calvin Coolidge, Harry S Truman and Lyndon B. Johnson.

Seven of these eight were judged in a *New York Times* survey conducted in 1962 by the noted historian, Arthur M. Schlesinger, Sr. (At the time of the survey, Lyndon Johnson was still vice-president; he did not become president until the following year, after the assassination of John F. Kennedy in November of 1963.)

Mr. Schlesinger requested seventy-five colleagues and fellow historians to rate the presidents in order of excellence. (John F. Kennedy, who was then in the second year of his administration, was not included because he was too current, and could not yet be fairly judged. William Henry Harrison, who served only for thirty-one days, and James Garfield, assassinated six months after taking office, were also omitted because their terms were too short.)

The thirty-one remaining presidents were rated by the experts in five categories, in descending order of excellence:

Great presidents: Abraham Lincoln, George Washington, Franklin D. Roosevelt, Woodrow Wilson, and Thomas Jefferson.

Near great: Andrew Jackson, Theodore Roosevelt, James K. Polk, Harry S Truman, John Adams, and Grover Cleveland.

Average: James Madison, John Quincy Adams, Rutherford B.

Hayes, William McKinley, William Howard Taft, Martin Van Buren, James Monroe, Herbert Hoover, Benjamin Harrison, Chester A. Arthur, Dwight D. Eisenhower, and Andrew Johnson.

Below average: Zachary Taylor, John Tyler, Millard Fillmore, Calvin Coolidge, Franklin Pierce, and James Buchanan.

Failures: Ulysses S. Grant and Warren G. Harding.

From this list, let's examine the seven accidental presidents, in chronological order and order of excellence.

John Tyler, Millard Fillmore, and Calvin Coolidge: below average.

Andrew Johnson and Chester A. Arthur: average.

Theodore Roosevelt and Harry S Truman: near great.

In five out of seven instances, the accidental presidents performed either on an average or a below average level.

These are poor odds for the electorate. Even in the cases of the two who were judged to be near great, Theodore Roosevelt and Harry S Truman, they were not initially selected to be vice-presidents because of their presidential qualities, which neither to that time had exhibited to the slightest degree. Their choices were motivated purely by practical politics.

In short, then, the United States was led by seven men who, on their records, did not deserve the high office thrust upon them. That two of these men did, in the end, prove themselves worthy does not tilt the odds in favor of the gamble. We were still left with three who were downright bad, and two were only fair.

Of the other vice-presidents, how many are familiar to you? Here are a few names, chosen at random:

Richard Mentor Johnson, William Rufus De Vane King, Henry Wilson, Levi Parsons Morton, Charles Warren Fairbanks, and Charles Curtis.

Unless you're an historian or a serious student of American history, it's doubtful that you know any of these gentlemen. Perhaps the last name, Charles Curtis, may ring a bell. If you're old enough, you may have voted for him. He was Herbert Hoover's vice-president from 1929 to 1933.

Mr. Curtis may have one other distinction. It is probable that he was the inspiration for the bumbling, lovable Vice-President Throttlebottom in the 1932 musical *Of Thee I Sing.* The only way Throttlebottom could get into the White House was to join a guided tour.

What about the others? How well have we fared with Richard Mentor Johnson, William Rufus De Vane King, et al? They were important enough to be chosen for the second highest office in the land, and while they served they were potential presidents; now they are less than footnotes and almost forgotten.

Why did these particular men, of all people, become the choices of their respective parties? The answers to that are complex and many, but chief among them are geography and expedience.

For the most part, the vice-presidency has been treated like a political football, to be kicked back and forth among the geographical regions where the presidential candidates are weakest. The theory behind this questionable reasoning is sadly single-minded: if a presidential candidate looks as if he might well lose a major state in a section of the country where he has the least support, then his party chooses a vice-presidential candidate from that state in the hope he will carry his home territory for the party.

How well has this principle worked? On the record, not well at all.

Since 1828, we have had thirty-seven national elections decided by popular vote. In one or two of those elections, the *sectional* strength of the vice-presidential candidate undoubtedly helped, but only three times did the winning presidential candidate need the *electoral* votes of his running mate: Zachary Taylor in 1848, James Garfield in 1880, and Benjamin Harrison in 1888. (Significantly, the running mate in each instance came from New York.) Not once, in the entire twentieth century, did the vice-president's home state swing an election.

But the questionable principle of geographical appeasement will undoubtedly continue, despite the overwhelming statistics showing how wrong it is. If we can judge by the past and continuing performances of our major parties, the second in command will not be the second best man, as he was originally meant to be.

The important question, one that has for the most part been consistently overlooked, is simply this: Is the man we choose to be our vice-president *our second choice* for the presidency? Is he indeed the second best man regardless of color, ethnic origins, religious beliefs, or geographical background?

We forget that the vice-president is exactly one heartbeat away from the presidency. No man in the world can be guaranteed immortality. Our presidents are as vulnerable as the ordinary man, and they die, as we all do, from causes both natural and violent. Their standbys must therefore be people who can take over the reins of government with leadership and strength.

Two dramatic examples of this often-overlooked principle involved the Roosevelts, Theodore and Franklin; Theodore as the choosee, and Franklin as the chooser.

President William McKinley's first vice-president was Garret Augustus Hobart of New Jersey. Hobart served only two and a half years; he died in November, 1899, at the age of fifty-five. McKinley's first term expired on March 4, 1901. He therefore served without a vice-president for almost a year and a half.

Choice of McKinley's second vice-president aroused controversy and dissension, and offered the only note of interest in the Republican nominating convention of June, 1900.

A number of men hoped to run with McKinley. Hobart, at President McKinley's express direction, had been far more than a figurehead. He had worked closely with the administration, and had helped to make the vice-presidency a functioning office. Whoever was to succeed him would have to be a man qualified for the position. This was the view of certain Republican bosses and McKinley advisers.

Mark Hanna, in particular, felt strongly on this point. Hanna, national chairman of the Republican Party and a long-time friend and advisor to William McKinley, tied the vice-presidential nomination to McKinley's health, as he indicated on more than one occasion.

When delegate sentiment in the Republican convention began swinging toward Governor Theodore Roosevelt of New York for vice-president, Hanna fumed:

"Don't any of you realize that there's only one life between that madman and the Presidency?"

A few days later, after the convention selected Theodore Roosevelt to be McKinley's running mate, Hanna reluctantly gave in, but again not without a note of warning for his friend, President McKinley, to whom he wrote:

"Your *duty* to the Country is to *live* for four years from next March."

Hanna's fears were tragically realized only six months after McKinley's second inauguration. The President was shot by a crazed anarchist on September 6, 1901, and died eight days later. But Hanna's misgivings about Theodore Roosevelt, whom he had so bitterly denounced as a "madman," were unfounded, for Roosevelt went on to become one of the country's memorable presidents.

During Franklin Roosevelt's third term, from 1941 to 1945, the state of his health showed an alarming deterioration. By 1944, it was obvious to those closest to him that FDR was a sick man, and even though they publicly continued to insist he was well enough to serve another four years, they suspected, with good reason, that he would never make it through a fourth term. His next vice-president, they knew, had to be chosen with the greatest care, for it was probable that he would succeed to the presidency itself.

President Roosevelt's first vice-president was John Nance Garner of Texas; Garner served from 1933 to 1941. Roosevelt's second vice-president, from 1941 to 1945, was Henry A. Wallace of Iowa. The idealistic Wallace expected to be renominated at the Democratic Party convention of July, 1944, meeting in Chicago. To his surprise and disappointment, Roosevelt and the convention chose, instead, Senator Harry S Truman of Missouri.

Wallace's failure to win renomination in 1944 raises intriguing questions that cannot possibly be answered. History is a fact that cannot be erased or made over (except by partisan distortion). Still, in Wallace's case, as in others, we can speculate that he may have done things differently had he succeeded to the presidency instead of Truman.

The framers of our Constitution approached the creation of the vice-presidency with a curious double standard. On the one hand, they wrote into the Constitution a free choice of the best man to be president, and the *second best* to be vice-president, as we see in Article II, Section 1.3 of the Constitution.

"The electors shall meet in their respective States and vote by ballot for two persons, of whom one at least shall not be an inhabitant of the same State with themselves. . . . The person having the greatest number of votes shall be the President, if such number be a majority of the whole number of the electors. . . . *After the choice of the President,* the person having the greatest number of votes of the electors shall be the Vice-President. . . ." (Author's italics.)

The intention is clear. The capable and generally omniscient writers of the Constitution wanted as president the man considered by the electors to be the *best* qualified for the position; the vice-president would be the electors' second choice.

In a most unfortunate oversight, however, the *duties* of the vice-presidency were not provided the same importance as its *raison d'être*, for the vice-president was given nothing else to do than to preside over the Senate, without participating in its debates or deliberations, and to cast the deciding vote in the event of a Senate tie. Beyond that, he was empowered to do nothing else. Little wonder the office had scant attraction for the top men of the country.

Rather, we have seen a succession of political hacks and mediocrities raised to the eminence of the vice-presidency, and in too many cases to the presidency itself.

1st Vice-President   John Adams—Federalist, Massachusetts, 1789–
1797 (President George Washington). Born: October 30, 1735, Brain-
tree, Mass. Died: July 4, 1826, Quincy, Mass.

Madmen and Geniuses

John Adams

Based upon the original wording of the Constitution, the early history of the vice-presidency for a brief period hewed to the intent of its framers. The first two elections went smoothly enough, much as predicted; but by the third election, problems inherent in the office became apparent.

In the first election, conducted in April of 1789 at New York City's Federal Hall, George Washington was unanimously elected president with a total of 69 electoral votes (he was the first choice of each of the 69 electors); of the 69 second choice votes, 34 went to John Adams of Massachusetts, and the remaining 35 were scattered among ten other candidates (no majority was required for the vice-presidency, only the greatest number of votes). There were as yet no political parties.

The second election, conducted in November of 1792, followed virtually the identical pattern, with Washington once again receiving all of the first choice ballots (there were 132 electors this time) and 77 of the second choice votes going to John Adams. A hint of things to come was evidenced by four electoral votes for Thomas Jefferson of Virginia and one vote for Aaron Burr of New York.

Although there were nominally no parties as such, both Washington and Adams were considered to be Federalists, advocates of a strong central government, while Jefferson and Burr subscribed to the thinking of those who favored more power for the individual states.

To John Adams, the vice-presidency was an office to be tolerated while he awaited his turn for the presidency itself, which he considered should be his in the normal course of events, after George Washington had completed service to his country. There were occasions, however, when Adams despaired of ever reaching the executive chair, for it sometimes seemed to him as if George Washington would live forever, and would serve forever.

Adams had no liking for the second chair; in his view, it was "laborious" and "wholly insignificant."

"My own situation (the vice-presidency) is almost the only one in the world," he wrote to a friend, "in which firmness and patience are useless."

Hardly a popular figure personally, John Adams was one of the most astute and knowledgeable politicians of his time. Even those who did not like him, and there were many who resented his remote stiffness, his prudish austerity, admitted that his devotion to his country and to the ideals of freedom warranted admiration, as did the keenness of his mind.

John Adams graduated from Harvard at the age of nineteen, served briefly as a schoolmaster in Worchester, Massachusetts, and had later become a lawyer.

Neither rebellious nor insubordinate by nature, Adams passionately believed in equal rights for the British colonies, as he demonstrated in an essay he wrote in 1765.

"British liberties are not the grants of princes or parliaments, but the original rights, conditions of original contracts, coequal with prerogative and coeval with government . . . many of our rights are inherent and essential, agreed on as maxims and established as preliminaries, even before a Parliament existed."

Parliament and the King did not agree, for they retorted that "the word *rights* is an offensive expression . . . (We) will not endure to hear the Americans talk of their *rights*."

Adams's essay brought him to the attention of much of the Massachusetts colony, for his words echoed sentiments that many of the colonists felt yet were fearful of expressing. In that same year of 1765, Adams helped to prepare a memorial from the city of Boston protesting the Stamp Act imposed by the British government. Confronted by a truculent and unified colony, the British backed down and repealed the Stamp Act. It was the first major victory in what was to become the American Revolution, and for John Adams began his ultimate conversion to independence from the Crown.

Devotion to the law was no less a passion to John Adams than devotion to equal rights. His participation in the trial following the Boston Massacre of 1770 brought a storm of abuse upon him from his own countrymen, but once having assumed a position he considered to be just and proper, he refused to budge, no matter what the cost to his popularity.

On March 5, 1770, British troops quartered in Boston fired upon a group of demonstrators who had gathered to protest the presence of the

British soldiers in their city. Five Americans were killed and a number of others wounded.

Enraged Bostonians demanded justice, but what they wanted was the Biblical injunction—"An eye for an eye"—in this case, the head of each Britisher who had participated in the massacre. Whether there were extenuating circumstances did not seem to matter. Revenge was the cry of the hour.

Eight soldiers and the officer of the day, Captain Thomas Preston, were arrested and placed on civil trial. When they asked John Adams to defend them, he quickly agreed, and accepted a guinea as a retainer.

His defense was based upon legalisms only, for he firmly believed that the demonstrators had been an unruly mob . . . "a motley rabble of saucy boys, Irish teagues and outlandish jack tars," as he told the jury.

The law itself, which John Adams cherished so highly, he defended as ringingly as he defended the British soldiers.

"The law," he proclaimed to the crowded courtroom, "in all vicissitudes of government, fluctuations of the passions or flights of enthusiasm, will preserve a steady, undeviating course; it will not bend to the uncertain wishes, imaginations and wanton tempers of men."

The jury agreed with him. His use of technicalities, eloquently presented, won the day for his clients, and they were all acquitted, except for two who were punished by having their thumbs branded.

Boston did not look kindly after that upon John Adams. Extremists, heaping a "torrent of unpopularity" upon him, were certain he had deserted the cause of the American patriots. Although pained by their misjudgment of him, John Adams continued to fight for justice in his own way.

But events would not permit John Adams to be removed from the mainstream of dissent. Affairs between the mother country and the American colonies degenerated to a danger point. What began as resentment of Parliament's unjust and continuing policy of "taxation without representation" became outright defiance, overt and deliberate.

By 1774, the aroused colonists had had enough. Through their committees of correspondence, an invention of John's cousin Samuel Adams, the colonies agreed to convene for the purpose of discussing their mutual grievances and to plan possible recourse against the Crown.

By this time, John Adams was once again openly involved in the cause of American patriotism. He and his firebrand cousin Samuel came to be known as "that brace of Adamses." When the First Continental Congress convened in Philadelphia in September of 1774, both John and Samuel were there as delegates from Massachusetts. And they were there again when the Second Continental Congress met the following year.

In July of 1776, the colonists finally achieved what they had been threatening for some time. Taking their cue from the English philosopher, John Locke, who had declared some hundred years before that man had an inherent right to "life, liberty, and property," the American

colonies issued an historic document. Prepared principally by Thomas
Jefferson, with an assist from John Adams and three others, the American Declaration of Independence proclaimed its own belief in "life,
liberty, and the pursuit of happiness," and formally severed the united
colonies from the British Crown.

Over the long years of the Revolution, John Adams did no fighting
in the field. He often wished he were part of his country's armed forces,
along with General George Washington, but he was far more important
to the United States as a diplomat. From 1776 to 1788, he spent more
time separated from his wife and family than with them, first as a
minister to France and Holland, and finally, after hostilities had ceased,
as a minister to England.

With the Constitution of the United States ratified in 1787, John
Adams was recalled from England the following year, and came back to
his country with the knowledge that he would most certainly be his nation's first vice-president. Alexander Hamilton of New York would have
wished otherwise, for he did not like Adams, and he himself hoped to
have complete control of the Federalists, still only a loose coalition of
aristocrats and property owners. But Hamilton could not keep the vice-
presidency from Adams; in April of 1789, John Adams joined George
Washington in New York City as the nation's first executive team.

Adams fretted continuously through the eight years of Washington's two terms. In the beginning, he constantly lectured the Senate in
his capacity as that body's presiding officer. When the senators openly
affirmed their resentment of his meddling, he retreated into a relative
silence. His restraint from that point on set the pattern for most of his
successors, who meekly accepted the restrictive dictates of the Constitution that required them only to preside over the Senate and to cast
tie-breaking votes, nothing more.

Some of Adams's other views did not sit too well with his peers,
for he toyed with the idea of an hereditary senate, with the seat of each
senator automatically going to the senator's first born son. And perhaps
a lifelong president, to be modeled upon a monarchy.

In one of his less illustrious projects, Adams fought for monarchical titles. Much to his delight, a Senate committee, in all gravity,
recommended a jaw-breaking title for the new head of state, George
Washington:

"His Highness, the President of the United States of America, and
Protector of their Liberties."

Adams was certain that a title of similar solemnity would have to be
bestowed upon the vice-president, but both Houses of Congress objected to any title, jaw-breaking or otherwise, for the chief executive and
his second in command. A senator from Virginia considered it strange
"that John Adams, the son of a tinker, and the creature of the people,
should be for titles and pre-eminences, and should despise the Herd and
the ill born. . . ." Another senator, Izard of South Carolina, summarized

the Vice-President's unfortunate proposals with his own title for the corpulent Adams: "His Rotundity."

In the end, Adams bowed to the wishes of the majority; the American executive would function without the benefit of fancy frills or royal trappings.

There were many times in the course of his two terms as vice-president that Adams wished he were elsewhere. He alternated between gloom and hope, wondering when, if ever, the presidency would be his. Nothing had been said in the Constitution to limit the number of terms a president could serve. Since George Washington was undoubtedly the most popular American of his time, he could easily have served for the rest of his life, if he so chose. Adams himself had advocated a lifelong president, so he could raise no objection if Washington decided to be exactly that. Adams often saw himself going no further than the vice-presidency, for he considered Washington, who was older, to be in far better health, and he was certain the President would outlive him. Adams, in his early fifties, was convinced he was already too old for the executive chair, and altogether too feeble for its duties. In fact, he was neither, as he later proved.

His wife, Abigail Adams, had her own reasons for not wanting her husband to serve as the country's second president. In one of her weekly letters to him, she spoke of the presidency as "a most unpleasant seat, full of thorns, briars, thistles, murmuring, fault-finding, calumny, obloquy. . ."

But John Adams, the unbending taciturn puritan, was as human as any man. When he learned, in 1796, that George Washington would not serve a third term, his "aging" body suddenly took on the resilience of youth, his spirits rose remarkably, and his health, which he had always considered delicate, he now looked upon as robust.

For John Adams, who was then fifty-four, the dream of his life was about to come true, although not quite in the way he had hoped.

2nd Vice-President   Thomas Jefferson—Democratic-Republican, Virginia, 1797–1801 (President John Adams). Born: April 13, 1743, Shadwell, Goochland County, Va. Died: July 4, 1826, Charlottesville, Va.

Madmen and Geniuses

Thomas Jefferson

Because of the lack of communication and the distances involved, the first national elections covered many weeks. In the third election, it was not until December of 1796 that the results could be examined. Political experts did not care for what they saw, for the inherent weakness of Article II, Section 1.3 of the Constitution suddenly became apparent.

When George Washington let it be known that he would retire after his second term (thereby establishing a two-term precedent that would not be broken until 1940), most of the country believed that Vice-President John Adams would automatically become the next president. As it happened, his election was not automatic at all, and for a-while seemed uncertain.

The nation had Alexander Hamilton to thank for the disorder and perplexity of its third presidential election. One of the most powerful men of his time, Hamilton had no chance for the presidency himself, and had learned to accept that unhappy fact. But he meant to take a hand in the election of the second president, who would not be John Adams, if he could help it. His candidate was Thomas Pinckney of South Carolina, who had been unofficially chosen by an informal group of Northern and Southern Federalists to be their *second choice*, after John Adams.

Hamilton had other ideas. He wanted the Southern Federalists to cast their *first* ballots for Thomas Pinckney and their second for any man other than Adams. The Northern Federalists, in the meantime, would dutifully cast their first ballot for John Adams, and their second for

Thomas Pinckney. In the final accounting, therefore, Pinckney would end up with more votes than Adams. (It must be remembered that, under the system then in effect, the electors voted *only for President*; in the election of 1796, there were 138 electors, with two votes each. Under Hamilton's plan, *all* of the Federalists would vote for Pinckney, while only *some of them* would vote for Adams.)

Hamilton's scheme backfired. Most Federalists voted as originally intended, for Adams first and Pinckney second, so that the final results showed Adams with 71, a majority of the 138 electors, thus giving him the presidency. But enough Federalists defected, under Hamilton's abortive plan, to lose the vice-presidency for the Federalists. Close on the heels of John Adams was Thomas Jefferson with 68 votes, and behind Jefferson were Thomas Pinckney with 59, Aaron Burr with 30, and the balance scattered among nine other gentlemen.

Thus it was that Thomas Jefferson, with the second highest total, was elected vice-president, and for the first time in our history, though not for the last, our country was administered by differing political philosophies.

This was a situation the framers of the Constitution had not expected, or considered, for they had not anticipated the development of political parties. The confusion that resulted was allowed to remain on the books for eight more years.

The rise of Thomas Jefferson to the country's second highest office was as inevitable as that of John Adams, for even as a young man in his twenties Jefferson had established himself as one of the distinguished men of Virginia. Like John Adams, Jefferson practiced law, although unlike Adams, he did not have to depend upon his income as a lawyer, for he had been born to wealth. When he left his family's home to build his own and far more famous mansion, Monticello, he became a successful planter and farmer, partly through inheritance, partly through marriage to an equally wealthy young lady, and partly by his own efforts. (Although Jefferson used slave labor, since it was the backbone of the Southern economy, he abhorred the practice of slavery and the importation of slaves. He directed, in his will, that a number of his own slaves were to be freed at varying times after his death.)

Thomas Jefferson differed from Adams in one other important respect. In spite of his wealthy background, his concern always was for the common man and this ideals of democracy, not just for the propertied aristocrat. He continuously championed the rights of the individual, as opposed to rule by a favored few, an approach preferred by most Federalists, including John Adams and Alexander Hamilton.

Jefferson's career as a lawyer covered only a few years. At the age of twenty-five, he was elected to the Virginia House of Burgesses, and continued as a delegate to that body from 1768 to 1775, when he went to Philadelphia as a member of the Virginia delegation to the Continental Congress. By then he had given up his law practice for the more satisfying pursuit of politics and study.

Never known as an orator, for he did not possess the fiery tongue of some of his peers, Jefferson nevertheless attracted considerable attention as far away as London by the supreme eloquence of his pen. In 1774, his twenty-three page pamphlet, *A Summary View of the Rights of British America,* created a minor sensation both in Virginia and England. Often intemperate, but always logical, his *Summary View* foreshadowed the document that would later place him in the temple of America's immortals.

When the Second Continental Congress looked around, some two years later, for the man to draft their assertions of independence from the British Crown, it was inevitable that Jefferson would lead the committee of five ultimately chosen. And it was inevitable that the other four, who included John Adams and the venerable Benjamin Franklin, should defer to the second youngest of their group, for the thirty-three-year-old Jefferson had amply demonstrated the soaring power of his pen.

The document that Jefferson presented to his committee for approval was debated by the Second Continental Congress until the evening of July 4, 1776, and was finally adopted with Preamble intact, but with major portions omitted or revised. The Congress as a whole objected to an entire section dealing with slavery, and softened another characterizing King George III as a tyrant. Still, even with the cuts and the changes, what resulted was the historic Declaration of Independence, one of the most important and eloquent documents ever conceived. Thomas Jefferson must be given the credit for the writing of this remarkable paper, although he did accept a few minor revisions offered by Franklin and one or two of the other committee members. Originally, Jefferson had written, "We hold these truths to be sacred & undeniable." Certainly cogent words, but how much more moving to read "We hold these truths to be self-evident. . . ." Whether the change was suggested by Benjamin Franklin or whether Jefferson made the change himself is inconsequential. They are words that, once heard, will never be forgotten. Similarly, the ending of the Declaration was accepted by the Continental Congress exactly as Jefferson had written it:

". . . With a firm reliance on the protection of Divine Providence, we mutually pledge to each other our Lives, our Fortunes and our sacred Honor."

With his reputation now firmly established by the Declaration, Jefferson returned to Virginia to serve in its legislature. In 1779, he succeeded to the governorship of his state. His two-year term in that office was marred by an unfortunate charge against him of cowardice in the face of the enemy. In June of 1781, a British force commanded by Lieutenant Colonel Banastre Tarleton pushed into the Virginia capitol of Charlottesville. They almost captured Governor Jefferson, but he managed to provide "for his personal safety with a precipitate retreat," as Colonel Tarleton later reported.

Whether the escape of the governor and his family was a panicky flight from the enemy, thus leaving behind the state government without making adequate arrangement for its safe removal, or whether Jeffer-

son's retreat before the British was a dignified and careful withdrawal
was debated long and angrily by the Virginia legislature. Finally, in
December of 1781, the legislature officially cleared him.

Jefferson's career as a statesman and politician next led him to
Europe as a minister to France, and then, in 1789, he returned to America as his country's first secretary of state, in President Washington's
cabinet. His four years in that position were often stormy, for he and
Secretary of the Treasury Alexander Hamilton continually differed on
official policy.

On the last day of 1793, just a few months short of completing
their first full term in office, President Washington accepted the resignation of his secretary of state in the interests of national harmony, for
Jefferson could not accept Hamilton's fiscal views regarding the United
States treasury and a national bank. Hamilton's views were supported
by the President; Jefferson realized he could no longer function in Washington's cabinet.

When Jefferson assumed the vice-presidency in 1797, under President John Adams, he once again found himself opposing the chief executive's point of view. This time his opposition was far more serious,
for he was running counter to the course set by his own president, whom
he had been elected to succeed in the event of the former's death. And
Jefferson, by his resistance to the President's actions, placed himself in
a vulnerable position that could have taken him to prison had he voiced
his opposition openly.

This struggle between the two (carried on by Jefferson behind the
scenes) was an historic one, for it helped to shape the future course of
democracy for the new nation. Even though Jefferson's role in the fight
was not known until decades later, it marked the only time that a vice-
president set out to nullify his president's policy, and succeeded.

Stung by the continuing barbs of the outspoken opposition press,
the Federalist-controlled Congress pushed through a series of measures
collectively known as the Alien and Sedition Acts. President Adams, who
had not actually sponsored the Acts, nevertheless readily signed them
into law. He had the help and advice of his wife Abigail, whose free-
wheeling pen castigated her husband's numerous enemies with every
other stroke.

The Alien and Sedition Acts were, purely and simply, a bald attempt to muzzle the opposition. As one pro-Adams newspaper put it:

"It is patriotism to write in favor of our government—it is sedition
to write against it."

Vice-President Jefferson swung into action. The Alien and Sedition
Acts were clearly an abridgment of the First Amendment and of free
speech; the Acts had to be nullified. But Jefferson had to work in secrecy,
for "the infidelities of the post office and the circumstances of the times"
could have landed him in prison under the provisions of the legislation
he was now fighting.

Jefferson prepared a series of resolutions. One copy went to Kentucky, where that state's legislature, after making some changes, adopted them as the Kentucky Resolutions of 1798 and called upon its senators and representatives in Congress to repeal the "unconstitutional and obnoxious acts." James Madison of Virginia further modified Jefferson's proposals, while leaving intact the Vice-President's intent, and in December of 1798, the Virginia Resolutions were adopted.

Between them, the Kentucky and Virginia Resolutions, largely authored by Jefferson, helped to arouse the nation to an awareness of the dangerous Acts promoted by the Federalists and the Adams administration. Although nothing was done at that time to abolish them, three of the four Acts were eventually allowed to expire, and the fourth was repealed when Jefferson assumed the presidency in 1801.

The Alien and Sedition Acts, ill-conceived and ill-begotten, managed only to split the Federalists and to bring about their disappearance as a party. Adams and his colleagues had miscalculated, for they had completely misinterpreted the mood of the country, and overlooked the influence of an antagonistic vice-president. There would be other such presidential miscalculations in the future, although never again would a vice-president risk his own freedom to fight for the freedom of others.

3rd Vice-President   Aaron Burr—Democratic-Republican, New York, 1801–1805 (President Thomas Jefferson). Born: February 6, 1756, Newark, N. J. Died: September 14, 1836, Staten Island, N. Y.

Madmen and Geniuses

Aaron Burr

The national election of November, 1800, saw the first signs of the classic party-to-party confrontation that would eventually become the hallmark of American politics. In the four years that Adams and Jefferson, as president and vice-president respectively, had shared the administration of the country, political factionalism had finally hardened into definite parties, so that by 1800 a man could claim to be either a Federalist or a Democratic-Republican; before then, he simply supported John Adams and Alexander Hamilton, or gave his allegiance to Thomas Jefferson and Aaron Burr, without claiming a party symbol.

With John Adams seeking reelection, the Federalists turned for their second choice to another Pinckney from South Carolina, Charles Cotesworth Pinckney, brother to the man Alexander Hamilton had hoped to elect four years before. Although the word "coalition" did not then have the relevance it has for us today, its implications were evident in the choice of Pinckney. Admittedly capable and admittedly a power in his home state, Pinckney's primary value to the Federalists lay in the fact that he represented a geographical area distinct and separate from their first choice, for there were certainly others in the North as qualified as he. Yet the Federalists, in what can only be described as an obvious appeasement of the Southern states, selected him for their second choice. Thus began the tradition of political strategy and coalition that has been an integral part of our system ever since.

Like the Federalists, the Democratic-Republicans also chose two sectional candidates—Thomas Jefferson of Virginia and Aaron Burr of

New York. Unlike the Federalists, however, the Democratic-Republicans faced a problem of priority; Aaron Burr, supposedly, was to be the Democratic-Republican *second* choice—that is, he was to be considered only as a possible vice-president. But as the election drew near, and certain bizarre developments took place in the Federalist party (with Burr himself lending a helpful hand), Burr decided he wanted the top spot and actively began to work for it. That he almost succeeded can be credited in part to his most bitter enemy, Alexander Hamilton.

As he had in the election of 1796, Hamilton once again plotted to deprive John Adams of the presidency. This time he schemed for the election of Charles Cotesworth Pinckney. In a blistering pamphlet entitled *The Public Conduct and Character of John Adams, Esq. President of the United States*, Hamilton charged that Adams was totally unfit for the presidency. Adams had "great and intrinsic defects," including "the disgusting egotism, the distempered jealousy, and the ungovernable indiscretion of (his) temper." If the Federalists knew what was good for them, they would not vote for Adams at all, but for Pinckney and others.

When Hamilton gave this pamphlet to the printer, he swore the printer to secrecy. Not a word of what Hamilton had written was to be revealed to anyone, nor was anyone to see the pamphlet. All copies were to be given to Hamilton, who intended to distribute them clandestinely to his Federalist friends and supporters. But Hamilton reckoned without fate and Aaron Burr, who somehow secured a copy. Burr made certain its contents were divulged, to the consternation of the Federalists. "It rent the party in twain," as one discriminating observer remarked, and it helped to seal the doom of John Adams and Charles Cotesworth Pinckney. They were both defeated by Thomas Jefferson and Aaron Burr, who tied for first place with 73 electoral votes each.

The tie vote between Jefferson and Burr was an unhappy development for the country and for the Democratic-Republicans, and elicited a cynical comment from Jefferson, as he wrote to Burr on December 15, 1800:

"It was badly managed not to have arranged with certainty what seems to have been left to hazard."

It was now up to the House of Representatives to break the tie between Jefferson and Burr, as provided for in Article II, Section 1.3 of the Constitution. Each state (there were sixteen at the time) would have one vote; the electors of each state would decide among themselves which candidate was to receive the one vote of that state. As it happened, the key state was Delaware, whose entire delegation consisted of only one man, Federalist James Bayard.

Like Hamilton, Bayard had little use for Aaron Burr, but he mistrusted Thomas Jefferson even more. To most Federalists, Thomas Jefferson was " an *atheist* in Religion and a fanatic in politics." Burr was no better, as Hamilton wrote to Bayard:

"Burr will certainly attempt to reform the government *à la Buona-*

parte. He is as unprincipled and dangerous a man as any country can boast—as true a Cataline as ever met in midnight conclave."

James Bayard faced his task with little enthusiam, but he reluctantly agreed "that Burr must be voted for by the Federalists as being the least of two evils." When the voting in the House of Representatives began on Wednesday, February 11, 1801, Bayard cast the Delaware vote for Burr.

At the end of the first ballot, it was discovered that the House was deadlocked, for only eight states had voted for Jefferson, with six going to Burr, and two undecided (the Maryland and Vermont delegations were equally divided, with exactly half of each state insisting upon Jefferson and the other half as insistent for Burr). Inasmuch as a majority of nine states was required for election, neither man was the winner.

The deadlock continued for thirty-five more ballots, and six more days. Finally, on Tuesday, February 17, Bayard of Delaware wearied of the fight, and announced he would change his vote. But, still unable to support Jefferson, he cast a blank. After that, the Burr supporters in the Maryland and Vermont delegations also gave up, and their states voted for Jefferson, who became the third president; and Aaron Burr of New York succeeded to the vice-presidency.

We have seen many controversial men emerge as leaders of our country, but none more so than Aaron Burr. Extremely capable, dangerously ambitious, Burr was a complicated man who took a wrong turn somewhere. To his detractors, he was a traitor and a murderer; to his supporters, he was a misunderstood genius. Whatever his true character, the United States executive saw the likes of Aaron Burr only once. In that respect the nation was indeed fortunate, for no democracy can long withstand the tortured machinations of its Aaron Burrs.

It is difficult to pin down precisely the influence and events that shaped the adult motivations of Aaron Burr. Certainly he had the advantages of birth and training. His maternal grandfather was Jonathan Edwards, one of the leading New England theologians of the colonial period. Burr's father, Reverend Aaron Burr, was a minister and teacher who settled with his family in Newark, New Jersey. In 1747, Reverend Burr helped to organize the College of New Jersey (later to become world-famous as Princeton) and served as its second president.

The boy Aaron Burr showed scant interest in religion as a career. Both his father and grandfather died within a few months of each other, when Aaron was barely a year old. The child was raised by an uncle and was given the best of private tutoring. At the age of thirteen, Aaron entered Princeton as a sophomore and graduated in September of 1772. Then he toyed with the study of theology for a few months, found he didn't care for it, and gave it up for good. Law, to the restless young Burr, had far more appeal, as did military service in the American Revolution.

Burr remained in the Revolutionary forces for three years; he acquitted himself creditably (much of his wartime activity centered on the gathering of intelligence), rising to the rank of lieutenant colonel by the time he was twenty-three. In the spring of 1779, he decided he'd had enough of war. Pleading illness, he resigned from the American army. General Washington never forgave Burr's desertion of his country at a time of desperate need.

But in 1779 Burr was not concerned with his commander-in-chief. He was far more interested in furthering his own ends. He studied law in Albany, was admitted to the bar in the spring of 1782, and began a practice that eventually took him to New York City and to prominence and money. By 1784, he was a member of the New York state legislature, and five years later, was the state's attorney general, appointed to that position by a man he sometimes supported and sometimes did not, Governor George Clinton. Within two years of that appointment, Burr achieved an even more notable success when the state legislature selected him as United States senator. Burr was then thirty-five.

Aaron Burr's political loyalties were as clouded as his motivations. He maneuvered back and forth between one faction or another as it suited his own needs. During the process he made many powerful enemies, including Alexander Hamilton. Nor did his numerous romances and affairs (some carried on while his wife was still alive) do his reputation any good.

To Alexander Hamilton, Burr was the worst kind of self-seeking politician, ". . . bold, enterprising, and intriguing. . . ."

Although there were countless others who shared Hamilton's distaste for Aaron Burr, the forty-four-year-old lawyer-politician had enough adherents in 1800 to make a positive try for the presidency. That he almost succeeded was evidence not only of his own supreme belief in himself, but of the untidiness of the electoral process as it had been established by the founding fathers.

Burr accepted the loss of the presidency without rancor, for he was young enough to wait for the proper time, when President Jefferson would retire and the mantle of presidential succession would fall upon the incumbent vice-president. It had already happened that way twice before, with John Adams and Thomas Jefferson both stepping up to the executive chair from the vice-presidency. There was no reason, in March of 1801, to suspect that it would happen otherwise for the country's third vice-president, Aaron Burr.

But Burr failed to consider the active hostility of his immediate superior, the President himself. His independent thinking often placed him in opposition to Jefferson, who had never attempted to hide his dislike for Burr. Jefferson now openly distrusted him as well, for Burr's attempt at the presidency had been too brazen and too blatant an example of raw ambition. One result of President Jefferson's unconcealed displeasure with his vice-president was to turn much of official Washington (the new federal capital) against Burr so that he found himself in almost complete isolation during the time he served with Jefferson.

Shut out of all important matters by the administration and shunned by most of the capital, Burr became more and more aware that the vice-presidency, at least for him, was to be a dead end. His appraisal was correct; when the Republican caucus met in Washington in February of 1804 to choose its candidates for the coming presidential election, Burr was not even considered for reelection as vice-president (President Jefferson of course was nominated unanimously).

"Mr. Burr had not one single vote," a caucus delegate later commented, "and not a word was lisped in his favor."

Burr was only temporarily disheartened by the result of the Republican caucus; he looked elsewhere for political glory, and settled upon the governorship of his home state, New York. There at least his reputation remained intact (or so he thought) for he had been one of New York's most successful lawyers.

But here, too, luck eluded him. The New York Democratic-Republicans followed the lead of their national counterparts and refused to give him their gubernatorial nomination. Burr therefore ran as an independent, with unofficial support from a number of New York Federalists.

As a party, the Federalists were heading for collapse, and they were not strong enough to swing the New York election to Burr. The final results of the balloting, in April, 1804, showed almost 31,000 for Morgan Lewis, the Democratic-Republican candidate, and only 22,000 for Burr. It was the most humiliating defeat any gubernatorial candidate had yet suffered in the state of New York, and it marked the start of Aaron Burr's rapid descent into disrepute and dishonor.

Not quite three months later, on July 12, Aaron Burr killed Alexander Hamilton on the dueling grounds at Weehawken, New Jersey. Burr was speedily charged with murder by a coroner's jury in the state of New York, where the duel had been arranged and where Hamilton had been brought to die. In October of 1804, a Bergen County grand jury in New Jersey returned an indictment against the Vice-President for the same murder. (The New Jersey indictment was dismissed in November, 1807, when it was proved that Hamilton had actually died in New York and not in New Jersey as had originally been presumed.)

This indictment against a sitting vice-president brought no protest from Aaron Burr. He did not use the argument of executive privilege, as did Spiro Agnew in 1973, and he did not claim that a sitting vice-president could not be indicted, again as Agnew did, in an attempt to escape the consequence of his actions.

Because of the double accusations hanging over him, the murder charge by his own state of New York and the indictment by New Jersey, the Vice-President had to run to avoid prosecution. He fled to the South, and then went back to Washington to take up his duties as presiding officer of the Senate. (He could not be extradited from Washington for the states had no jurisdiction in the District of Columbia.)

The tragic result of the Burr-Hamilton duel created an incredible and unparalleled situation—the second most important man in the United States was charged with a capital crime. Yet, despite this, he behaved officially as if nothing had happened.

"We are indeed fallen on evil times," wrote a senator to a friend. "The high office of President is filled by an *infidel*, that of Vice-President by a *Murderer*."

Accused killer, sitting vice-president, the supremely ambitious Aaron Burr had not yet given up. As his vice-presidential term was coming to an end, he began to concoct a grotesque scheme to create his own empire in Louisiana and parts of Mexico. Even while this traitorous dream was forming in his mind, Burr gave a farewell address to the Senate that told of his high regard for that body.

"(It is) a citadel of law, of order, of liberty; and it is here—it is here—in this exalted refuge; here, if anywhere, will resistance be made to the storms of political phrensy and the silent arts of corruption. . . ."

When his term as vice-president ended two days later, Aaron Burr's career and life went downhill. His grand scheme for a personal empire came to naught. He was captured and tried for treason in 1807. But the government failed adequately to prove its case, and Burr was released on technical grounds. From that moment, he was a beaten man. He spent the rest of his life vainly trying to recapture the glory he had known briefly both in New York and Washington. He died in a Staten Island hotel at the age of eighty, penniless, virtually forgotten, and utterly defeated.

The elections of 1796 and 1800 demonstrated that Article II, Section 1.3 of the Constitution had a serious flaw; it was therefore decided to separate the electoral voting for the president and the vice-president. To this end, the Twelfth Amendment was proposed to Congress in December of 1803 and ratified into law in September of 1804, in time to affect the presidential election of that year.

Under the new provisions of the Twelfth Amendment, the electors were to cast separate and distinct ballots for the presidency and the vice-presidency. The president would be chosen in one separate ballot, and the vice-president would be chosen in a second separate ballot. Never again would a man not intended for the presidency come so close to winning that high office as Aaron Burr almost did. In addition, the vice-president would now have to have a *majority* of the electoral votes, not simply the *greatest number*, as in the past.

As a reform measure, the Twelfth Amendment improved the *voting procedure* for the executive offices, but did nothing for the caliber of the second in command. The amendment itself cannot be entirely blamed for the subsequent poor showing of the vice-presidency, for the country's leaders and party chieftains continually downgraded the office, as was clearly demonstrated in the years immediately following Aaron Burr's term.

Many historians insist that the very separation of the two executive offices confirmed the apparent unimportance of the vice-presidency, so that only unimportant men were willing to accept vice-presidential nominations. But the unimportance of the office was more imagined than real, as we were to see on many later occasions. In the end, it was the cynical attitude of the politicians, and not the office itself, that gave us the near disasters we have stoically endured in the vice-presidential chair.

Fate, in the form of sturdy constitutions, was kind to us for the first fifty years. We can only shudder to think what might have happened to our country if Thomas Jefferson, James Madison, and James Monroe had not been healthy and long-lived.

4th Vice-President George Clinton—Democratic-Republican, New York, 1805–1809 (President Thomas Jefferson), 1809–1812 (President James Madison). Born: July 26, 1739, Little Britain, N. Y. Died: April 20, 1812, Washington, D. C.

Madmen and Geniuses

George Clinton

With Aaron Burr out of the way, the path was now clear for the Democratic-Republican caucus of 1804 to choose a man more pliable to serve as vice-president for Jefferson's second term. The newly-enacted Twelfth Amendment certified, for the first time, that the vice-presidential candidate could not then aspire to the presidency (except by the death of the president, which no one considered possible, so why worry about it?). The man to run with President Jefferson had only to be willing to serve, and he had to live in the North, preferably New York, for that state controlled many electoral votes. (The Virginia-New York axis, instituted with Jefferson and Aaron Burr, continued for twenty-four years, through the administrations of Madison and Monroe.)

The Democratic-Republicans found their perfect vice-presidential candidate in George Clinton, seven-time governor of New York. He had dominated the politics of his state for more than two decades, and had cherished the notion that he might one day become president. Now that he was to be chosen for the vice-presidency, he was certain it would be a stepping-stone to the executive chair itself.

How wrong he was. At the time of the election in 1804, he was sixty-five. Many of the country's leaders, during his day, remained active and alert long past their sixties. President Jefferson was only four years younger than he, while former President John Adams, his intellectual acuity unimpaired, was four years older.

But Clinton at sixty-five was an old man; not just aging, he was elderly, and probably suffering from senility. After a distinguished service as governor of New York State for eighteen uninterrupted years, he had finally retired from that office because of "the declining condition of my health," as he advised the New York voters in January of 1795. But he was not too ill, in his own mind, to aspire to the presidency, as he did for a number of years.

In his youth a robust and vigorous man, George Clinton had come to government with a revolutionary and independent spirit, a democrat in every sense of the word. His father had emigrated from Ireland and had settled in New York's Ulster County, not the most promising of areas to make a fortune. Denied the benefit of inherited wealth or a college education, George Clinton managed to become a lawyer, and by the time he was twenty-eight represented Ulster County in the colony's General Assembly. Within a few years, he had complete control of politics in his county, and, after the Revolution, the entire state.

The early part of Clinton's career was marked by a fervent hatred of the British. He particularly despised the Loyalists, those Tories who remained loyal to the Crown throughout the Revolution. By then the most powerful man in Ulster County, George Clinton made no effort to mask his intense dislike either for the King or his followers. One anti-Clintonian described Clinton's methods of handling the Loyalists in his county:

"They were by his orders tarred and feathered, carted, whipped, fined, banished, and in short, every kind of cruelty, death not excepted, was practiced by this emissary of revolution."

This appraisal may have been too harsh, but Clinton did press his revolutionary ideals with zeal and energy. During the war, he served as a brigadier general in command of a section of the Hudson River highlands. He did not distinguish himself in the field for he knew nothing of military matters, and he was consistently outmaneuvered by his British counterpart, Sir Henry Clinton, a distant cousin and a far better soldier.

Yet George Clinton's military service during that period rewarded him politically. Many of his troops, who were empowered to vote for statewide offices under New York's newly enacted constitution, helped to elect him as the state's first governor, much to the consternation of the aristocrats, who had placed their hopes on two of their own, John Jay and Philip Schuyler. Clinton defeated them decisively.

From that point, George Clinton came as close to being a political boss as it was possible to be in those days, before there were parties and before the advent of party organizations. He served six successive terms as governor, from 1777 to 1795, and only in his last three-year term, which he won in 1792, was there a question as to his dominance. In that year, the Federalists and their candidate John Jay clearly won the election, but Clinton saw to it that the votes of three counties, which would have given the election to Jay, were invalidated on the most trivial of technicalities, and Clinton barely won reelection.

Partly because of the erosion of his former popularity, and partly because of his poor health, Clinton retired from the governorship at the end of his sixth term in 1795, when he was fifty-six. In the meantime, despite the fact that he was too ill for the governorship, he made plans for national office. If the presidency were to be denied him, as seemed likely, since both Thomas Jefferson and Aaron Burr were far stronger candidates for the executive chair, Clinton could at the least hope for the vice-presidency.

When it became apparent in 1800 that Burr would beat him out for the second spot on the Democratic-Republican ticket, the infirm Clinton once again returned to the governorship of New York. Patronage and the continuing prestige of the Clinton political hierarchy were both at stake. Clinton's nephew, DeWitt Clinton, had become a New York power in his own right. In an effort to regain the spoils of office, which had begun to slip away during Clinton's interregnum, the younger Clinton and his Republican colleagues easily manipulated the elder Clinton to their own ends. With only a minimum of difficulty, the Clintonians took the governorship back from the fading Federalists, who had held it for six years.

Clinton's seventh and final term as the chief executive of New York State lasted from 1801 to 1804. Aaron Burr's political decline placed the New York governor in line for the vice-presidency for Jefferson's second term, despite Clinton's own admission that his faculties were failing, as he wrote to his nephew, DeWitt Clinton, in September of 1803:

"You will have some Leisure before your departure for Congress. Will you employ a part of it in drafting a communication to the Legislature for the next session. Your knowledge of the present Situation of our Affairs will furnish you with Materials and from my former Communications you will be able to collect my sentiments on the different Subjects. I have been so long dealing in Speeches that I found it extremely difficult to draft one for the last session without committing Plagiarism."

We can well imagine how the present-day voter would react to an admission of that kind from a potential president, for that's how Clinton still regarded himself. The Democratic-Republicans looked upon him as fit only for the second spot, and when the caucus of 1804 nominated him for the vice-presidency, Clinton quickly accepted.

When the election results were announced on February 13, 1805 (the opening and counting of the ballots were supervised by the outgoing vice-president, Aaron Burr), it was found that Jefferson and Clinton both had received 162 electoral votes, while the defeated Federalist slate of Charles Cotesworth Pinckney and Rufus King of New York could muster only fourteen votes. Pinckney and King knew they had not a chance, and made only a token, half-hearted try for the executive.

Clinton's seven years in the vice-presidency were ludicrous. John

Quincy Adams, who was then a senator from Massachusetts, early recognized Clinton's inadequacies. In a letter to his father, Adams wrote
about the Vice-President:

"Mr. Clinton is totally ignorant of all the most common forms of
proceeding in the Senate, and yet by the rules he is to decide every
question of order without debate and without appeal. His judgment is
neither quick nor strong; so there is no more dependence upon the cor-
rectness of his determinations from his understanding than from his
experience. . . . In this respect a worse choice than Mr. Clinton could
scarcely have been made."

Another senator, William Plumer of New Hampshire, had even
harsher criticism.

"He is old, feeble & altogether uncapable of the duty of presiding
in the Senate," Plumer wrote. "He has no mind—no intellect—no memory—He forgets the question—mistakes it—& not infrequently declares
a vote before its taken—& often forgets to do it after it is taken. . . ."

In spite of these all too apparent deficiencies, Clinton was renominated for vice-president in 1808. He still felt himself capable of assuming
the presidency itself, but few agreed with him. Even his most faithful
followers now accepted the widely-held belief that Clinton, by then in
his sixty-ninth year, was indeed a doddering and feeble man, too inexperienced in the all important area of foreign affairs for the top executive
office.

When the Democratic-Republican caucus of 1808 bypassed him for
the presidency, a furious Clinton spluttered that he had been "treated
with great disrespect and cruelty by the gentlemen of his own party."
Nevertheless, he swallowed his pride and his anger, and agreed to serve
as vice-president under James Madison of Virginia, who had been Jefferson's personal choice as his successor.

Clinton's renomination and subsequent reelection to the vice-presidency demonstrated the universal indifference to that office. Although
Clinton was too old and too infirm for the presidency itself, he was good
enough to be vice-president. That he was also the potential president
seems not to have occurred to anyone.

The aging, senile Clinton never forgave his colleagues for refusing
to give him the presidency he thought he deserved. He opposed President Madison's policies, refused to cooperate, and generally made a
shambles of administration unity. Cantankerous and bitter to the end, he
proved a liability to his party, and when he finally died in April of 1812,
many in the country privately heaved a sigh of relief, while publicly
praising the "old patriot."

Death came to George Clinton, at the age of seventy-three, as a
result of "the general decay of Nature," and a severe attack of pneumonia. His children raised a monument in his honor, bearing an inscription
more faithful to his past service to the state of New York than to his more
recent efforts as vice-president. Had he been content to retire with his

gubernatorial achievements alone, the words on his monument would have been far more relevant.

"While He lived, His Virtue, Wisdom, and Valor Were the Pride, the Ornament and Security Of his Country, and when He Died, He Left an Illustrious Example of a Well Spent Life, Worthy of all Imitation."

5th Vice-President Elbridge Gerry—Democratic-Republican, Massachusetts, 1813–1814 (President James Madison). Born: July 17, 1744, Marblehead, Mass. Died: November 23, 1814, Washington, D. C.

Madmen and Geniuses

Elbridge Gerry

The death of George Clinton left the vice-presidency vacant for the first time. A month later, the Democratic-Republican caucus assembled to choose its candidates for the presidential term that would begin in March of 1813.

Many of the delegates leaned toward Clinton's nephew, DeWitt Clinton, to be the next vice-president, but that wily gentleman had seen how the second office had led absolutely nowhere for his uncle, and he therefore declined. So once more, the Democratic-Republicans chose an elderly man, seventy-year-old John Langdon of New Hampshire. But Langdon, too, disappointed them, because of "poor health," and the caucus finally chose Elbridge Gerry of Massachusetts. It should be noted that all three of the possibilities were Northerners (President Madison of Virginia represented the South).

Although Gerry was almost four years older than George Clinton had been at the beginning of his first term, he was a geriatric improvement, if not political. Independent in his views, on occasion to the point of stubbornness, Elbridge Gerry had devoted his entire life to the service of his home state and to his country.

Unlike most of his colleagues, Gerry did not come to politics through the study and practice of law. A graduate of Harvard at the age of eighteen, Gerry went into the family business, the shipping of dried codfish out of the Massachusetts port of Marblehead. During the Revolution, Gerry added to the family fortunes by the judicious use of privateering.

Elbridge Gerry's intense interest in politics sprang from a meeting with Samuel Adams in 1772; from that time on, the young Gerry (he was then twenty-eight) devoted himself to freedom and "republicanism." He served in various capacities in Massachusetts, and went to Philadelphia in 1776 as a member of the second Continental Congress, along with the "brace of Adamses." One of the fifty-six signers of the Declaration of Independence, Gerry did not actually place his signature on that document until September 3, some two months later.

As a delegate to the Constitutional Convention that met in Philadelphia in 1787, Elbridge Gerry made one of his more lasting impressions upon history, although not because of his membership in that body. Rather, his fame as one of the framers of the Constitution rests more upon his opposition to the finished product than to his contributions. As one fellow delegate disgustedly put it, Gerry "objected to everything he did not propose."

It may not have been quite that bad, but Elbridge Gerry did exhibit inconsistencies that annoyed his colleagues. On the one hand, he advocated a strong centralized government, but ended by opposing such a government because of his commitment to "republicanism." Gerry failed to realize that the "republicanism" he had in mind had a far more graphic significance in 1776, when he so passionately favored "separation from the prostituted Government of G. Britain," than it did in later years.

On other points he was just as inconsistent. He feared "the friends of Aristocracy," yet because of his own position as a man of wealth, he could not bring himself to support popular suffrage, despite his avowed belief in "republicanism." He did not care for parties, particularly the "one devoted to democracy," the worst, he thought, of all "political evils." In the end, he refused to sign the Constitution in the belief that it would lead to civil war. He had hoped for a plan "in a more mediating shape...."

In 1797, President John Adams appointed Gerry to be part of a three man mission to France, along with Charles Cotesworth Pinckney and John Marshall (later to be hailed as our first great Chief Justice of the Supreme Court). This mission to France was the result of a prolonged episode that was to achieve fame as the notorious "XYZ Affair."

The XYZ Affair was a blatant attempt by the French to extort protection money from the fledgling American republic. The French had been harassing American shipping; they advised the three Americans that the harassment would stop upon the payment of monies both to the French government and some of its officials (one of whom was Maurice Talleyrand, minister of foreign affairs).

When Pinckney heard this outrageous demand, delivered to the Americans at various times by three Talleyrand emissaries who came to be known as Messrs. X, Y, Z, he exclaimed in righteous anger:

"No! No! Not a sixpence!"

This cry was dramatically converted by an affronted American public to a slogan cherished by every schoolchild:

"Millions for defense but not one cent for tribute!"

With this refusal to knuckle under to the French demands, the American mission failed, and Pinckney and Marshall went back to the United States. Gerry, however, remained behind, hoping to bring about a solution on his own, for he had carried on secret negotiations with Talleyrand. Pinckney accused the Massachusetts politician of playing a different kind of game.

"I never met a man of less candor," said Pinckney, "and as much duplicity as Mr. Gerry."

The Gerry negotiations led nowhere, but he always claimed that his mere presence in Paris, with his two colleagues back home, averted a possible war with France. Although the French government had made many threatening gestures, it had never seriously meant to go to war with the United States. Gerry returned to the United States far less than a hero, for his motives in remaining behind in France had been misunderstood by most of his countrymen.

But the Democratic-Republicans in Massachusetts regarded him as the man who had prevented war with France, and they nominated him in 1800 to run for governor. He was defeated in a close race. Over the next three years, Gerry was defeated three more times, in each campaign by a wider margin. After that, he refused to run again, until 1810, when the Jeffersonians persuaded him to try once more. Despite his lack of popularity and his age (sixty-five), and despite his obvious distaste for the common man, he managed to defeat his Federalist opponent, who had even stronger aristocratic ties. Gerry won reelection the following year, and soon after, the Democratic-Republicans nominated him to run for vice-president.

There is some irony in Gerry's eventual acceptance of the vice-presidency under the stipulations of the document he had once said he could not "pledge himself to abide by." During the final two weeks of the Constitutional Convention, in September of 1787, Gerry had actively opposed adoption of the vice-presidency.

As vice-president, Elbridge Gerry performed in a competent if uninspired manner. He insisted upon attending diligently to his duties as presiding officer of the Senate, despite a continuing siege of bad health. He aroused no enmities, contributed little of note, and provoked no one to denunciation, as had his unfortunate predecessor.

A year or so after assuming the vice-presidency, sixty-nine-year-old Elbridge Gerry faced a crisis, along with the rest of the country. In June of 1813, President James Madison suffered a serious illness. Louis Serurier, the French Minister, described the concern evident everywhere at news that President Madison was critically ill of bilious fever.

"The thought of his possible loss strikes everybody with consternation," Serurier wrote to a friend. "It is certainly true that his death, in

the circumstances in which the Republic is placed, would be a veritable
national calamity. The President (Elbridge Gerry) who would succeed
him for three and a half years is a respectable old man, but weak and
worn out."

After a number of weeks, President Madison recovered with no apparent loss of vigor, and both he and the United States survived his illness. A potential crisis of presidential succession had been providentially
averted.

On November 23, 1814, after serving about a year and a half of his
term, Vice-President Elbridge Gerry was stricken with a fatal hemorrhage as he rode in his carriage from the Capitol to his Washington
home. He was seventy years old.

With the death of this "Worthy of the Revolution," the United
States found itself without a vice-president for the second time in less
than three years. James Madison thus became the only president to
lose two successive vice-presidents through natural causes.

Few Americans remember Elbridge Gerry. Neither his service as
vice-president, nor his doubtful opposition to the Constitution ever made
him a household symbol. Not even his participation in the XYZ Affair
elevated him to the American pantheon.

But of all the politicians our country has known, not one can take
credit, as can Elbridge Gerry, for the addition of a new word to the
English language, and, at the same time, for the creation of a time-
honored though questionable political maneuver.

During Gerry's second one-year term as governor of Massachusetts,
there were eleven districts in the state that were largely Federalist.
(While the Federalists had virtually disappeared in the rest of the
country, they remained a potent force in Massachusetts for a number of
years.) In order to insure victory for the Jeffersonian Republicans, it
was necessary to rearrange these Federalist strongholds so that the small
areas where their strength was concentrated would become entire districts. Conversely, the rest of the former districts would be stretched out
into long and grotesque shapes deliberately devised to give the majority
in those areas to numerically inferior Jeffersonians.

This highhanded rearrangement, to satisfy partisan necessities, thus
permitted the Federalists to win only a few small crowded districts,
while the thinly spread out Jeffersonians won the others. In the end, this
practice enabled the Jeffersonian Republicans to take away enough of
the formerly Federalist districts to guarantee continued Jeffersonian
dominance in the state legislature.

Elbridge Gerry's contribution to this device was indirect. The bill
creating these new districts was pushed through the Massachusetts legislature by the Jeffersonian majority and signed by Governor Gerry.
With his signature on that bill, Elbridge Gerry thereby immortalized
himself.

A disgruntled Federalist, viewing a map of the newly designed districts, compared the long and fantastic shape of one of them to a salamander.

"No," replied another disgusted anti-Jeffersonian, "better call it a Gerrymander."

Both the word and the practice took hold, and have since been used with telling effect in many European countries as well as in most parts of the United States.

6th Vice-President Daniel D. Tompkins—Democratic-Republican, New York, 1817–1825 (President James Monroe). Born: June 21, 1774, Fox Meadows, N. Y. Died: June 11, 1825, Tompkinsville, Staten Island, N. Y.

Madmen and Geniuses

Daniel D. Tompkins

The successive losses of two elderly vice-presidents sobered the Democratic-Republicans. For their next choice, a running mate for James Monroe, who had been selected to succeed James Madison, the Jeffersonian Republicans turned to a much younger man, forty-two-year-old Daniel D. Tompkins of New York. Like his predecessors, Tompkins was a professional politician and also a governor. He was elected governor of New York in 1807, when he was thirty-three, and continued to serve in that post until his election as Monroe's vice-president in the winter of 1816.

Elevation of the young and capable Tompkins to the national executive held out hope for a rebirth of the vice-presidency, which had slipped badly under Clinton and Gerry. But Tompkins was to prove more of a disappointment to his friends and colleagues than either of the elderly gentlemen who had preceded him. A man of natural abilities and charm, Tompkins never fulfilled his potential, for he was plagued by a combination of bad luck, a tenacious rival, and poor judgment.

Daniel D. Tompkins was born in the Westchester village of Scarsdale, in 1774. The son of a well-to-do farmer, he received an adequate elementary education, graduated from Columbia College in 1795, and was admitted to the bar in 1797. Exactly seven years later, when he was thirty, he became a justice of the New York State Supreme Court.

Tompkins' rapid rise in the New York hierarchy was indeed impressive. Even his detractors were forced to praise him. A biographer of DeWitt Clinton, for example, grudgingly admitted that Tompkins had a knack "of securing by his affability and amiable address, the good opinion of the female sex, who although possessed of no vote, often exercise a powerful indirect influence."

There is no evidence that Tompkins needed the support of the female sex, but there is ample cause to suspect that he would never have reached the governorship of New York without the sponsorship of DeWitt Clinton and Ambrose Spencer. These two gentlemen, acknowledged leaders of the New York Democratic-Republicans, fully expected Tompkins to bend to their will, as had DeWitt Clinton's aged uncle. But Tompkins refused to submit to the orders or wishes of these political bosses. His independent course infuriated DeWitt Clinton, who, from that time, became an unremitting enemy, although he failed to keep Tompkins from reelection to the New York executive chair.

Tompkins' governorship during the War of 1812 revealed a firm hand and a generous nature, both of which the state and the country desperately needed at that point. The federal government was virtually bankrupt, without funds to advance to the various states for the mustering of troops to defend their borders. Many states refused to use their own money, or to raise any for the national cause. New York, under Governor Tompkins, was a notable exception.

New York's long border with Canada placed that state in a vulnerable and exposed position. To mobilize the needed manpower for a proper defense, Governor Tompkins himself raised an estimated $4 million (at an exceptionally high rate of interest, which everyone was then paying—England had to repay £45 million for a loan of £27 million). The only collateral required of the governor was his word, and no more.

When Tompkins was nominated for the vice-presidency in 1816, his popularity in New York had reached a peak. He had hoped for the presidency itself, but the Democratic-Republican caucus refused to consider him for the top spot because he was little known outside of his own state. He was perfectly acceptable, however, for second in command. He and James Monroe, with 183 electoral votes each out of a total of 217, easily defeated a number of opponents.

The next election, in 1820, was almost a repeat, except that James Monroe received every electoral vote but one out of 232, and Tompkins received 218.

Tompkins' reelection to the vice-presidency was most peculiar. He had spent as little time as possible in Washington, and on the occasions when he did officiate in the Senate, he behaved as if he wanted to be elsewhere. Money problems were beginning to trouble him; he had always lived well beyond his means, often depending upon providence and the generosity of a solvent relative to bail him out temporarily. With his creditors haunting him, and a New York State investigation subjecting him to a public ordeal, Tompkins took to drink.

The investigation by the state of New York had at least been inspired by DeWitt Clinton and his followers, if not actually started by them. In an effort to remove DeWitt Clinton from the governor's chair, which he had occupied since 1817, New York anti-Clintonians had nominated Vice-President Tompkins for the governorship in 1820. As a counter move, the Clintonians brought out into the open a matter that had been quietly simmering behind the scenes—Tompkins' wartime accounts.

Tompkins had made the mistake, during the War of 1812, of not keeping adequate vouchers for the disbursements he had made of the $4 million he had raised for his country and his state. The exigencies of the moment had taken precedence, and Tompkins spent the money without worrying about accountability. With a war on, and most of the governmental machinery in chaos, or nonexistent, Tompkins had no time to worry about vouchers. So the millions poured out, and somehow, it was suggested, his "family finances" had been mixed in with the official funds. As a result, his wartime accounts were $120,000 short.

No one really believed, or so it was originally said, that he had deliberately defrauded the state. If he erred, it was on the side of necessity. In April of 1819, the New York legislature authorized the state comptroller to balance Tompkins's shortage of $120,000 by allowing him a commission of twelve percent on $1 million of the money he had raised, thereby wiping out exactly the amount of the shortage. The matter would have ended there, except that the Vice-President demanded a commission of *twenty-five percent,* meaning the state owed him $130,000 above the $120,000.

Even this might have been resolved in Tompkins's favor, since he had a sizeable segment of support in the Legislature. In fact, a New York Senate committee headed by Martin Van Buren recommended the $120,000 be canceled and Tompkins be paid, as a bonus, $11,780.50. But Tompkins's candidacy for the governorship in opposition to DeWitt Clinton turned out to be a major mistake. The Clintonian controlled New York Assembly rejected the Van Buren recommendation, and instructed the comptroller to sue the Vice-President for any balance due the state.

For Daniel Tompkins, this was a period of agony and defeat. He lost the governorship to Clinton, and the public wrangling by the New York legislature over the monies he owed or did not owe only deepened the presumption of fraud.

He did have one major and surprising success, for in the midst of all this, the Democratic-Republican caucus once more chose him to run for vice-president with President James Monroe. That he stood accused, at least by implication, of a possibly serious crime against his state did not seem to matter to the Democratic-Republicans, nor, as it later developed, to the entire body of electors, for he was reelected almost by acclaim. (Such a forgiving attitude can only be a source of wonder to us today. We have destroyed brilliant careers for far less.)

But reelection to the vice-presidency brought little comfort to Tompkins. He did not bother to come to Washington, or even to take his oath of office there. He stayed in New York, where he was sworn in privately.

By all accounts, the Vice-President had become a drunkard of the worst sort. One letter writer said of him:

"Mr. Tompkins has degenerated into a degraded sot."

Another man wrote of him in early 1822:

"The Vice-President left this city yesterday. I don't think he was perfectly sober during his stay here. He was several times so drunk in the chair that he could with difficulty put the question."

Tompkins spent his few remaining years attempting to clear his name. The New York legislature subsequently passed a bill wiping out its claim against him, and the United States government helped by declaring he was owed certain monies as commissions for his wartime fund raising. But these monies were never paid while he was alive. (By a number of years too late, the state of New York finally decided that it did indeed owe the former governor $92,000.)

Technically, Tompkins's name had been cleared, but life had become more of an unbearable disappointment than ever. His creditors would not let him be, and his usual sources for funds had dried up. To ease the pain and the burden, he drank more heavily than ever. As one biographer noted:

"He began to drink too freely even for those days of deep drink. His eye lost its lustre; deep lines furrowed the round, sunny face; the unruffled temper became irritable."

Tompkins spent almost no time attending to his vice-presidential duties during his second term. He was too ill and too tired, and too drunk most of the time, to stay in Washington. The Senate, at his own request, elected another man in early 1823 as president *pro tempore.* Tompkins never again officiated in that body.

At last, worn out from what he himself characterized as "toilsome days, sleepless nights, anxious cares, domestic bereavements, impaired constitution, debilitated body, unjust abuse and censure, and accumulated pecuniary embarrassments," Tompkins died on June 11, 1825, at the age of fifty-one. The cause of death was never specified, but his heavy drinking had to be a contributing factor.

The story of Daniel D. Tompkins has a fitting epilogue, which took place a few years after he died.

In January of 1817, in one of his last official acts as governor, before he resigned to assume the vice-presidency, Tompkins requested and signed a bill finally abolishing all slavery in the state of New York. The bill was to take effect ten years later.

When a grateful multitude gathered in 1827 finally to celebrate the legal abolishing of slavery in the state, they shouted for a memorial to the man who had been responsible for eliminating this ugliness. What better way to remember him than by the naming of a street or thoroughfare in his honor?

The New York City Board of Aldermen dragged their feet, but by 1833 the demand had become overwhelming. The aldermen did what the public asked and renamed an area on East Seventh Street "Tompkins Square," a name it still retains. The former name of this area had been "Clinton Square."

7th Vice-President   John C. Calhoun—Democratic-Republican, South
Carolina, 1825–1829 (President John Quincy Adams), 1829–1832
(President Andrew Jackson). Born: March 18, 1782, Abbeville District,
S. C. Died: March 31, 1850, Washington, D. C.

Madmen and Geniuses

John C. Calhoun

If Clinton, Gerry and Tompkins represented a low point for the vice-presidency, the next two gentlemen to occupy the office amply illustrated its potential, for they were both in the front rank of America's political leaders. That they were willing to accept the second spot demonstrated the importance they attributed to the vice-presidency; each of them looked upon it as a necessary step to the top. Only one reached the coveted executive chair; the other had to settle for a less exalted place in history.

By 1824, the Federalist party had disappeared from the scene, and with it the rule of the Virginia-New England aristocracy. Of the country's political leaders, only John Quincy Adams retained a philosophical tie with the Founding Fathers; he was nominally a Democratic-Republican, as was everyone else, for that was the only party, but his sympathies and his heritage were unquestionably Federalist.

With expansion of the country beyond the Appalachians, a new breed of frontiersman made his presence known in Washington. One of them was John C. Calhoun of South Carolina. He was no crude, brawling illiterate with a musket and a taste for violence. His family had been among the first settlers in the South Carolina interior; they had accumulated both prestige and property, although they had to do without a formal education. John Calhoun inherited a good name, a slave-owning philosophy, and a fierce loyalty to his fellow planters. As a young congressman during the War of 1812 (he was twenty-nine at his first election), he quickly gained prominence, along with Henry Clay and others, as one of the fiery and impatient War Hawks from the South and West who helped to force the United States into a second round of hostilities against the British.

From Congress, Calhoun went into President Monroe's cabinet as secretary of war. When the jockeying began for the 1824 presidential nominations, Calhoun was one of the more prominent possibilities. But his presidential hopes were shattered when the Pennsylvania caucus gathered in 1824 and chose, instead of Calhoun, the immensely popular hero of the Battle of New Orleans, "Old Hickory," Andrew Jackson.

There then began one of the more curious episodes in our political history. Determined to secure the vice-presidency, now that the presidency itself was temporarily out of his reach, Calhoun courted both major candidates, Andrew Jackson and John Quincy Adams. He offered to support *both* of them for president, provided each supported *him* for vice-president.

Apparently the vice-presidency was of vast unimportance to Jackson and Adams, and although they must have been amused at the spectacle of Calhoun's complicated juggling act, each nevertheless accepted his support in return for their support of his candidacy as vice-president. The result was a runaway victory for Calhoun; he was elected vice-president with a total of 182 electoral votes out of 260, with the balance scattered among five other candidates.

The presidential election of 1824 was not one of our more glorious moments. With four major candidates in the field, Andrew Jackson of Tennessee received the highest popular vote, but he did not have the required majority of the electoral votes. Second behind him, in both popular and electoral votes, was John Quincy Adams of Massachusetts, and badly trailing were William Crawford of Georgia and Henry Clay of Kentucky.

Because no one candidate had received a majority of the electoral votes, the race had to be decided by the House of Representatives. In a maneuver that had the Jackson forces angrily shouting "collusion," Henry Clay threw his support to John Quincy Adams, and the House finally chose Adams to be our sixth president. Whether or not a deal had been made between Adams and Clay was never conclusively proven, but Adams quickly appointed Clay secretary of state.

Calhoun's interest in the vice-presidency was minimal; in his view, it was only a stepping stone to the higher office that he still hoped to achieve. Nevertheless, he did his best to preside over the Senate in a judicious manner; he sat impassively through long-winded debates and tried not to upset the established routine of the senatorial body. He even endured without visible flinching irrational tirades directed against him personally, much like the outburst produced one day by Senator John Randolph of Virginia, who addressed the chair:

"Mr. Vice-President, and would-be Mr. President of the United States, which God in his infinite mercy prevent."

President John Quincy Adams expected his vice-president to be, at the least, neutral if not cooperative. But Calhoun did everything possible, in his limited capacity, to thwart Adams's program. In 1826, animosity between our two chief elected leaders erupted into open warfare, with each attacking the other in his favorite newspaper. But they both took the precaution of hiding behind pseudonyms (a popular journalistic artifice of that day), "Patrick Henry" for the President, and "Onslow" for the Vice-President. Patrick Henry and Onslow hurled a barrage of charges at each other, not the least of which were "despotism" and "anarchy."

When the newspaper feud finally ran its course, Calhoun faced another and potentially more damaging ordeal. He was accused of having illegally profited from the Rip Rap deal, a military contract for stone perches negotiated ten years before while he had been secretary of war in the cabinet of President James Monroe. A new fortification, to be named for Calhoun, was to be built above the Rip Rap Shoal in Hampton Roads, Virginia, where it was necessary to use stone perches to shore up the fort. A contract was negotiated by Calhoun's chief clerk to buy 150,000 perches at $3.00 each. The contractor, as it happened, was the clerk's brother-in-law.

Calhoun's enemies decided, in December of 1826, to go after him by claiming he had participated in profits from the Rip Rap contract. Calhoun immediately demanded that the House of Representatives conduct an investigation into the charges.

"An imperious sense of duty, and a sacred regard to the honor of the station which I occupy, compel me to approach your body," Calhoun wrote to the House leaders.

His request for an investigation was granted. A seven man committee, all but one hostile to Calhoun, was appointed and Calhoun himself took a temporary leave from his duties as presiding officer of the Senate while the investigation was being conducted.

After forty days, the House committee issued a report clearing Calhoun officially of wrongdoing in the Rip Rap matter, yet leaving him, as some of his opponents claimed, "much worse than he was before moving the business." To Calhoun, however, the equivocal verdict of the hostile committee was a clear vindication and he returned to his duties as presiding officer of the Senate.

(In September of 1973, during his tortured campaign to avoid prosecution for his criminal acts, Spiro Agnew tried to keep his own case out of the courts by forcing the House to investigate him. Agnew was aware that a House investigation would take many months, perhaps longer, and he therefore cited the Calhoun matter of 1827 as a precedent.

There were parallels for Agnew to point to, for in each instance each man was sitting as vice-president when the charges were brought against him, and the charges related to matters that had taken place before each had become vice-president. But there the parallels ended, for the charges against Agnew represented felonies, while the only crime that could have been attributed to Calhoun, in the lack of a specific statute covering his case, might have been "misjudgment," hardly an impeachable offense ten years later. In that connection, it should be pointed out that it could never be proven that Calhoun did profit from Rip Rap.

While the House in 1827 acceded to Calhoun's request for an investigation, it rejected a similar request from Agnew in 1973, proving that precedents in politics are not absolute.)

By 1828, when it was time for another presidential election, Calhoun had deserted Adams completely and had joined the Andrew Jackson faction, which now called itself the Democratic Party. In the first election decided entirely by popular vote, Jackson and Calhoun easily defeated the opposing ticket of John Quincy Adams and Richard Rush of Pennsylvania. Adams thus joined his father as the only two presidents who had failed up to that day to win reelection.

Calhoun's tenure as vice-president under Andrew Jackson should have been a time of warm cooperation and understanding, for in some respects the two men were remarkably similar. They were both Southerners, and both were totally dedicated to the welfare of their home states and territories. But they differed in one important area. Jackson was a nationalist; he believed firmly in the Union before individual state. To Calhoun, it was the other way around. He too had been a nationalist in his earlier days, but he had now moved in the direction of states' rights. Inevitably this basic divergence in political philosophy would lead to a head-on clash between president and vice-president, and would help to foil Calhoun's ultimate ambition.

Oddly, it was a woman who started Calhoun's downfall. In January, 1829, three months before Jackson's inauguration, Senator John Eaton of Tennessee, a Jackson friend and protégé, married Peggy O'Neale Timberlake. The young widow Timberlake had a tarnished reputation, much of it due to Senator Eaton himself. Eaton boarded at the O'Neale Tavern; while Mr. Timberlake was away at sea, Eaton and Peggy had a fine time in each other's company. When Timberlake died aboard ship, either of a mysterious malady or by his own hand, Andrew Jackson urged his young friend Eaton to marry Peggy at once. Eaton did, without delay, for Peggy was a handsome and provocative woman.

When President Jackson appointed Eaton to his cabinet as secretary of war, the outcry in Washington social circles was agonized and immediate, particularly from the women. Peggy O'Neale Timberlake Eaton would now have to be accepted as an equal, and that the women would never do, for Peggy had "left her strait and narrow path" too often and indiscriminately. Or so it had been rumored.

President Jackson refused to believe these stories, for he considered Peggy to be "chaste as a virgin." He ordered the wives of his associates to attend Mrs. Eaton as a social equal. One who refused was Floride Calhoun, stubborn wife of the Vice-President. When Calhoun insisted that he could not change his wife's mind (or would not), President Jackson himself called upon the obstinate Floride, who listened politely to his tongue-lashing, and then calmly instructed her butler:

"Show this gentleman to the door."

The affair of Peggy Eaton was the beginning of Jackson's disillusionment with Calhoun. It took other and more powerful forces, most notably the nullification crisis, to provoke a final break between Jackson and Calhoun, but the Peggy Eaton episode and Floride Calhoun's refusal to accept her as a social equal provided the opening wedge that eventually widened into an outright breach between president and vicepresident.

Calhoun had been refining the theory of nullification for a number of years. (The concept had been advanced more than once by Jefferson and others.) Calhoun had long been troubled by the supremacy of the federal government, for he believed it was the natural right of each state to decide for itself what direction it was to take, without interference from Washington. His position, and the position of his home state as well, was made clear in 1828 in a declaration issued by South Carolina during a continuing fight over protective tariffs, which the South firmly believed benefited the North to the injury of the South:

"Whatever is to be done by South Carolina ought to be so done as to impress upon the minds of the Congress of the United States that she does not at this conjuncture approach the national legislature as a suppliant or as a memorialist, but as a sovereign and an equal."

Calhoun was not a secessionist; he did not want to destroy the Union. But to him, South Carolina and the welfare of his fellow planters (he owned a large plantation with many slaves) were all-important. If the federal government instituted legislation inimical to the interests of any state, that state then had the right to nullify these laws and refuse to obey them. In short, the individual state, as a "sovereign body," superseded the authority of the federal government.

This was the heart of the nullification doctrine that Calhoun slowly and carefully nurtured over the years. Although he was careful to point out that nullification did not suspend a law for the entire country, but only for the protesting state, elements of his doctrine spelled treason to many and a desire to destroy the Union.

Calhoun fully expected his fellow Southerner, President Jackson, to subscribe to his views. But Calhoun forgot that Andrew Jackson the President of the United States was a far different man than Andrew Jackson the gentleman planter of Tennessee. Calhoun learned the difference at a Jefferson Day dinner on the night of April 13, 1830.

It had long been rumored that Calhoun was about to declare publicly his support of nullification. Jackson meant to find out if that were so and he meant to do it in a way that would force Calhoun's hand.

The banqueting hall for the Jefferson Day dinner was crowded with Democrats of every persuasion. After twenty-four prepared toasts, President Jackson rose to offer the first of some eighty additional toasts. Looking straight at Calhoun, he said, in a firm voice that carried to every corner of the hushed hall:

"Our Union—it must be preserved."

With that short phrase, he had flung the challenge to his vice-president. All eyes were now on the South Carolinian, who sat pale and motionless. How would he reply? Would he here and now reveal his true feelings at last about nullification, secession, and the republic? Or would he back away?

After a few tense moments, Calhoun raised his glass in response to the President.

"The Union," he said. "Next to our liberties, most dear."

So he had finally committed himself to South Carolina before country. From that moment, he was never again an effective force in the United States executive. The presidency was lost to him forever.

At the end of 1832, South Carolina declared the federal tariff acts to be void and not "binding upon this State or its citizens." Although Calhoun's name was never mentioned in connection with this declaration, without question he was fully in sympathy with it.

Jackson answered in a stern reply that included these words: "If this doctrine had been established at an earlier day the Union would have been dissolved in its infancy." He announced his intention to fight South Carolina with every means at his disposal. A threat to dispatch two hundred thousand volunteer troops to the truculent Southern state brought an end to the short-lived rebellion. South Carolina withdrew its ill-fated declaration and returned to the republican company of states.

Shortly after, exactly nine weeks before his second term as vice-president was to expire, John Calhoun resigned, the only man ever to do so until Spiro Agnew resigned in 1973. Calhoun accepted appointment as senator from South Carolina, and, except for one year as secretary of state in the cabinet of President John Tyler, he served in the United States Senate for the remainder of his life. He continued to hope the presidency might still be his, and at one point attempted to secure the Democratic nomination, but after the nullification crisis he was never again a serious contender.

A brilliant orator and perceptive politician, Calhoun was one of the Senate's outstanding members. During the first half of his career, he wavered between nationalism and sectionalism, but once he left the vice-presidency, he became an outright advocate of slavery and states' rights.

In the light of Calhoun's unswerving dedication to Southern partisanship, which he ultimately made no effort to conceal, and considering Andrew Jackson's precarious health, a question inevitably arises: what kind of president would Calhoun have made?

Not even his most ardent admirers and indefatigable biographers know the answer. The presidency has sometimes had a peculiar and marked effect upon its officeholders. A few presidents surprised their colleagues, opponents, and the country by a sudden broadening of their vision and liberalization of their views, apparently brought on by the office itself. Perhaps the presidency would have done the same to Calhoun. Perhaps not.

    · No one can say for certain what course John C. Calhoun would have taken. But if, as president, he had clung to the sectionalism that marked his career after 1832, we can be sure that the Civil War would have been fought many years earlier.

8th Vice-President   Martin Van Buren—Democrat, New York, 1833–
1837 (President Andrew Jackson). Born: December 5, 1782, Kinderhook, N. Y. Died: July 24, 1862, Kinderhook, N. Y.

Madmen and Geniuses

Martin Van Buren

The collapse of John Calhoun's hopes for the presidency thrust the mantle of succession upon the shoulders of Martin Van Buren. As early as December of 1829, a few months after the Peggy Eaton episode had begun to embroil and titillate most of Washington, President Jackson privately admitted his preference for Van Buren over Calhoun.

As happened frequently during his two terms, Jackson was dangerously ill in the fall and winter of 1829. At the urging of an associate, Jackson wrote a political will in the form of a letter to an old friend, to be used only in the event of Jackson's death.

Jackson's letter said of Van Buren, who was then his secretary of state: "Permit me to say here of Mr. Van Buren that I have found him everything that I could desire him to be, and believe him not only deserving of *my* confidence but the *confidence* of the *Nation*. . . He, my dear friend, is not only well qualified, but desires to fill the highest office in the gift of the people, who in him, will find a true friend and safe repository of their rights and liberty. I wish I could say as much for Mr. Calhoun."

The old warrior's tenacity pulled the President through that illness, and the letter was never made public. But its unmistakable endorsement of Van Buren clearly indicated Jackson's growing disenchantment with Vice-President Calhoun.

Van Buren's emergence as heir apparent to Andrew Jackson was not accidental. He had plotted his rise to the top in a carefully planned and executed campaign. As a youthful lawyer learning the ropes in New

York City, he had early committed himself to a career in politics, with success his only possible goal. Everything Van Buren did was calculated to further his own ends; he was the *compleat* politician, as his colleagues and opponents soon became aware. They described him variously as "The Red Fox of Kinderhook," "The Little Magician," and "The American Talleyrand." He was all of these, yet he was scrupulous. If he manipulated, it was for the furtherance of his career, not to the detriment of his state or country.

Van Buren was born in 1782, in the hamlet of Kinderhook, New York, not far from Albany. After a brief apprenticeship in a Kinderhook law firm, he went to New York to complete his studies. There he allied himself with a recently organized group that called itself "The Tammany Society" (later known by its more familiar name of "Tammany Hall").

From the beginning, Van Buren demonstrated an unerring ability to pick the winning side. He supported the Clintonians when they were on top; when they began to slide, he went over to their enemies. And with every move, he consolidated his own position. In 1808, when he was twenty-five, he was rewarded with his first public office; Governor Daniel Tompkins appointed him surrogate of Columbia County. It was a minor office, but of major significance to Martin Van Buren, for it demonstrated the rewarding possibilities in politics.

Within five years, Van Buren had worked his way into the New York senate, and two years later he added to his growing luster by assuming the attorney generalship of the state. During this period, he had begun to create, along with other New York Democratic-Republicans, a remarkable political organism called the "Albany Regency."

The Albany Regency was a carefully contrived assemblage of state leaders, hack politicians, Van Buren followers, county and local functionaries, and anyone else who might help to consolidate the Van Buren statewide position. One of Van Buren's associates in the creation of this mélange was William L. Marcy, who has one memorable sentiment to his credit: "To the victor belongs the spoils of the enemy!"

With the help of the Regency, which was held together by the dispensing of thousands of political jobs, many of them with nonexistent duties, Van Buren made his first bid for national attention in 1821. The New York state legislature, controlled by Van Buren minions and friends, dutifully appointed him to the United States Senate in place of the incumbent, an able man who deserved reelection. Van Buren served in the Senate for a total of eight years.

His unquestioned leadership in the state of New York helped Van Buren to rise quickly in the Washington hierarchy, despite a listless record as a senator. He dutifully attended Senate sessions, as well as committee meetings, but he did little to enhance his public image as a member of that body. He was content to wield his influence behind the scenes.

As one of the acknowledged powers in the federal capital, Van Buren's support was much sought after, but for a number of years he studiously avoided commitment to any one faction or leader, for he was wise enough to realize that no one man in Washington at that time towered over all others. He was willing to see which way the political winds were blowing before permanently allying himself with a single candidate.

The canny young politician from Kinderhook annoyed President John Quincy Adams; the President preferred more openness than Van Buren was willing to demonstrate. In the eyes of President Adams, the New Yorker was "a combination of talent, of ambition, of political management, and of heartless injustice."

Adams's opposition helped to strengthen Van Buren's growing conviction that Andrew Jackson was a man of destiny, and a man therefore to follow. By 1827, when Van Buren's friends in New York reelected him to a second six-year term as United States senator, Van Buren began openly supporting Jackson, as President Adams grumbled in his diary: "Van Buren is now the great electioneering manager for General Jackson."

In a strictly political move, designed to thwart the remnants of the Clintonian faction in New York State (DeWitt Clinton had died in February of 1828), Van Buren decided to run for governor of New York in the fall election of 1828. He had no intention of serving more than a few weeks, for he expected to be appointed to Jackson's cabinet should Old Hickory win the presidential election that year. Both elections ended in triumph for Van Buren; he was elected govenor of New York, and his man, Andrew Jackson, swept to victory over incumbent President John Quincy Adams.

Van Buren served as governor of New York for exactly two months and three days. On March 4, 1829, he went to Washington to be sworn in as secretary of state in Andrew Jackson's new cabinet.

His status was considerably enhanced by the Peggy Eaton affair, which had begun a few weeks before, and which he knew exactly how to exploit. As a widower with four sons, he had no disapproving female to cluck her dismay. He therefore went out of his way to be courteous to Mrs. Eaton; he included her in social and official functions; and he made no secret of his personal acceptance of her as an important member of the Jackson circle. At no time did Van Buren bring his friendship for Mrs. Eaton to the attention of President Jackson, but it was apparent the crusty old warrior was fully aware of it, and heartily approved.

Martin Van Buren extracted maximum advantage from the affair of Peggy Eaton. By 1831, it was painfully obvious that both Eatons had become a liability to President Jackson, politically and socially, but Jackson was too loyal and too stubborn to remove either of them from the Washington scene. He had backed himself into a corner. Van Buren found an answer for the President.

Van Buren recommended that the entire cabinet, including himself and Secretary of War Eaton, would resign. Such a mass resignation would be a face-saving device for Eaton and the President both. Jackson agreed to this proposal on condition that Van Buren accept appointment as minister to England.

There were those who did not look upon Van Buren's plan as totally unselfish. A newspaperman who had formerly supported him editorialized:

"Well indeed may Mr. Van Buren be called the great magician for he raises his wand and the whole Cabinet vanishes."

The appointment of Van Buren as minister to England was an interim one only, for the Senate was not in session at the time. When the Twenty-second Congress convened in December of 1831, President Jackson sent Van Buren's name to the Senate for confirmation to the ministerial post.

By now Vice-President John Calhoun had become an avowed enemy to Van Buren. The South Carolinian knew that the New Yorker had usurped his place in the Jacksonian scheme of succession, and he used every available device to curb Van Buren's growing influence. He was determined that Van Buren would not be minister to England. He and his associates contrived a tie vote on Van Buren's confirmation; Calhoun, therefore, as president of the Senate, would cast the deciding vote.

When Calhoun descended from his dais to vote an enthusiastic "Nay!" his glee was evident.

"It will kill him dead, sir," he exclaimed, "kill him dead. He will never kick, sir, never kick!"

Not all senators agreed with him. Thomas Hart Benton of Missouri commented acidly: "You may have broken a minister, but you have elected a Vice President."

"Good God!" said the man nearest him, Senator Gabriel Moore of Alabama. "Why didn't you tell me that before I voted?"

Senator Benton's assessment was correct. The Jacksonian Democratic-Republicans (popularly shortened to the "Democratic Party") met in Baltimore in May of 1832 to choose their presidential slate for the coming election. Jackson of course was renominated unanimously. At Jackson's insistence, the convention adopted the two-thirds rule—nomination required two-thirds of the delegates, not just a simple majority. Under this rule, Martin Van Buren easily defeated Calhoun and three others, with a total of 208 votes out of 283.

Van Buren's four years in the vice-presidency illustrated perfectly the political opportunism that infected many holders of that office. With his eye on the presidency, which he knew would be his in 1836 if he did nothing to throw it away as had Calhoun, Van Buren refused to rock the boat. Although he disagreed with some of Jackson's program, he would not so publicly declare. He equivocated on the nullification question. On the one hand he assured Southern Democrats that in his opinion Congress must at all times consider as paramount the rights of a minority group, such as the state of South Carolina; but then, when President Jackson insisted upon his support, the Vice-President managed a lukewarm statement that satisfied Jackson yet did not fully desert the principle of states' rights.

The Bank of the United States was another prime example of Van Buren's fence straddling. Although it seemed a contradiction, the nationalist-minded President Jackson disapproved thoroughly of the federal bank, for he believed that only the individual states could determine where to deposit the monies under their control. Conversely, Van Buren privately supported the federal bank, but again he would not jeopardize his standing with the President, so once more he did as Jackson asked, and publicly acquiesced in Jackson's attacks against the bank.

Nor would Van Buren take a positive stance on slavery. Whatever his personal feelings on the matter, he dared not risk antagonizing his Southern colleagues, for 1836 was fast approaching, and with it the next nominating convention of the Democratic Party. Despite the abolitionists, who were beginning to be heard, Van Buren defended the institution of slavery, and vowed that he would "go into the White House the inflexible and uncompromising opponent" of legislation to abolish slavery in the District of Columbia.

Van Buren's rigid program of satisfying everyone without really antagonizing anybody paid off handsomely, for he won the 1836 Democratic nomination for president on the first ballot, and went on that fall to defeat four sectional candidates offered by the newly organized Whig Party.

Van Buren was not a popular president. He inherited the Panic of 1837 from Jackson, whose fiscal policies and crusade against the Bank of the United States helped to bring on a period of financial uncertainty and misery. The Van Buren administration had no answers, but hoped (as would other administrations in the future) that the problems would go away by themselves.

9th Vice-President   Richard Mentor Johnson—Democrat, Kentucky, 1837–1841 (President Martin Van Buren). Born: October 17, 1780, Floyd's Station, Ky. Died: November 19, 1850, Frankfort, Ky.

Madmen and Geniuses

Richard Mentor Johnson

Andrew Jackson's control of the Democrats was absolute. When he chose Martin Van Buren as his successor, there was little opposition from within his party. Nor was there more than a half-hearted attempt to dissuade Old Hickory from choosing the new vice-president as well.

Jackson's choice of Colonel Richard Mentor Johnson of Kentucky to be Van Buren's running mate was astonishing. Johnson had little to recommend him as a possible president; worse, in his private affairs, which he made no effort to keep from the public, he evidenced a total disregard for propriety.

Fortunately for Colonel Johnson and the Democrats, the anti-Jacksonians, who were just beginning to coalesce as the Whig Party, were not yet strong enough to overcome President Jackson's magnetic appeal to the common man. Jackson's immense popularity spilled over to the benefit of Richard M. Johnson and thereby assured the Kentuckian a tenuous place in American history.

Why had Jackson insisted upon Colonel Johnson? Perhaps because Johnson had long been a loyal Jacksonite, and Andrew Jackson liked to reward his faithful followers, sometimes even to the point of stubbornness. Or perhaps because of Johnson's record as an Indian fighter during the War of 1812. With the sudden emergence of the aging William Henry Harrison as a certified Whig hero and bona fide Indian fighter in his own right, the Democrats needed a counter figure. The wily Jackson found him in Richard Mentor Johnson, who claimed to be the actual slayer of the fierce Indian chief Tecumseh some two decades before.

Despite Johnson's unusual mode of life, which many in the country, particularly in the South, considered outrageous, he fulfilled Jackson's assessment by managing a victory over three other candidates, including John Tyler of Virginia.

Of a total of 294 electoral votes, from 26 states, Richard M. Johnson received 147, far more than his nearest rival but not a majority. Selection of the vice-president devolved therefore upon the United States Senate, the first and only time this ever happened in the country's history. With 49 to 52 senators attending, the Senate voted 33 to 16 in favor of Richard M. Johnson to be the ninth vice-president.

Richard Mentor Johnson's climb to the vice-presidency was slow and steady. The son of a wealthy Kentucky landowner, Johnson had begun his political career in 1804, when he was elected to the Kentucky House of Representatives at the age of twenty-four. Over the next thirty-three years, until his inauguration on March 4, 1837, as Van Buren's vice-president, he served variously in the United States Congress as a representative and senator from the state of Kentucky. He did well enough in both capacities to warrant constant reelection, but it was his role in the War of 1812 and his private life that brought him fame and notoriety on a national level.

During his third term in Congress when he was thirty-two, Johnson gained some renown along with his fellow Kentuckian, Henry Clay, and John Calhoun, as the expansionist "War Hawks" who were insisting upon a second war with England. It was partially through their intense efforts that the United States did at last embark upon the War of 1812.

At about this same time, Johnson's mother reportedly broke up a romance between her son and a poor seamstress. In a fit of pique, Johnson took up with a handsome mulatto slave woman named Julia Chinn, whom he had inherited from his father. He made Miss Chinn his mistress, established her in his home as his wife in fact if not in name, and had two daughters with her, Adaline and Imogene.

Johnson educated the two girls, treated them as if they were his legal children, and expected society in general to accept them as peers. Although outraged neighbors and acquaintances refused to recognize the girls as his daughters, Johnson stubbornly kept them under his roof. Both of the girls were fair-skinned and attractive. When each daughter married a white man, Johnson gave them large tracts of his property for wedding gifts.

Julia Chinn died in 1833 during a cholera epidemic. Johnson later had two other slave women as mistresses, but not with the single-minded intensity he had devoted to Julia.

Johnson's long relationship with Julia Chinn became a short-lived *cause célèbre* in 1835 when Andrew Jackson decided the Kentucky colonel was to be the next vice-president. Some of Jackson's closest aides advised against Johnson because many influential Southerners objected to him; his outlandish and open miscegenation offended them. Editor

Duff Green, a former Jackson supporter who had defected to the opposition, hysterically bleated in his *United States Telegraph* that Johnson had a "connection with a jet-black, thick-lipped, odoriferous negro wench, by whom he has reared a family of children whom he had endeavoured to force upon society as equals."

In the end, southern opposition and Editor Duff Green were not enough. Johnson managed to win the vice-presidency despite the open hatred of many of his fellow landholders.

Vice-President Richard M. Johnson brought no honors to his office. He did no more than was expected of him. At one point in 1839 he took an extended leave so that he could devote his time to the management of a hotel and tavern at White Sulphur Spring, a resort and watering spa he had built on his property. One enthusiastic visitor to the spa reported that he had "found a fashionable company of between 150 and 200 happy mortals, quaffing the water and luxuriating in the shade of the forest trees."

Others were less rhapsodic. One disapproving guest at "Col. Johnson's Watering establishment" wrote to a member of President Van Buren's cabinet that the Vice-President of the United States "seems to enjoy the business of *Tavern-Keeping* . . . even giving his personal superintendance to the chicken and egg purchasing and water-melon selling department."

Nor was that the worst of it. The letter writer mentioned "a young Delilah of about the complection of Shakespeares swarthy Othello," who was said to be Col. Johnson's third "wife."

Still others objected to Johnson's growing carelessness and his messy personal habits. To many, the "old gentleman" (he was then fifty-nine) was becoming too slovenly and ill-kempt.

By 1840, when the Democrats were once again to convene for the purpose of selecting their presidential and vice-presidential candidates, Andrew Jackson had gotten the message. He now insisted that Johnson would become a "dead wait" upon Van Buren's popularity.

"If Col. Johnson is the nominee," Jackson contended, "it will loose the democracy thousands of votes. . . ."

The Democratic convention, meeting in Baltimore in May of 1840, overwhelmingly gave its endorsement to Van Buren to run for reelection, but refused to renominate Johnson for vice-president. Enough individual states, however, did endorse Colonel Johnson so that, in the end, he was once again Van Buren's running mate.

The Whigs, in the meantime, had selected the old Indian fighter, William Henry Harrison of Ohio, to be their presidential candidate, and John Tyler of Virginia to be vice-president.

With the major candidates finally chosen, the election campaign of 1840 swung into high gear. The months that followed featured a frenzied array of campaign songs and sloganeering. "Tippecanoe and Tyler Too!" was shouted from one end of the country to the other.

It was a catchy phrase, constantly reminding the voters that the old soldier, Whig candidate William Henry Harrison, had dealt a decisive defeat to Tecumseh and his people at the Tippecanoe River in Indiana, in November of 1811.

The Democrats were not to be outdone. They had their hero as well, this one an even more genuine article, as they boasted in their own masterpiece of nonsense rhyme:

> Rumpsey dumpsey, Rumpsey dumpsey,
> Colonel Johnson killed Tecumsey.

No one had ever actually witnessed the death of Tecumseh, which supposedly took place at the Battle of the Thames in October of 1813. The Americans, under the command of General William Henry Harrison, had crossed from Fort Detroit into Ontario, Canada, to face an enemy force composed of British soldiers supported by Tecumseh and his Indians.

A regiment of mounted infantry, led by Col. Richard M. Johnson, stormed the Indian ranks. What happened next is described for us by G. P. Quackenbos, Ll. D., in his *Illustrated School History of the United States and the Adjacent Parts of America* (published in 1877):

"Suddenly the fearless Shawnee (Tecumseh) sprang to his feet and sounded the shrill war-whoop. A hundred rifles were aimed at the undaunted Kentuckians as they rode swiftly down, and many a saddle was emptied. Col. Johnson, ever foremost in danger, was wounded, and borne from the field by his milk-white charger, which was itself bleeding profusely.

" 'Leave me,' gasped the fainting hero to the comrades who supported him; 'don't return till you bring me tidings of victory.'

"Just at the critical moment when the Kentuckians reached their foes and the battle raged most fiercely, a bullet, said to have been fired by Col. Johnson himself, struck Tecumseh in the breast. He shouted his last word of command, stepped forward, and then calmly sunk at the foot of an oak and expired."

There were other accounts of the battle that made virtually the same unsupported claim. Supported or not, the Democrats exploited the story to its fullest in 1840.

Unfortunately for Van Buren and Johnson, "Tippecanoe and Tyler Too!" proved more effective than "Rumpsey dumpsey and Tecumsey." Harrison and Tyler easily defeated their Democratic rivals.

For Richard Mentor Johnson, that was the end of his dream, for he had on more than one occasion voiced the opinion that he ought to be president.

He returned to Kentucky, forgotten by the country, but not by his home state; he was elected to the Kentucky House of Representatives for the term of 1841–1842. Two years later he was a badly beaten favorite son candidate for the presidency at the Democratic convention in Baltimore. He then retired to his White Sulphur estate.

In 1850, he once again was elected to the Kentucky House of Representatives, but he was by then much too ill to discharge his duties. A Louisville newspaper reported:

"Col. R. M. Johnson is laboring under an attack of dementia, which renders him totally unfit for business."

Johnson died a short time later of a paralytic stroke, at the age of seventy. Except for two brothers, he had spent the last years of his life alone, as recorded in the Fayette County Order Book, No. 13:

". . . He left no widow, children, father or mother living. . . ."

10th Vice-President John Tyler—Whig, Virginia, 1841 (President William Henry Harrison). Born: March 29, 1790, Charles City County, Va. Died: January 18, 1862, Richmond, Va.

Madmen and Geniuses

John Tyler

The Panic of 1837, which Martin Van Buren and the Democrats were powerless to stop or slow down, gave the rapidly growing Whig Party its first significant opportunity. Hundreds of banks failed, thousands of bankruptcies were recorded, prices rose and wages plummeted. The resultant financial disorder brought unemployment and misery to most of the country.

Van Buren's administration responded to the crisis with a petulant complaint that people were "prone to expect too much from the Government." Little wonder that disaffected voters began shouting:

"Down with Martin Van Ruin!"

The outs at last had a real chance to oust the ins.

To achieve this goal, a crazy quilt amalgam of divergent ideologies convened in Harrisburg, Pennsylvania, in December of 1839 to choose presidential and vice-presidential candidates to oppose the incumbents. The Whig Party was composed of a bewildering array of social and political opposites. Aristocratic descendants of Hamiltonian federalism joined with nullifiers, who in turn linked hands with northern merchants and industrialists, who gladly joined southern plantation owners and states' righters, who in their turn accepted alliance with abolitionists. The only thing they all had in common was a mutual hatred of Andrew Jackson.

To one observer, the Whigs comprised "a discordant combination of the odds and ends of all parties." The president of the Harrisburg convention had a different interpretation, as he proudly proclaimed to the wildly cheering assemblage:

"Lo! the Avalanche of the people is here!"

In one respect, he was right, for the Avalanche swept Van Buren and Richard Mentor Johnson out of office in a vote that was close on the popular side (only 146,000 votes separated the two major parties) but was far more decisive in the electoral count. The Whig candidates, William Henry Harrison of Ohio for president and John Tyler of Virginia for vice-president, amassed 79.60 percent of the electoral votes for a convincing win.

By any criterion, the Whig Party choice of sixty-seven-year-old William Henry Harrison was unfortunate. As one Democrat caustically noted, the only ability the Whigs were looking for in 1840 was "availability." Not much more can be said of Harrison. On the important issues of the day, he was noncommittal, but that's the way the Whigs wanted it. Because of their motley membership, the Whigs could not create a unified policy; they therefore decided on none. Harrison's non-position dismayed them not in the least. But to make certain he did not embarrass them, they muzzled him through the entire campaign and would not permit him to make public statements without prior clearance.

For a counterweight to the rough-hewn, frontier-raised Harrison, the Whigs turned to a man his opposite both geographically and philosophically. They selected, to be Harrison's vice-presidential running mate, the patrician, aristocratic John Tyler of Virginia.

He was, they thought, a perfect choice. Harrison was against slavery (although not rabidly so); John Tyler was for it. Harrison was from the West and the North—Ohio; Tyler, from Virginia, represented the South and the East.

It was a ticket ideally balanced, and became the forerunner of many more presidential slates chosen for the same dubious reason.

An ardent advocate of states' rights, John Tyler began his career as a Jeffersonian before converting to the Whig cause in the 1830s. He had served in politics for more than three decades, since his first election to the Virginia House of Delegates in 1811. From 1827 to 1836 he had been a member of the U. S. Senate. During much of that period, the Jacksonites thought of him as a Democrat, for he frequently hewed to the policies and decisions of the Jackson administration. On some occasions however, particularly when he considered his own convictions to be paramount, Tyler betrayed an independence that should have forewarned the Whigs of possible danger.

In 1834, Senator Tyler voted in favor of a resolution, offered by Henry Clay of Kentucky, to censure President Jackson for his tenacious opposition to the National Bank. Two years later, the Virginia legislature instructed its senators, including John Tyler, to vote in favor of expunging that censure resolution from the Senate *Journal*. Tyler believed these instructions to be "villanous," for he did not think that anything could, or should be expunged from the *Journal*. He therefore resigned from the Senate, in February of 1836, rather than submit to instructions that violated his principles, as he explained in his letter of resignation.

". . . I shall set an example for my children which shall teach them to regard as nothing, place and office, when either is to be attained or held at the sacrifice of honor."

Tyler's resignation, which brought him into conflict with the Jackson forces, was at least partially responsible for his choice by the Whigs four years later to be Harrison's vice-president. His selection was neither unanimous nor universally applauded by his new party, for a number of influential Whigs still believed him to be spiritually, at least, in sympathy with the Democrats.

But misgivings on the part of a few did not matter; in a campaign as colorful and wacky as any the country has ever seen, the Whigs bamboozled the electorate into believing that "Tippecanoe and Tyler too" were not only the men of the hour but the men for the next four years as well.

Unfortunately for the Whigs, their standard bearer served far less than four years. On a cold and stormy Inaugural Day, March 4, 1841, William Henry Harrison, the ninth president of the United States, insisted upon participating in all of the outdoor ceremonies without a hat and coat. He then proceeded to read the longest inaugural address on record—8578 words—one hour and forty-five minutes. Exactly one month later, the sixty-eight-year-old Harrison was dead of pneumonia.

The country was stunned; so were the Whigs. No one had ever dreamed that the President might die, or anticipated the possibility. John Tyler had never been intended as a replacement, as John Quincy Adams gloomily noted in his diary.

Tyler was hastily summoned from his home in Williamsburg, Virginia, where he had spent most of his vice-presidency. On April 9, he made an inaugural speech that set the stage for a bitter controversy. He said the following:

"For the first time in our history the person elected to the Vice-Presidency of the United States . . . has had devolved upon him the Presidential office."

Strict Constitutional constructionists, including John Quincy Adams, refused to accept this view. They argued that Tyler had inherited only its powers and duties, not the office itself. But still others insisted Tyler was correct.

The trouble arose from a vagueness in the wording of the pertinent clause in the Constitution, Article II, Section I: "In Case of the Removal of the President from Office, or of his Death, Resignation, or Inability to discharge the Powers and Duties of the said Office, the Same shall devolve on the Vice President. . ."

What had the framers of the Constitution intended that the word "Same" was to modify? Was it to refer to the "said Office," as Tyler and his supporters contended, or had it been meant to apply only to the "Powers and Duties," as Adams and others insisted?

Tyler frostily stuck to his guns. Any letter that came to him at the White House (where he had moved his family) addressed to "Acting President," or "Vice-President Acting as President," he returned unopened.

The dispute went on for weeks. The matter came to a head finally in June when the House of Representatives sent a message to the Senate bearing a resolution that both houses were "to wait on the President of the United States, and to inform him that a quorum of the two houses is assembled. . ."

A Whig senator from Connecticut moved that a similar Senate resolution be adopted. In a spirited debate, a Democratic senator from Ohio attempted to amend the motion by substituting for the words "the President of the United States," another phrase—"the Vice President, on whom, by the death of the late President, the powers and duties of the office of President have devolved."

But the Democratic move failed, and the original Whig motion was adopted by a comfortable margin. Congress at last had recognized John Tyler as president in fact, not just as acting president. Although John Quincy Adams held out until the end, he too finally gave up, and the most significant principle of presidential succession was thus established. Since that date, seven other vice-presidents succeeded to the presidency upon the death of the president, but never again was the right of the vice-president to assume the presidency challenged.

(In order to clarify the fuzzy wording of the original Article, the Twenty-fifth Amendment to the Constitution, ratified on February 23, 1967, included a section that settled the question once and for all:

"In case of removal of the President from office or of his death or resignation, the Vice President shall become President.")

Tyler had the shortest vice-presidency on record, thirty-one days. His completion of Harrison's presidential term, three years and eleven months, thus comprised the longest single period during which the country had no vice-president.

The Tyler administration was a troubled one. His refusal to knuckle under to the Whig leaders infuriated them. When he vetoed a number of their pet projects, they angrily voted him out of their party, and he thus set another precedent that has never been broken—he became the only president without a party.

Tyler has at least one other accomplishment to his credit that has never been matched by any other chief executive. During his two marriages (his first wife died in 1842 and he married Julia Gardiner, thirty years his junior, a year and a half later), he had a total of fifteen children—eight with his first wife and seven with his second.

When Tyler left the presidency in March of 1845, he was never again a serious contender for a federal office. In 1861, with the country ready to be torn apart, he briefly attempted to stem the onrush of civil war by presiding at a peace conference that was unfortunately doomed from its inception. After its failure, Tyler openly cast his lot with his fellow slaveowners and actively worked for Southern secession. He helped to create the government of the Confederate States, and he was elected to the Confederate House of Representatives as a member from the state of Virginia.

He died a short time later, in January of 1862, at the age of seventy-one. For the first time in its history, the United States federal government ignored the death of a former president. He had become, in the eyes of Washington, a non-person. To the Confederacy, he was a fallen hero; the South gave him a state funeral.

The United States Congress, in 1911, rectified the 1862 slight to the tenth president by authorizing a monument to be erected in his memory. Congress appropriated $10,000 for the memorial, which was dedicated at Hollywood Cemetery, Richmond, Virginia, on October 12, 1915, with five United States senators and five congressmen in attendance.

Officially, John Tyler had become a person again.

11th Vice-President   George Mifflin Dallas—Democrat, Pennsylvania, 1845–1849 (President James Knox Polk). Born: July 10, 1792, Philadelphia, Pa. Died: December 31, 1864, Philadelphia, Pa.

Madmen and Geniuses

George Mifflin Dallas

By late spring of 1844, the Whigs and the Democrats were once again ready to choose their presidential candidates. Incumbent President Tyler had no chance at all of being nominated by the Whigs; they turned to the man they had spurned twice before, the "Great Pacificator," Henry Clay of Kentucky. For his running mate, the Whig convention dutifully followed the geographical principle by selecting Theodore Frelinghuysen of New Jersey for vice-president.

The Democratic frontrunner, Martin Van Buren, in the meantime had weakened his chances by taking an evasive position on the annexation of Texas when popular opinion was for it. And even more unlucky for him was the two-thirds rule that had been created eight years before.

This time, Van Buren had a majority of the Democratic delegates, meeting at Baltimore's Odd Fellows' Hall in May of 1844, but he could not muster the necessary two-thirds. On the ninth ballot, the weary delegates turned to a dark horse, little-known James Knox Polk of Tennessee, who not only favored annexation of Texas, but also had the backing of the elderly and ailing Andrew Jackson, who had finally turned in disappointment from his protégé Van Buren.

On the afternoon of May 29, the third day of the Democratic convention, the delegates cast their eyes northward for their vice-president, as had the Whigs. They chose hard drinking, forty-nine-year-old Senator Silas Wright of New York to be James Polk's running mate.

Out flashed the word over Samuel F. B. Morse's newfangled invention, the "electromagnetic telegraph." Morse and his partners had set up their telegraph between Baltimore and Washington for a test run to report the results of the Democratic convention. One of Morse's partners, Alfred Vail, was on the third floor of the warehouse at Baltimore's Pratt Street railroad depot, while Morse was waiting, with his instruments, in a room below the Senate chamber in Washington.

When Vail flashed the news of Wright's nomination to Morse's room in the Senate Building, word was quickly relayed to Wright, who was then in the Senate Chamber. Senator Wright was furious. If the convention did not want Van Buren, they could not have him. Under no circumstances, Wright insisted, would he "ride behind on the black pony (of slavery) at the funeral procession of his slaughtered friend," Martin Van Buren, to whom he remained fiercely loyal.

Wright instructed Morse to telegraph back to the convention that he refused the nomination. The delegates were startled. Never before had anyone ever rejected an actual nomination for the second highest office in the land. The convention requested him, by telegraph, to reconsider. Back came the same answer, again by telegraph.

The incredulous delegates thought the newfangled telegraph was garbling the message. They could not believe that Wright actually meant no. They immediately sent a committee, by train from Baltimore to Washington, to find out for themselves. Wright finally convinced them that he indeed did not want the vice-presidential nomination. He wrote a formal letter of rejection, which had to de dispatched to Baltimore by horse and wagon since it was now night and trains were no longer running, and the committee did not trust Morse's telegraph.

At seven-thirty the next morning, the delegates reconvened to discover they did not have a vice-presidential candidate, and the job had to be done all over again. With a sparse attendance (many delegates had already gone home, and Ohio, with 23 votes, had only one member left to represent the entire delegation), the convention chose, on the second ballot, fifty-four-year-old George Mifflin Dallas of Pennsylvania.

When election time rolled around some months later, it was apparent Henry Clay's star was beginning to dim. In a close race, James Knox Polk and George Mifflin Dallas defeated their Whig opponents to become, respectively, the eleventh president and the eleventh vice-president of the United States.

Dallas left no spectacular mark in history; he was neither a very good nor a very bad vice-president. On a vice-presidential scale, he would rate somewhere in the middle. But he has not been forgotten by posterity, even though he is unknown to the average American. In 1846, the annexed state of Texas named in his honor both the newly laid out village of Dallas and the county.

Educated as a lawyer, the wealthy Philadelphia born Dallas preferred politics and diplomacy. He served, in 1813, as private secretary to Albert Gallatin, U. S. minister to Russia. Over the next three decades, he was a mayor of Philadelphia, a U. S. district attorney, United States senator, attorney general of Pennsylvania, and then was himself made minister to Russia from 1837 to 1839. He was always considered a power in Pennsylvania politics, but it was his constant misfortune to play second fiddle to his state's number one figure, James Buchanan. Buchanan wanted the presidency; he therefore kept aloof from the office he and so many others considered insignificant—the vice-presidency. For George M. Dallas, who vainly kept his eye on the top spot, the second executive chair would have to do.

In a sense, history regards Dallas as an opportunistic puppet who obediently supported the President regardless of his own views. Dallas often said that it was the duty of the vice-president to cooperate in every way with his chief, for it was the president who created and implemented the country's policy. In short, the vice-president had no right to take an independent position, nor should he.

Yet, as if in contradiction to his compliant behavior, Dallas uttered sentiments that spoke of a loftier view. Of the vice-president, he said: ". . . (He) is the direct agent and representative of the whole people . . . elected by the suffrages of all the twenty-eight States, and bound by his oath and every constitutional obligation, faithfully and fairly to represent, in the execution of his high trust, all the citizens of the Union."

Whatever he may have been, an opportunist, a lackey, or a sincere statesman, Dallas faithfully served President Polk, even to the point of destroying his future chances in his home state. A crucial moment for George M. Dallas came in July of 1846, when the Tariff Act of that year was brought before the Senate for a final showdown vote.

Over the years, the tariff had become a festering and contentious issue between North and South. Originally conceived as a source of revenue for the federal government and later as a means of protecting America's young and struggling industries, the tariff, which imposed duties on foreign imports, seemed more and more to favor the industrial North to the harm of the cotton-growing South. Manufacturers and mercantile interests insisted upon continuing protection, while plantation owners clamored for free trade.

For industrial Pennsylvania, protective duties were a must; George Dallas had been deliberately chosen by the Democrats, in 1844, to calm the apprehensive Pennsylvanians. Polk was a known advocate of free trade; Dallas supported a protective statute. His presence on the ticket helped to win his own state for the Democrats and James Polk.

But the Pennsylvanians were to be abandoned by the man they had helped place in the vice-presidential chair. Reform of the tariff in the direction of freer trade was a continuing goal for President Polk. After much maneuvering and behind-the-scenes politicking, the Tariff Act of 1846 was presented to the Senate for a decisive vote on July 29. As expected, the senators split exactly down the middle, 27 for and 27 against. It was now up to Vice-President Dallas to break the tie.

It was a moment Dallas had dreaded. He did not fully agree with the terms of the Act, but there was more on his mind than the sentiments of his state and duty to his fellow Pennsylvanians. Polk had previously announced he would not run for reelection; with the field thus wide open, Dallas had hopes of winning the next Democratic presidential nomination himself. For that he would need the support of the South and the West.

Both senators from Pennsylvania had voted against the Polk-sponsored measure, but Dallas did not follow their lead, despite his solemn assertion that the bill "deals with some pursuits and resources of my native Commonwealth less kindly than she might well expect."

He voted "aye" and the measure passed, 28 to 27.

The uproar from Pennsylvania was immediate and frenzied. Fearing for the safety of his family, Dallas sent the Senate sergeant-at-arms to Philadelphia with instructions for his wife "to pack up and bring the whole brood to Washington." Newspapers raged against "Pennsylvania's recreant son," and Dallas was hanged in effigy. One editor undoubtedly echoed statewide feeling when he wrote:

"Farewell to all Vice-Presidents from Pennsylvania for the future . . . We have had enough of one to last us while all who live now shall continue to breathe. . ."

His words proved to be strangely prophetic, for never again has a major party's vice-presidential nomination gone to a Pennsylvanian.

George M. Dallas reached his zenith with his one-term vice-presidency. In the Democratic convention of 1848, he received three votes for president on the first ballot, but that was all. He never again held a public office, although he did serve his country once more as minister to Great Britain for five years, from 1856 to 1861. He died in Philadelphia, in December of 1864, at the age of seventy-two.

A eulogy delivered before the Bar of Philadelphia by Charles J. Biddle on February 11, 1865, was frankly laudatory, and may have stretched the truth somewhat, as eulogies of that kind often do. Biddle attempted, at one point, to create the impression that Dallas as vice-president had been a statesman of independent opinion, not as subservient to President Polk as it may have seemed.

Biddle referred to "a strange intrigue" that took place during the Mexican War. President Polk and the Democratic hierarchy, obviously concerned about the tremendous popularity of the two top Whig generals in the field, Winfield Scott and Zachary Taylor (a popularity that increased with each American victory over the Mexicans), searched for a way to get rid of Scott and Taylor. It wouldn't do for either of these Whig generals to steal the limelight from the Democrats in the 1848 presidential election. (That did, of course, happen with Zachary Taylor.)

At the suggestion of Democratic Senator Thomas Hart Benton of Missouri, President Polk recommended a new military rank, that of Lieutenant General, "who should be General in chief" to supersede the Whig commanders in the field, Scott and Taylor. The new civilian commander of the American armies in Mexico would be none other than Senator Benton himself, who had previously served as a lieutenant colonel thirty years before in the War of 1812.

The opposition Whigs immediately set up a howl of protest. The new rank was an "ulterior and covert design" deliberately rigged to boost its holder for the presidency in 1848. Besides, it was unthinkable to bestow the rank of "Lieutenant General" on anyone else when its only previous holder had been George Washington.

Polk's recommendation, passed by the House, was defeated in the Senate. A bitter Benton charged that three members of Polk's cabinet, Secretary of State James Buchanan of Pennsylvania, Secretary of the Treasury Robert James Walker of Mississippi, and Secretary of War William Learned Marcy of New York, had conspired behind the scenes to defeat the President's proposal. Charles Biddle claimed that Vice-President Dallas too had worked against Polk and Benton. Perhaps so, although no one else ever made claim for Dallas. In any event, both Buchanan and Dallas would have had a strong motive for beating back this attempt to place Benton in the front rank of presidential hopefuls, since each of them wanted the presidency for himself.

Whatever the truth of Biddle's statement, Dallas's opposition to the Polk-Benton plan did him no good at all, for the only support he received at the Democratic convention of 1848 came from his home town of Philadelphia.

One phrase in Biddle's eulogy does, however, deserve retelling. He spoke of the vice-presidency as "this high and peculiar position." How right he was.

12th Vice-President Millard Fillmore—Whig, New York, 1849–1850 (President Zachary Taylor). Born: January 7, 1800, Summerhill, Cayuga County, N. Y. Died: March 8, 1874, Buffalo, N. Y.

Madmen and Geniuses

Millard Fillmore

To the outspoken Horace Greeley, the presidential nominations of 1848 were twin disasters. The famed editor of the *New York Tribune* dipped his pen in vitriol when he wrote of the Democratic nominee: ". . . The country doesn't deserve to have as President that pot-bellied, mutton-headed cucumber."

He was slightly less caustic when he attacked the Whig choice as a "journeyman throat-cutter." Greeley was, after all, a Whig; he was expected, as a matter of course, to lend the considerable influence of his newspaper to his party's candidate. But it was not until the end of September, barely a few weeks before the election, that the free-wheeling editor finally suggested to his readers "that, as there was only a choice of evils, they should vote the Whig ticket."

While Greeley's criticisms were extreme, his opposition to both candidates pointed up the unfortunate atmosphere that dominated the two major nominating conventions of 1848. Neither party had learned a lesson from the past.

The Democrats, meeting at Baltimore's Universalist Church toward the end of May, chose the earnest but colorless Lewis Cass of Michigan for their presidential candidate; for his vice-presidential running mate, again they allowed geography to rule by selecting a politically incompetent general from the South, William O. Butler of Kentucky. The best to be said for Butler was that "he looked well on a horse."

Selection of Lewis Cass was to have repercussions the Democrats did not expect, for in the process of nominating him it was necessary to

85

reject once more the bid of former President Martin Van Buren. Dissatisfied Democrats, particularly radicals, reformers, and abolitionists, bolted the regular ranks, organized a splinter party, the Free Soilers, and made their own executive nominations—Martin Van Buren for president and Charles Francis Adams (son of John Quincy Adams) for vice-president.

The Democrats were to regret bitterly both the Free Soilers and the Free Soil presidential ticket.

In the meantime, the Whigs outdid the Democrats in electoral folly. They selected one of the heroes of the Mexican War, "Rough and Ready" General Zachary Taylor. Old Zack had never held an elective office, had never voted, and in fact did not even know his party affiliation. When pressed, he finally supposed he was a Whig, "but not ultra-Whig."

Despite his total lack of qualifications, Taylor easily defeated Henry Clay for the nomination. The eminent Kentuckian thus went down to defeat for the fifth and last time.

Choice of their vice-presidential candidate presented somewhat more of a problem to the Whigs. Altogether fourteen names were placed in nomination, but it was soon evident that Millard Fillmore of New York was the popular favorite.

Fillmore had the necessary requirements; he was from the North, while Taylor, from Louisiana, represented the South. Taylor owned three hundred slaves, and he was therefore presumed to be proslavery, while Fillmore was presumed to be antislavery (as it later turned out, the Whigs were wrong on both counts). Even better, Fillmore was neither brilliant nor forceful, so there was no chance he would overshadow the well-meaning but totally inadequate Zachary Taylor.

With all of this in mind, the Whig delegates stampeded to Fillmore's cause and nominated him on the second ballot.

If the two major conventions produced no particular surprises, the election results the following November most certainly did. Taylor and Cass each won fifteen states; Martin Van Buren and the Free Soil Party won none. But in the pivotal state of New York, which the Democrats would have carried under normal circumstances, Van Buren took enough popular votes away from Cass to give the state's thirty-six electoral votes to Taylor and the Whigs. These thirty-six made the difference, for they gave Taylor a total of 163 to Cass's 127. If Cass had won New York, the result would have been reversed.

To Millard Fillmore, the vice-presidential nomination had been "an honor as unexpected as it was unsolicited." (It could not have been either, for his friends and associates had encouraged him to seek the second chair as early as 1844.) When it was evident in November that he and Taylor had won the election, Fillmore wholeheartedly pledged his support to the old soldier, even though he was forced to admit:

". . . I have never had the honor of taking him by the hand, or of meeting him face to face, but I have studied well his character and I feel, therefore, that I know him well; for it is a character plain and open, to be read by every body and not of that complex nature that deludes and puzzles the observer."

But President Zachary Taylor did not return the compliment. He simply disregarded his Vice-President. Even worse for Fillmore was the President's willingness to permit the patronage prizes of New York State to go to Senator William H. Seward (and through him to the Whig party boss and state leader, Thurlow Weed) rather than to the Vice-President, as Fillmore had come to expect.

The first six months of his vice-presidency could not have brought joy or comfort to Fillmore. The Thirty-first Congress was not yet in session, and would not meet until December. It was a period of frustrating inactivity for the Vice-President, who did not even have the solace of providing cushy sinecures for his grateful supporters. Many of them, disgruntled at his impotence, deserted to the Seward and Weed camp. Nor did it help the Vice-President's reputation and peace of mind to have Thurlow Weed's newspapers chortle:

"We could put up a cow against a Fillmore nominee and defeat him."

When the Senate finally convened on December 3, 1849, it soon became apparent that more important matters than patronage confronted Fillmore. There was agitation, surprisingly encouraged by President Taylor, for the Territory of California to be admitted to the union as a free state.

Angry Southerners rallied to oppose Taylor's recommendations. The South had looked upon him as one of their own. But he refused to follow the script; he was in favor of immediate admission of California as a free state, with no conditions attached.

The aroused South condemned the President's position as a sellout. And one of the critical legislative battles in the country's history began to develop, with the dying Calhoun on one side, Daniel Webster on the other, and Henry Clay in the middle, once more trying to shape a compromise that would temporarily satisfy both factions.

For Millard Fillmore, who could do no more than fidget helplessly in his chair as president of the Senate, the bitter and often acrimonious debate that raged for the first months of 1850 was a spectacle he could watch but not join.

Yet, as the issue approached a showdown, it appeared as if Fillmore might after all play a central role.

A careful head count of pros and cons revealed a possible tie on the measures suggested by Clay. If that were so, the deciding vote would be cast by the Vice-President. Suddenly his views on the entire matter became all important. Antislavery forces were certain he would support their position, but he would not yet commit himself.

Henry Clay's proposed legislation, which came to be known as the Compromise of 1850, contained the following:

Admission of California as a free state; organization of territorial governments in the other areas acquired from Mexico, including New Mexico and Utah, without making mention of slavery (this was intended to appease proslavery elements, who chose to believe that slavery might therefore be possible in these new territories, even though the hot climate and arid soil made it an unlikely prospect); and a new and more stringent fugitive slave act.

President Zachary Taylor did not approve of the Compromise, for he saw no reason to tie the admission of California as a free state, which he supported, to legislation he did not support.

The President had no chance to put his disapproval into effect.

On July 4, 1850, a hot and blistery day in the federal capital, President Taylor endured a grueling afternoon of long-winded tributes to our first President at the dedication of the new Washington Monument. After the endless speeches were finally over, Taylor hurried back to the White House, where he consumed huge quantities of iced milk and cherries, despite the protests of his alarmed physician. That night he was seized with violent cramps, and five days later, at the age of sixty-five, Zachary Taylor, the twelfth president of the United States, died of acute gastroenteritis.

Again, without warning, the country had an accidental president no one had really wanted. Fifty-year-old Millard Fillmore, bland, smooth faced, self-made veteran of New York politics, had reached the top almost through no effort of his own. Within the space of only ten years, the nation suffered four presidents it should never have had—William Henry Harrison, John Tyler, Zachary Taylor, and now Millard Fillmore.

President Fillmore confounded his associates in the North by signing into law the Compromise that his southern predecessor had vowed he would not. With his signature on the omnibus package, including the reprehensible Fugitive Slave Act, Fillmore destroyed any hopes he may still have held for future office.

But Fillmore's acceptance of the Compromise brought an uneasy peace to the country—at least for eleven years. No one can say whether Zachary Taylor might have accomplished the same had he lived.

How had a man like Millard Fillmore, with little to recommend him for one of the important positions in the world, managed to achieve what should have been impossible? How could he have reached the presidency with nothing in his background or training to indicate that he, above all others, was the man for the job?

As happens all too frequently in the often shoddy record of American politics, Fillmore was the lucky beneficiary of fortunate circumstances and political cynicism. He got where he did simply because he was in the right place at the right time.

Self-made and virtually self-educated (with the help of his wife), Fillmore had risen from a life of poverty on a rocky New York farm to prominence and middle class comfort as a Buffalo lawyer, and then as a politician. In 1829, at the age of twenty-nine, he was elected to the New York State Assembly; he later served a number of terms as a congressman. In 1844, he unsuccessfully ran for the governorship of his state.

That should have been the end of his career as a politician. But he once more sought public office, this time successfully, winning the comptrollership of New York in the state election of 1847. It was hardly an office to command national admiration. Yet apparently it was enough for the Whigs, who elevated him the following year to the vice-presidency without a second thought.

Fillmore's two and a half years in the presidency, however, gave the Whigs time to consider their actions. At their convention in June of 1852, they rejected him, after fifty-three ballots and four days, in favor of another military man, General Winfield Scott, Zachary Taylor's commanding officer during the Mexican War.

But Fillmore was not yet licked. In 1856 he tried for the presidency once more, when he joined with the superpatriotic, ultraconservative "Know Nothings" to run as a third party candidate. Surprisingly, he received 875,000 votes, as against 1,838,000 for the winner.

The main thrust of the "Know Nothings," who officially called themselves the American Party, was anti-Catholic and antiforeign. Their platform contained these inflammatory words:

"*Americans must rule* America; and to this end *native-born* citizens should be selected for all state, federal, and municipal offices of government employment, in preference to all others."

That almost a million voters agreed with sentiments such as these is shocking. But fortunately for the nation, the "Know Nothings" quickly disappeared.

Fillmore, who lived another eighteen years, stolidly endured a reputation that was, perhaps, undeserved. He came to be known as our first "doughface" president—an opprobious term to describe a Northern politician with Southern ideas on slavery.

13th Vice-President   William Rufus De Vane King—Democrat, Alabama, 1853 (President Franklin Pierce). Born: April 7, 1786, Sampson County, N. Y. Died: April 18, 1853, Cahaba, Ala.

Madmen and Geniuses

William Rufus De Vane King

For the first third of its existence, the vice-presidency had a spotty record. Both able men and mediocrities filled the chair, usually with indifference or boredom. Intrinsically, the office offered little of value, despite the unexpected ascension of two vice-presidents to the top spot.

There had been those, like the capable Calhoun and the ineffectual Richard Johnson, who had seen the vice-presidency as a necessary stop en route to the White House, but most qualified leaders spurned the position as leading nowhere.

When the second chair was offered to Daniel Webster in 1848, he rejected the prospect with a scathing denunciation that epitomized the general lack of regard for the office.

"No, thank you," he declared, "I do not propose to be buried until I am really dead and in my coffin."

Four years later, James Buchanan was just as emphatic in his refusal to accept the second chair. In a letter to a supporter, written during the Democratic convention of June, 1852, Buchanan said:

". . . I shall not, under any circumstances, consent to the employment of my name in connection with that office. Indeed should I be nominated for it by the convention, *I would most assuredly decline.* It is the very last office under the Government I would desire to hold. . . ."

The scorn that men like Webster and Buchanan held for the second executive chair was reflected in the generally undistinguished parade of party regulars who were placed in nomination during the second half of the nineteenth century. In its first phase, the vice-presidency at least had the distinction of having been served by John Adams, Thomas Jefferson, John C. Calhoun and Martin Van Buren. It was not to be so fortunate again for decades.

By the time the two major parties were ready to convene in 1852 to choose their new presidential tickets, it was evident that the coming campaign would be fought on the basis of personalities, not partisan platform or national issues. The Compromise of 1850 had brought a shaky stability to the country. For the moment, the potentially explosive issue of slavery was quiescent. The Whigs and the Democrats both were content to leave the question where it was—simmering beneath the surface; they preferred not to rock the boat.

Both parties held their conventions at the Maryland Institute Hall in Baltimore, with the Democrats meeting first, from June 1 to June 5. The Democrats had a number of contenders for the top spot—Lewis Cass of Michigan, trying once again, James Buchanan of Pennsylvania, William Learned Marcy of New York, and the magnetic "Little Giant" of Illinois, thirty-nine-year-old Stephen A. Douglas. After a few ballots, it was evident that none of these four could muster the necessary two-thirds majority.

On the thirty-fifth ballot, a new name was injected into the voting— forty-seven-year-old Franklin Pierce of New Hampshire. Little attention was paid to him until the forty-sixth ballot when a few more delegates swung over to the comparatively unknown politician from New England.

By the forty-ninth ballot, it was all over; with a sudden bandwagon surge, the Democrats chose Franklin Pierce to be their presidential candidate with a final tally of 283 votes out of a total of 289.

For the second time in eight years, the Democrats had chosen a dark horse—a strange and unusual selection, for Pierce was little known to the country at large. But that's the way the Democrats wanted it; his unfamiliarity to the electorate was an asset, they believed, and strength rather than weakness.

Pierce had no record to explain, and therefore no unpopular positions to defend. For 1852, a time of noncommittal caution, he was the perfect candidate. (He had one serious flaw, however; he was close to being an alcoholic. During the campaign, the opposition called him "a hero of many a well-fought bottle.")

The Democrats' vice-presidential choice was even more remarkable. Because their number one candidate was from the North, they looked to the South for their number two man, and chose the proslavery Senator William Rufus De Vane King, from the cotton-rich, slave-supported Black Belt of Alabama. Except for this geographical and philosophical consideration, and a lengthy experience as presiding officer of the Senate, King had no real qualifications as a potential president.

The selection of King set a standard for the middle phase of the vice-presidency, and represented the universal indifference of party leaders to the office. There had long been whispers about his personal life that should have left him far more vulnerable to attack than Richard Mentor Johnson had ever been.

A more serious mark against him, which the Democratic delegates cheerfully overlooked, was the state of his health, for King was ill with tuberculosis and obviously dying. But neither his age nor his health nor rumors from the past seemed to matter. It took the convention only two ballots to nominate the sixty-six-year-old Alabamian for vice-president.

On the other side, later that month, the Whigs made their last hopeless reach for the White House by nominating for the presidency their third general, "Old Fuss and Feathers" Winfield Scott. His decisive defeat that November led to the collapse of the Whig party.

A wealthy planter, William Rufus De Vane King came to politics at an early age. He was elected to Congress in 1810, when he was twenty-four, and began a long career as a United States senator in 1819.

King never married. For many years, he and James Buchanan were inseparable companions. They met when Buchanan was himself elected to the Senate in 1834.

(In the same year that King first entered the United States Senate, Buchanan's beautiful and wealthy fiancee died suddenly—her friends were convinced she had committed suicide because of Buchanan. The truth of the incident was never revealed, for Buchanan's private papers relating to the matter were burned unopened shortly after his death in 1868, at his specific instructions.

After his fiancée died, Buchanan's name was never again seriously linked with another woman. When he served in the White House, from 1857 to 1861, as the country's first bachelor president, his niece, Harriet Lane, acted as his official hostess. It should be added that William Rufus De Vane King also used a young niece as his hostess.)

Whatever the extent of the relationship between King and Buchanan may have been, there were many in Washington who believed the worst. A biographer of James Knox Polk noted that King's "fastidious habits and conspicuous intimacy with the bachelor Buchanan gave rise to some cruel gibes" in the federal capital. Andrew Jackson had dubbed the prissy senator "Miss Nancy"; to John Quincy Adams the unmarried Alabamian was "a gentle slave-monger."

Aaron Brown, a prominent Tennessee Democrat, had even more positive opinions of King and Buchanan, for he referred to King as Buchanan's "better half," and described the Alabama senator as "*Aunt Fancy* . . . triged out in her best clothes. . .".

In 1844, President Tyler appointed William R. King United States minister to France. Shortly before he sailed for Europe, King wrote to Buchanan:

"I am selfish enough to hope you will not be able to procure an as-

sociate who will cause you to feel no regret at our separation. For myself,
I shall feel lonely in the midst of Paris, for there I shall have no Friend
with whom I can commune as with my own thoughts."

He came back to the United States in 1846, and returned to the
Senate in 1848. When Vice-President Fillmore succeeded to the presidency upon the death of Zachary Taylor in 1850, King was elected
president *pro tem* of the Senate. He was a logical choice for the job, since
he had served in a similar capacity at various times through four other
administrations.

After his nomination by the Democrats in 1852, Senator King
neither campaigned for the vice-presidency nor served in the office. By
then he was much too ill, and lacked both the well-being and the stamina
for the rigors of stumping and speechmaking.

His rapidly declining health, however, did not deter the electorate
from voting for him. The final results of the November election gave the
Democratic ticket of Franklin Pierce and William Rufus De Vane King
a resounding triumph, with 85.81 percent of the electoral vote.

The people had chosen an alcoholic and a dying man.

Vice-President King never made it to Washington for his inauguration. In a futile attempt to regain his strength, he had gone to the more
temperate and soothing climate of Cuba. By March of 1853, when he
should have been in the federal capital, he was too ill to travel. A special
act of Congress permitted him to take the oath of office in Havana. He
was the first and only executive officer of the country to take the oath in
a foreign country.

It was a strange background for the inauguration of the thirteenth
vice-president. Inaugural day in Washington was raw and cold with a
blustery northeast wind blowing over the federal capital. The new Vice-
President had a much more exotic setting, as a witness described it:

". . . The clear sky of the tropics over our heads, the emerald carpet
of Cuba beneath our feet, and the delicious sea breeze of these latitudes
sprinkling its coolness all over us."

When King realized he had little time left to live, he was determined that he would die at home in his native land. A vessel of the
U. S. Navy, the steamer *Fulton*, was dispatched to Cuba to return him
to the United States.

After a voyage of some five hundred miles through the Gulf of
Mexico, King arrived in Mobile, Alabama on April 11. While the *Fulton*
remained at anchorage, the Vice-President was put ashore at Government Street Wharf with "an immense assemblage of citizens" awaiting
him (as reported by the Mobile *Register*).

But there was no demonstration from the crowd. Perhaps the "feeble and attenuated" Vice-President thought of himself as a triumphant
statesman returning to well-deserved plaudits, for he glanced around as
though expecting a chorus of huzzahs. To the muted onlookers, however,
this was no moment for cheering, for it was apparent to all that the Vice-
President, "thus enfeebled by the heavy hand of disease, thus stricken

by the arrows of sickness," was a dying man. The crowd could only watch in sad and respectful silence as King was supported into a waiting carriage by two officers of the *Fulton*.

King remained in Mobile long enough to regain some strength for the return to his plantation, one hundred and twenty miles to the north and six miles east of Cahaba. He arrived at "King's Bend" on Sunday, April 17, 1853, and died the following day at the age of sixty-seven.

Vice-President King had filled his office for exactly six weeks. His death once again left the vice-presidency vacant for almost an entire term. Within a space of sixteen years, William Henry Harrison through Franklin Pierce, the second chair was occupied only for a total of five years, nine months, and two weeks, leaving it vacant for more than ten years.

In all that time, no one seemed to care.

Of all the inglorious and unknown vice-presidents, the thirteenth must surely lead the list. William Rufus De Vane King must be, by all odds, the least remembered man in American history, and the most neglected. He had been a senator for twenty-nine years, and, according to contemporary reports, had some influence in Washington. An editorial in one metropolitan newspaper attempted to summarize the life and character of the departed Vice-President with these obligatory words of praise:

"(He was) warmly esteemed in the Senate, because of his sterling personal worth and fine amenity of manner, and kindness of heart."

But not even his former colleagues in the Senate could find anything else in his career to eulogize except for the length of his service in that body.

14th Vice-President   John Cabell Breckenridge—Democrat, Kentucky, 1857–1861 (President James Buchanan). Born: January 21, 1821, Lexington, Ky. Died: May 17, 1875, Lexington, Ky.

Madmen and Geniuses

John Cabell Breckenbridge

The years immediately following the Compromise of 1850 were peaceful only by definition. The Fugitive Slave Act was constantly defied by protesting abolitionists. Antislavery anger, never far from the surface, erupted without provocation. In 1852 it was fanned to a feverish pitch by a novel that sold more than 300,000 copies within a few months of its publication.

Uncle Tom's Cabin, written by Harriet Beecher Stowe, a minister's daughter, gave a picture of wickedness and immorality in the slave-owning South that horrified millions of people. Many of her readers must have shuddered with tangible dread at the cataclysmic prophecy that ended her book:

"This is an age of the world when nations are trembling and convulsed. A mighty influence is abroad, surging and heaving the world, as with an earthquake. And is America safe: Every nation that carries in its bosom great and unredressed injustice has in it the elements of this last convulsion."

Indeed it was a troubled time for the United States. The country needed a leader of the broadest vision and the most temperate yet daring wisdom. It got, instead, Franklin Pierce. His administration accomplished nothing except to aggravate an irritation that needed no more flaying or wounding.

The nervous concord that had evolved out of the Compromise of 1850 was shattered by the Kansas-Nebraska Act of 1854. It was legislation ill-conceived, and in the end, disastrous for the entire nation, although it brought delight to the South. It enraged the North, destroyed the Whig Party, split the Democrats, led to the organization of the new Republican Party, and finally, seven years later, to the Civil War itself.

In a way, the Kansas-Nebraska Act was inevitable, for it was inspired by the mushrooming settlement of western lands. Proslavery people, handcuffed by the Missouri Compromise of 1820, which restricted slavery only to those areas below the line of 36° 30' (roughly bisecting the country from east to west beyond the slave state of Missouri), saw in the new frontiers an opportunity to extend their "peculiar institution" northward.

Under the Kansas-Nebraska Act, which repealed the Missouri Compromise of 1820, the *people* in these two newly organized territories would decide whether they wanted slavery; under the old legislation, only the *Congress* could so decide. When the Kansas-Nebraska Act was voted into law on March 4, 1854, popular sovereignty was born. The senator from Georgia exulted:

"We have relumed the torch of Liberty on the altar of slavery!"

President Pierce wasted no time in signing the Act. Nor did he delay in recognizing a proslavery government that set itself up in Kansas, while declaring an opposition, antislavery government illegal. Kansas became a battleground; thousands for and thousands against poured into the new territory. There was fighting, and burning, and looting. Hundreds of men, women, and children were shot, or stabbed to death, or lost their lives by fire.

"Bleeding Kansas" became a symbol of the country's divisiveness. By June of 1856, when it was once again time for the national conventions to choose their presidential candidates, it was clear that anyone connected with the passage of the Kansas-Nebraska Act could never hope to win. The Whig Party had dissolved and by the end of 1854 its antislavery remnants began to form the emerging Republican Party. Within two years they were strong enough to hold their own convention and to nominate their own candidate for president, the California "Pathfinder," John Charles Frémont.

Through a queer twist of fate, the Democrats had one man who could not be tied to the Kansas-Nebraska Act, since he happened to be serving in England at the time of its passage, as United States minister. James Buchanan of Pennsylvania was therefore untouched. The Democrats nominated him on the seventeenth ballot, over their incumbent President, Franklin Pierce, and Stephen Douglas.

For vice-president, the Democrats chose thirty-five-year-old John Cabell Breckenridge of Kentucky; his choice was both regional and therapeutic, an effort to appease the disappointed Southern followers of Stephen Douglas.

Finally, the superpatriotic, ultraconservative "Know Nothings" threw former President Millard Fillmore into the race.

Out of 4,000,000 votes cast, the victorious Democrats, Buchanan and Breckenridge, received only 1,838,000—less than a majority—but they had enough electoral votes, 58.79 percent, to win the election.

The new vice-president, John Cabell Breckenridge, at thirty-six the youngest man ever to serve in that office, had a curious ideology. On the one hand he insisted he would always yield to established law, and he expressed the fervent hope that his home state of Kentucky would "cling to the Constitution while a shred of it remains. . . ." But he could then declare, as passionately:

"The Constitution and the equality of the States! These are the symbols of everlasting Union. Let these be the rallying cries of the people."

He was, in short, a zealous states' righter. Like his president, he was the wrong man at the wrong time. But John Cabell Breckenridge was a far more colorful man than his immediate predecessor, William Rufus De Vane King; his career was filled with adventures and miscalculations that placed him in a class with Aaron Burr. He deserves to be remembered for that alone.

A tall, well-formed gentleman with a square face and aggressive jaw, John Cabell Breckenridge exuded a supreme confidence that spoke of inevitable success. Even as a young lawyer practicing in Lexington, Kentucky, he carried himself with an air of assurance that impressed enemies and admirers alike. By the age of twenty-eight, he was serving in the Kentucky State House of Representatives. Although a Democrat, he had won his seat in a district controlled by the Whigs. Henry Clay, on the opposite side of the political fence, openly admired this young man who defended slavery where it existed while maintaining that it should not be extended elsewhere.

In 1851, enough respectful Whigs joined with Democrats to help Breckenridge win election to Congress. Five years later, he headed the Kentucky delegation to the Democratic convention, and placed in nomination for vice-president Linn Boyd, a favorite son of his state. Instead, the convention chose him.

Breckenridge's presence on the Democratic ticket undoubtedly helped win the election of 1856 for James Buchanan. Much of the country feared the strong antislavery position taken by the Republicans, and preferred instead the more conciliatory attitude of the Democrats. The nation was not quite ready for Frémont or Abraham Lincoln.

John Cabell Breckenridge's vice-presidential term was neither more nor less spectacular than many others of the nineteenth century. He presided over Senate sessions with impartiality and patience, and accepted without public dissent the legislative matters and constitutional questions that were being decided by others. As he told the legislature in his home state of Kentucky:

"Gentlemen, I bow to the decision of the Supreme Court of the United States upon every question within its proper jurisdiction, whether it corresponds with my private opinion or not; only I bow a trifle lower when it happens to do so. . . ."

In the four years that Breckenridge served as the second highest elected officer of his country, the nation seethed with wild talk for or against secession. The inevitable conflict was rapidly approaching.

The Vice-President expressed the fervent hope that the Union might be preserved, but he did nothing to prevent the breakup of the country, for he considered secession to be constitutional and proper. Stephen A. Douglas assessed the Vice-President's views with derisive accuracy:

"Breckenridge may not be for disunion, but all the disunionists are for Breckenridge."

In 1860, Breckenridge was nominated as the presidential candidate of the Southern wing of the Democratic Party, while the Northern Democrats selected Senator Douglas of Illinois. The Republicans, in their second try for national office, had earlier chosen Abraham Lincoln as their standard bearer. As a further complication, former Whigs and other conservatives calling themselves the Constitutional Union Party nominated John Bell of Tennessee.

The result of this calamitous split amongst the Democrats plus the appearance of a fourth party was a minority victory for Abraham Lincoln and the Republicans.

At the end of his term as vice-president, in March of 1861, Breckenridge began serving as United States senator from Kentucky. When the Civil War started only a few weeks later, Kentucky did not secede, as Breckenridge had expected. Despite intense antagonism from his Northern colleagues, Breckenridge used his senatorial forum to condemn President Lincoln and to defend the principle of separation.

In September, the armies of the North and South invaded Kentucky. The more numerous Union forces won control of the state. For Breckenridge, the time of fateful decision had arrived, and he finally fled to the Confederacy.

The federal government immediately indicted him for treason, since he had gone over to the rebel side from a state that had not seceded. John Cabell Breckenridge thus gained for himself the unhappy distinction of joining the luckless Aaron Burr as one of two vice-presidents to be charged as traitors.

Jefferson Davis and the Confederacy received him gratefully. For three years, Breckenridge fought in the Southern army, rising to the rank of major general. In February of 1865, Jefferson Davis, president of the Confederate States, named Breckenridge his secretary of war.

When the war ended, after the surrender of Robert E. Lee at Appomattox in April of 1865, Breckenridge and others made a desperate attempt to escape capture by the Federal troops. Of the entire Confederacy, he was the most vulnerable, for he was still under indictment as a traitor.

For more than two months, Breckenridge and his little band played a terror-filled game of hide and seek with government forces. Through backroads and wilderness, travelling by night, they made their way across southeast Georgia into Florida, down the coast, and across the ocean to Cuba.

As Breckenridge later described his flight, he had endured "adventures which may be termed both singular and perilous."

For almost four years after that, Breckenridge wandered through England and Canada (where his wife and family joined him), back to England, across Europe and the Middle East. All this time English admirers and more prosperous Southern expatriates supported him, while he waited for the charge of treason against him to be lifted.

On Christmas, 1868, President Andrew Johnson issued a General Amnesty Proclamation, and Breckenridge's long years of exile were over. He returned to Kentucky in March of 1869, to find tumultuous crowds cheering him all along the way. As one historian succinctly stated it, Kentucky waited until the end of the war to secede.

Breckenridge did not again seek public office, but instead devoted himself to the practice of law and to his private affairs. On May 17, 1875, he died in Lexington, at the age of fifty-four, after two unsuccessful operations for a liver ailment.

In its obituary, the *New York Times* wrote:

"The General, in his last hours, awaited death with wonderful composure, passing away quietly and peacefully."

Among the many eulogists, one speaker said:

"Kentucky could but mourn her loss and teach her sons to imitate his virtues."

But it was not until January, 1958, that the stigma that had hung over Breckenridge's final years was wiped away. A Kentucky Circuit Court judge dismissed, at long last, an 1862 indictment for "treason and conspiracy" against John Cabell Breckenridge and other Kentuckians.

15th Vice-President Hannibal Hamlin—Republican, Maine, 1861–1865 (President Abraham Lincoln). Born: August 27, 1809, Paris, Me. Died: July 4, 1891, Bangor, Me.

Madmen and Geniuses

Hannibal Hamlin

Within a space of two years, Abraham Lincoln became a national figure. During the 1858 senatorial contest in Illinois, he engaged in a series of debates on the slavery issue with his opponent, Stephen A. Douglas. Quotes from both men were widely printed throughout the country and aroused controversy and enthusiasm on both sides.

Lincoln suddenly found himself in demand as a speaker. In February of 1860, he was invited to address the Young Men's Central Republican Union at New York's Cooper Institute. It was this speech that launched him as a serious contender for the presidency.

Many of his words were pointed to the South. His tone was neither accusatory nor vindictive; he was simply asking for understanding and patience. But he warned that the Republican Party would not swerve from its principles:

"Wrong as we think slavery is, we can yet afford to let it alone where it is . . . but can we, while our votes will prevent it, allow it to spread into the national Territories, and to overrun us here in the free States? If our sense of duty forbids this, then let us stand by our duty, fearlessly and effectively. . . . Let us have faith that right makes right, and in that faith let us to the end dare to do our duty as we understand it."

Republican newspapers reprinted his speech with high praise; Horace Greeley of the New York *Tribune* was especially enthusiastic. Both the speech and the resultant publicity helped to nominate Lincoln for the presidency when the Republicans held their second national

103

convention in Chicago three months later. Lincoln's principal rival for the nomination was Senator William H. Seward of New York; it took only three ballots for Lincoln to defeat him.

Nomination of the Republicans' vice-presidential candidate consumed one ballot less. Popular choice of the rank and file delegates for vice-president was Cassius M. Clay of Kentucky.

But the party leaders were not disposed to allow the rank and file any real voice in the selection of the second man. (The same kind of cynical high-handedness was to be repeated in later conventions.) Besides, the Sewardites, angry at the defeat of their man for first place, had to be appeased. A New Englander was therefore the obvious choice for the vice-presidency.

The bosses had their eye on a party loyalist, a man acceptable to Seward, and a man who unflinchingly believed that duty to party transcended all other considerations. This faithful regular was Senator Hannibal Hamlin of Maine, a fifty-one-year-old professional politician whose complexion was swarthy enough to invite suspicion of his ancestry. His other particularities, however, were entirely proper. As one observer pointed out, Hamlin was "the exact complement of the ticket headed by Mr. Lincoln, in respect to locality, political antecedents, and manifest fitness for the office."

Geographically, Hamlin was indeed ideal, for the Republicans had to write off the South, and a Southern man would not have helped at all. A vice-presidential candidate from Maine was therefore a perfect balance for the presidential candidate from Illinois. Politically, Hamlin was a former Democrat who had defected to the Republicans (but it should be added, only when it was right for his career and not before).

Then what of Hamlin's "manifest fitness for the office"? In a sense, he was even more qualified for the executive chair than Lincoln, for Hamlin had a long history of legislative and executive experience, both in Washington and his home state, while Lincoln could boast only of one term as a congressman and no executive experience whatsoever. At least one Republican leader, however, had misgivings about the politician from Maine, as he noted in his diary the day after the convention:

"Mr. Hamlin is not the right person."

(Three years later, the editor of the Cincinnati *Commercial* put it far more harshly, in an angry letter he wrote to a member of Lincoln's cabinet:

"I do not speak wantonly when I say there are persons who feel that it was doing God's service to kill [President Lincoln], if it were not feared that Hamlin is a bigger fool than he is.")

Hamlin's nomination for the vice-presidency on the second ballot involved him in little obligation for extensive campaigning. Beyond a few speeches in his native state of Maine, he did no electioneering whatsoever, remaining, for the most part, silent and unavailable, as did Lincoln.

Others were both vocal and vituperative. Embittered Southerners, who despised Hamlin for his antislavery inflexibility, attacked him on any grounds they could find. An editor from South Carolina chose Hamlin's dark complexion as a point of vulnerability. The "Black Republicans," he thundered, "(have put) a renegade Southron on one side for President, for Lincoln is a native Kentuckian, and they put a man of colored blood on the other side of the ticket for Vice-President of the United States."

The divided Democrats assaulted and accused, but they could not win. When all the votes were finally counted, Abraham Lincoln had eked out a minority victory to become the sixteenth president of the United States, and Hannibal Hamlin of Maine was the fifteenth vice-president.

Hamlin's family were among the first settlers in the District of Maine, before it had become a state. His father was a successful doctor specializing in children's diseases, and doubling as a farmer, town clerk and county sheriff. Hannibal Hamlin, born in August, 1809, was himself a farmer and during the rare occasions when he was out of public office, he worked in his fields.

After admission to the bar in 1833, Hamlin turned his entire attention to politics. In 1836, at the age of twenty-seven, he won election to the Maine House of Representatives as a Democrat, and over the next twenty-four years served as a congressman, a senator, governor of Maine, and finally, in 1857, once again as United States senator.

He was happiest in the Senate, for it was there that he had power, especially the power of dispensing patronage. He frequently spent more time in the distribution of spoils and attending to the demands of thousands of hungry job-seekers than taking care of his senatorial duties. In his view, the system of spoils was correct and justifiable, and a natural outgrowth of American politics. For Hamlin the dispensing of jobs was not only a means to an end, but often the end itself.

Hannibal Hamlin was reelected to the United States Senate in 1857, this time as a Republican. His election to the vice-presidency three years later removed him from an office he enjoyed to one he did not, for he knew that as vice-president he would have little patronage at his disposal.

Although Hamlin had earlier admitted, in a letter to his wife, that the duties of the vice-presidency "will not be hard or unpleasant," he presided for exactly two and a half weeks after his inauguration. Then, "in conformity with established usage," he requested the Senate to choose a president *pro tempore* so that he could return to Maine.

Hamlin repeated this pattern consistently throughout the next four years. He would come back to Washington to preside at the opening of a new Senate session, only to leave well before the session officially ended. He considered himself "the most unimportant man in Washington, ignored by the President, the Cabinet, and Congress."

But Vice-President Hamlin has two conspicuous actions to his credit: (1) he banned the sale of liquor in the Senate chambers and thus exposed himself to the wrath and indignation of every hard-drinking senator, which meant most of them; and (2) in the summer of 1864, at the age of fifty-five, he enlisted as a private in Company A of the Maine Coast Guards, and during his sixty days service he stood guard duty and worked as a cook. (He was the highest elected official ever to serve in so low a military capacity while in office).

Despite the assertion of Hamlin's first biographer, his grandson Charles Eugene Hamlin, that Lincoln wanted Hamlin to be renominated for vice-president in 1864, there is evidence that indicates otherwise. Lincoln was a political realist; he was well aware that Hamlin had done nothing to enhance his prestige during his vice-presidency. (Much of this was due to Lincoln himself, who gave Hamlin nothing to do at a time of great emergency when the beleagured President should have been delighted to have anyone's help.)

Lincoln was concerned about his own chances for reelection. New England, with or without Hamlin on the ticket, was safely his. But Lincoln and the Republicans needed someone to help win the doubtful states; therefore a War Democrat (one who had remained loyal to the Union—a Southerner if possible) was his choice. The man settled on was Andrew Johnson of Tennessee.

(The post was first offered to the aggressively cocky Major General Benjamin F. Butler, who turned down the suggestion with these words:

"Ask him what he thinks I have done to deserve the punishment, at forty-six years of age, of being made to sit as presiding officer over the Senate, to listen to debates, more or less stupid, in which I can take no part nor say a word.")

Hamlin was shocked by the results of the Republicans' 1864 convention. Lincoln of course won renomination easily, as expected. The vice-presidential balloting, however, did not work out as Hamlin had hoped. His own solid New England deserted him; at the end of the first ballot Andrew Johnson had 200 votes, and Hamlin 150.

Before a second roll could be called, state after state stampeded to Johnson. Even Hamlin's own state of Maine changed its entire vote to Johnson. Hamlin did not then know, and only learned many years later, that his president had actively worked behind the scenes to depose him.

In 1868 Hamlin won his second reelection to the Senate and served as a senator for twelve more years, through the administrations of Ulysses S. Grant and Rutherford B. Hayes.

By 1881, Hamlin had had enough of the political struggle, and finally retired at the age of seventy-two, after having served his state and his country over a period of forty-five years. But he was not quite through with the government. He wangled an appointment as United States Minister to Spain.

He had always wanted to travel through Europe, but had considered himself too poor to do so, even though he was worth $148,000 at his retirement. An old hand at making the most of governmental largesse, Hamlin spent most of his eighteen-month ministerial appointment happily jaunting with his wife from one European country to another, all the while allowing his government to foot the bills. He did manage to get to Madrid from time to time to meet the King and Queen of Spain and to administer to his token duties.

He returned to the United States at the end of 1882, and spent nine quiet years farming, fishing, and reading. He died on July 4, 1891, of heart trouble and dyspepsia. He was seven weeks short of his eighty-second birthday.

16th Vice-President   Andrew Johnson—Democrat, Tennessee, 1865
(President Abraham Lincoln). Born: December 29, 1808, Raleigh,
N. C. Died: July 31, 1875, Carter's Station, Tenn.

Madmen and Geniuses

Andrew Johnson

Abraham Lincoln had once said that "only events can make a president." He might have added that often it is time alone that recognizes greatness. There were many in his day who thought of Lincoln as a failure. His fellow Republican, Senator Charles Sumner of Massachusetts, was deeply disappointed in the President:

"How vain to have the power of a god," said Sumner, "and not use it godlike."

Even the Gettysburg Address, a moving and memorable document, was dismissed as trivia by many newspapers who described it as a series of "dull and commonplace sallies" over which "the veil of oblivion" should be dropped, or as "silly, flat, and dishwatery utterances."

As the Civil War progressed, with its mounting toll of horror and tragedy, Lincoln himself became convinced that he would not be re-elected in 1864. Although his renomination by the Republicans, who convened at the Front Street Theatre in Baltimore on June 7 and 8 of 1864, was certain, it was the vice-presidency that concerned him and other leaders of his party.

By choosing a border-state Democrat who had remained loyal to the Union, they hoped that enough Democrats and doubtful votes would be swung to Lincoln so that election of the Republicans, who temporarily referred to themselves as the National Union Party, would be assured.

The vice-presidential nomination therefore went to Andrew Johnson, military governor of Tennessee and a life-long Jacksonian Democrat. He was chosen not because he was against slavery, for he was not, but because of his spirited defense of the Union. He fought against his own South though most Southerners reviled him for it; Andrew Johnson thought the Union had to be preserved above all else.

Some ten weeks later, the Democrats chose as their candidates General George B. McClellan of New York and George Hunt Pendleton of Ohio.

The Republican nominations brought a flood of abuse from anti-Lincoln newspapers. The New York *World* snapped at Lincoln and Johnson as "a railsplitting buffoon and a boorish tailor . . . men of mediocre talents, narrow views, deficient education, and coarse, vulgar manners. . . .

"In a crisis of the most appalling magnitude, requiring statesmanship of the highest order," the *World* caustically noted, "the country is asked to consider the claims of two ignorant, boorish, third-rate backwoods lawyers, and to the highest stations in the government! . . . God save the Republic!"

Whether Johnson's presence on the ticket materially helped Lincoln is a matter of conjecture only. In the early fall of 1864, the mood of the Republicans was pessimistic; the war had bogged down, and the Union forces urgently needed a major victory.

As if by the hand of providence, the victories came, beginning with the fall of Atlanta on September 3. Others Northern triumphs followed. After that, McClellan and the Democrats were doomed. Final totals of the November election count showed a thumping 90.99 percent of the electoral vote for Lincoln and Johnson (eleven Southern states did not take part in the election).

Two men of the most ordinary birth and with the poorest of prospects were now filling the highest elective offices in the country.

There have been many views of Andrew Jackson, both flattering and condemnatory, as there have been of most major political figures. But one fact in his life stands out—he was an outsider who remained an outsider to the day of his death.

Unlike Lincoln, Andrew Johnson could not join the establishment of his day. He had been born into poverty, as had Lincoln: he was self-educated, as was Lincoln; by his own efforts he rose to prominence, and so, too, did Lincoln. But through all his years of struggle and success, Andrew Johnson hated the aristocracy and refused to join its ranks in any guise.

Early in his career, he had said of the leaders in his town:

"Some day I will show the stuck-up aristocrats who are running the country. A cheap purse-proud set they are, not half as good as the man who earns his bread by the sweat of his brow."

On another occasion, during the Civil War, he revealed a double prejudice in his answer to a visitor who had expressed concern for Southern slaves as "human chattels."

"Damn the negroes," Johnson replied. "I am fighting these traitorous aristocrats, their masters!"

Andy Johnson took pride in being a "plebeian," and spoke of it constantly; he never forgot his humble birth, and made of it a passionate credo that ruled his life.

An early biographer of the sixteenth vice-president had written of him that he had been "born in the midst of degrading influences (and) brought up in the misery of the poor white class." Nor did his luck or his lot improve as a child. In 1822, when Andy was fourteen, he and his younger brother were apprenticed to a tailor.

A regimen of hard work, day and night, with no pay was too much for the boys and two years later they ran away. Despite an offered reward of ten dollars for their return, Andy and his brother evaded capture.

A needle and thread and a hot goose iron had become Andrew Johnson's tools. At the age of nineteen, he set himself up as a tailor in the small town of Greeneville, Tennessee.

With the help of his young wife, the illiterate Andrew Johnson learned to read and write. His industry and unflagging stamina soon brought him prosperity (including, in time, eight slaves) and a measure of local fame. In 1829, he won his first election, when his fellow townspeople, the working men in particular, chose him as an alderman.

The Greeneville gentry were astounded that a tailor had been elected to their town council.

It was not the last time the lowly-born tailor shocked the aristocratic establishment. In 1830 he was elected mayor of Greeneville; from there he went on to the Tennessee legislature, to the United States House of Representatives, to the governorship of Tennessee, and finally, in 1857, to the United States Senate.

When talk of secession swirled through the Senate halls after the election of Abraham Lincoln in 1860, Andrew Johnson made an impassioned plea in defense of the Union and against separation.

"Without regard to consequences," he said to his fellow Southerners, who were infuriated now at his betrayal of their cherished convictions, "I have taken my position . . . in the language of the patriot Emmet, 'I will dispute every inch of ground; I will burn every blade of grass, and the last entrenchment of freedom shall be my grave.' Then let us stand by the Constitution; and, in saving the Union, save this, the greatest government on earth."

President Lincoln was impressed enough with Senator Johnson's continuing defense of the Union and the Constitution to appoint him military governor of Tennessee in early 1862. When Lincoln recommended him for the vice-presidency two years later, there was almost no dissent from the Republicans, even though Johnson had always been a Democrat, and had no intention of switching his affiliation.

Vice-presidents normally attract little attention at inaugurals. It is the president who is the man of the hour. But Inauguration Day, March 4, 1865, was monopolized by Johnson, unintentionally. He arrived at the Senate Chamber to take his oath of office either drunk or ill.

There were many witnesses at the new Vice-President's unfortunate performance. And there were almost as many versions of what had taken place and why. Interpretation of Johnson's behavior depended upon whether you were for him or against him.

Apparently, Johnson had been ill with typhoid. When he arrived at the Vice-President's office shortly before the oath was to be administered, he complained to outgoing Vice-President Hannibal Hamlin that he was not well and could do with a drink of whiskey. The teetotaling Hamlin was exactly the wrong man to ask, but Johnson so obviously needed a bracer that Hamlin sent a page to bring back a bottle. Johnson poured himself either two or three stiff and ample drinks (there are differing versions of the number he actually consumed, but even two, in the quantity all onlookers described, would have been enough to stagger him).

By the time he was ready for his induction speech, Johnson had been thoroughly overcome by a combination of illness, whiskey, and an overheated Senate Chamber. He launched into an embarrassingly befuddled oration that became a maudlin ramble through his humble past. He gloried in being a plebeian. He went on and on, making little sense, affronting his listeners and bringing anguish to his friends.

By any standard, Andrew Johnson had disgraced himself. The New York *World*, which had earlier lamented Johnson's vice-presidential nomination, loosed a venomous attack against him:

". . . To think that one frail life stands between this insolent, clownish creature and the presidency! May God bless and spare Abraham Lincoln!"

But Abraham Lincoln was not spared. He was assassinated six weeks later by John Wilkes Booth, and Andrew Johnson, the humble tailor from Tennessee, woke up on the morning of April 15, 1865, to learn that he had become the seventeenth president of the United States. During his brief term as vice-president, he had done little more than seclude himself in an attempt to overcome the disgrace and disaster of his inauguration.

Andrew Johnson is most remembered for the impeachment proceeding against him in 1868. The reasons for the impeachment were many and complex; they were tied to the unhappy failure of Reconstruction and the desire of a Congress dominated by Republicans to appropriate additional power at the expense of an unpopular Democratic president. Johnson agreed with Lincoln's announced policy of moderation and leniency towards the South, a policy that many radical Republicans angrily opposed. But Johnson lacked Lincoln's keen sense of awareness and reality; he took an inflexible, obstinate position on Reconstruction, and refused to compromise. When the Republican Congress passed more stringent Reconstruction legislation than Lincoln had envisioned, Johnson promptly vetoed every such measure that came to his desk.

Perhaps if Johnson and Congress both had given a little, a reasonable policy on reconstructing the shattered South might have been possible. But Johnson would not waver. By February of 1868, the radical Republicans had had enough of this despised and defiant Democrat. Congressman Thaddeus Stevens of Pennsylvania warned the President: ". . . Unfortunate, unhappy man, behold your doom."

The effort to remove Johnson from office took place in the United States Senate over a period of two and a half months, and culminated in a final vote on May 26, 1868. Of fifty-four senators, thirty-five voted "Guilty" on the charges that had formally been brought against the President and nineteen voted "Not guilty."

Two-thirds of the total, or thirty-six, were needed for conviction and subsequent removal of the President. By one vote, therefore, the radical Republicans failed to prove their case and failed to establish their sought-for precedent to remove any president who refused to cooperate with the Congress.

As a titillating addendum, it should be noted that the man who defeated Hannibal Hamlin of Maine in that state's senatorial election of early 1865, William P. Fessenden, voted "Not guilty." Hamlin won reelection to the United States Senate only after Johnson's trial, but, in the words of his most recent biographer:

"Hamlin's defeat in the 1865 senatorial race took on a new dimension, since, if elected, the former Vice-President would certainly have voted to oust President Johnson."

17th Vice-President Schuyler Colfax—Republican, Indiana, 1869–1873 (President Ulysses S. Grant). Born: March 23, 1823, New York, N. Y. Died: January 13, 1885, Mankato, Minn.

Madmen and Geniuses

Schuyler Colfax

If not for the assassination of Abraham Lincoln, historians would have given as little attention to Andrew Johnson as they had to William Rufus De Vane King and to Hannibal Hamlin. But the assassin's bullet had done more than murder a president; it had transformed, with dramatic suddenness, an unimportant Tennessean into a man watched by the entire world. From that moment on, Johnson's life, his thoughts, his policies, his every phrase and action, would be studied and dissected and analyzed.

For better or worse, Andrew Johnson of Tennessee had become the seventeenth president of the United States, and as such he could not be ignored.

The rise of the former tailor typifies the essence of American politics. Too much of our power relies upon chance; we allow ourselves to be governed by accident, not by choice for surely Andrew Johnson could not have been proposed as the dominant and most influential man in the country. He was, simply, another entrant in a long list of unimpressive politicians who had but "one frail life" between them and the presidency, as the New York *World* stated it with biting pertinence.

The country's political leaders continued to exhibit a total lack of comprehension after the expiration of Johnson's almost four years in the White House. These gentlemen, practical in so many other matters, blithely dismissed the painful examples of the previous quarter century as if they had been unhappy episodes that could not possibly happen again.

115

Despite a recent record that included no less than three chief
executive officers acquired through tragedy and misfortune, and despite
the uninspiring, lackluster performance of each, the Republicans selected for the nation's next vice-presidents two men with even less to
recommend them than had Andrew Johnson.

Schuyler Colfax of Indiana and Henry Wilson of Massachusetts,
both of whom served with Ulysses S. Grant, are two more of the un-
familiar, faceless politicians who served as leaders, yet are important
only to their descendants and their home towns. But Colfax and Wilson
left an impact on their times virtually unmatched by any previous vice-
presidents (barring perhaps Aaron Burr and John C. Breckenridge).
They were both involved in a major scandal of the Grant administration
and should have been politically destroyed as a result.

That each man survived, and with one, in fact, going on to additional honors, is a measure of the scornful cynicism that has marked
much of Americans politics.

In 1868, Ulysses S. Grant of Illinois was the most popular and idol-
ized man in the country. His role in the Civil War, as commander of the
victorious Union armies, brought him fame and adulation, and assured
him a unanimous Republican nomination for president.

With General Grant to lead their ticket, the Republicans of 1868
were euphorically optimistic. So certain were they of success they didn't
even bother with the traditional principle of geography when it came
to the selection of Grant's running mate. Horace Greeley's New York
Tribune commented that "no geographical reasons should weigh against
the imperative wisdom of putting forward our two best men."

Ten favorite sons agreed, and allowed their names to be entered
in the race for the vice-presidency. The two most prominent were Schuyler Colfax, Speaker of the House, and Senator Benjamin Wade of Ohio,
president *pro tempore* of the Senate.

Wade had desperately worked for the removal of Andrew Johnson
during the impeachment proceedings; as the Senate's president *pro
tem*, Wade would have filled the balance of Johnson's presidential term,
which was to expire on March 4, 1869. The senator from Ohio had no
illusions about the next presidency; he knew it was to go to General
Grant. But a few months in the White House, he reasoned, should have
made him an odds-on favorite for the second chair.

Schuyler Colfax, no less a behind-the-scene power, had his own
plans. Looking toward 1872 (assuming Grant would serve only one
term), Colfax and his associates did their own maneuvering for the vice-
presidency; Senator Wade led on the first four ballots, but on the fifth,
the voting broke wide open in favor of Colfax, and he was nominated
to run with Ulysses S. Grant on a Republican platform that embodied
the last phrase of Grant's letter of acceptance:

"Let us have peace."

Colfax added nothing to the Republican ticket. An amiable gentleman with a perpetual grin that seemed frozen in place, Colfax had been

characterized by Lincoln as a "friendly rascal." To many of his colleagues, he was "Smiler" Colfax, a name that had more of menace in it than friendliness.

But the moment was Grant's. His running mate neither helped nor hurt; nor was the general's candidacy harmed by his more capable opponent, Horatio Seymour, former governor of New York. Ulysses S. Grant and Schuyler Colfax defeated the Democrats by a comfortable margin.

As vice-president, Colfax exhibited little of the sagacity and canny shrewdness that had seen him rise in political circles at an early age. Although he had studied law, he was never admitted to the bar. He made up for this lack by an astute manipulation of the *Free Press* of South Bend, Indiana, a newspaper he acquired in 1845, when he was only twenty-two. Under its new name of the *St. Joseph Valley Register*, Colfax's paper became the organ of the Whigs in northern Indiana.

He attended two national conventions of the Whig Party, and campaigned on behalf of Whig candidates. He later took an active role in the organization of the Republican Party in Indiana. In 1855, at the age of thirty-two, Colfax won his first elective office when he entered the Thirty-fourth Congress as a Republican representative from Indiana. He served in the House continuously for fourteen years, the last six as Speaker.

Colfax's lengthy tenure in the Speakership brought him both prominence and power. He even had a town named for him, as had George M. Dallas, although with vastly different results.

In the summer of 1865, Speaker Colfax, the former newspaperman, headed a party of journalists traveling to the Far West to witness the building of the Central Pacific Railroad. The Central Pacific, which began in Sacramento, California, was to traverse the Sierra Nevada Mountains and travel 690 miles eastward to link up with the Union Pacific.

When the Colfax party arrived in northern California, they were fascinated by the army of Chinese laborers who were "laying siege to Nature in her strongest citadel," as one of the journalists described the scene.

"The rugged mountains looked like stupendous anthills," the journalist wrote. "They swarmed with Celestials, shoveling, wheeling, carting, drilling and blasting rocks and earth, while their dull, moony eyes stared out from under immense basket-hats, like umbrellas."

Not far beyond this spot was the settlement of Illinois-town. Leland Stanford, president of the Central Pacific and former governor of California, promptly changed the name of this hamlet to Colfax, in honor of the Speaker, who was, to quote a railroad historian, "most appreciative." (In its most recent census, the entire population of Colfax, California totaled 915.)

This first exciting exposure to the world of railroading may have had more of a profound effect upon Colfax than he could have imagined at the time. Not quite eight years later, an investigation of another railroad entangled Colfax in a web of lies and greed that should have been impossible for him to escape.

Almost from the moment of his inauguration on March 4, 1869, Vice-President Schuyler Colfax assumed an unaccustomed role. President Grant assigned him no tasks; with long, tedious spells between sessions of Congress, Colfax had little opportunity to demonstrate the adroit behind-the-scenes maneuvering that had brought him the Speakership of the House. He therefore turned his attention to other matters—specifically, the presidency, which he hoped would be his in 1872.

Colfax mistakenly assumed that Grant would not run again, and he permitted talk of his own availability to be heard by announcing that he would retire from the vice-presidency after his first term. His announcement was the signal for his friends within the Republican Party (and he had many) to begin a Colfax-for-president campaign.

Grant put an end to that by revealing that he would indeed run for a second term. And it was soon apparent that he was looking for someone else to replace Colfax as his next running mate.

The Vice-President immediately tried to regain his past status by a reverse announcement that he would be available for a second term in the vice-presidency if he were drafted. But Grant wanted no more of the ambitious Colfax, and the Republican convention of 1872, dutifully fulfilling the President's dictate, dumped the smiler from Indiana and chose, to be the next vice-president, Senator Henry Wilson of Massachusetts.

That, however, was not the end of Colfax.

Exactly three months after the Republican convention, in September of 1872, the New York *Sun* headlined a sensational story:

"THE KING OF FRAUDS—How the Credit Mobilier Bought its Way Through Congress."

Beneath that glaring lead were two others in slightly smaller type—"COLOSSAL BRIBERY" and "HOW SOME MEN GET FORTUNES."

In a revelation that the *Sun* described as "the most damaging exhibition of official and private villainy and corruption ever laid bare to the gaze of the world," the newspaper claimed that both the outgoing Vice-President and the man whom the Republicans hoped would replace him had received, along with a number of influential congressmen, "from 2,000 to 3,000 shares each" in a gigantic swindle.

As with so many affairs of this kind, the Credit Mobilier scandal had its roots in a complex tangle of intrigue, financial juggling, and use of influence in high places. The syndicate that had been formed a few years before to build the Union Pacific Railway had later established the Credit Mobilier as a holding company, to own the railroad's stock.

Since the Union Pacific was to be built with government funds with almost none put up by the syndicate (contrary to law) and, beyond that, since there would be enormous profits realized, the directors of the railroad and of the Credit Mobilier had to make certain they had the proper congressional support. One of them later testified:

"We wanted capital and influence."

The directors therefore entrusted a few hundred shares of Credit Mobilier stock to one of their officers, Oakes Ames, who happened also to be a congressman from Massachusetts. Representative Ames said of these shares:

"I shall put (them) where they will do the most good to us."

He sold them, in 1867, at ridiculously low prices to a number of his fellow congressmen, who either were too obtuse to realize they were literally being bribed or were too hungry for a bargain to care. Schuyler Colfax, who was then Speaker of the House, received twenty shares, as did Senator Henry Wilson. (The *Sun's* original charge of "2,000 to 3,000 shares each" was a fantastic exaggeration.)

When the House of Representatives decided in early 1873 to investigate the shoddy dealings of the Credit Mobilier, Vice-President Colfax made the dreadful mistake of denying the whole thing. If he had simply stated that he had been an innocent investor, as did many of the other congressmen who were implicated, he probably would have been absolved of wrongdoing, at least in the public's view. But throughout forty-two pages of weaseling testimony, shot through with lies and contradictions, the Vice-President continued to maintain that he had withdrawn from his contract with Ames some years before.

Unfortunately, the principal culprit, Representative Ames himself, had a differing version.

"I intended to make it as favorable as I could to Mr. Colfax," Ames reported, "but when I heard it was said they intended to break me down I could not do otherwise than state everything."

Ames's story, obviously much closer to the truth, revealed Colfax as a man guilty, at the least, of greed and poor judgment, if not prejury. Not only had Colfax retained the twenty shares of stock, he had also been paid rather largish sums as dividends and interest, as attested to by a carefully annotated page in Oakes Ames's little black memorandum book.

In one respect Colfax was lucky. Although the committee of inquiry did not officially clear him, it did no more than slap him lightly on the wrist, with a convenient explanation that his questionable conduct had taken place before he became vice-president. There had been talk of impeaching him, but this idea was dropped, since he was to leave office in a few weeks. Congressional brotherhood was a handy thing to have in a time of trouble.

For Schuyler Colfax, political life had ended. But, remarkably, he was offered the editorship of the New York *Tribune*. When that plan fell through, he took to lecturing, and managed to make a comfortable living for his remaining years. He became, in the words of an earlier historian, " a successful popular lecturer, touring the country from one end to the other."

On one of his lecture tours, in January of 1885, when he was sixty-one, the former Vice-President had to change trains at Mankato, Minnesota. With the temperature at thirty degrees below zero, he walked three-quarters of a mile from one railroad depot to another. Five minutes after he reached Manakato's Omaha Station, he collapsed and died.

According to the news dispatch reporting his sudden death, it was supposed that exposure to the extreme cold, plus overexertion and the subsequent heat when he got to Omaha Station, brought on "a fatal derangment of the heart's action."

18th Vice-President Henry Wilson—Republican, Massachusetts, 1873–1875 (President Ulysses S. Grant). Born: February 16, 1812, Farmington, N. H. Died: November 22, 1875, Washington, D. C.

Madmen and Geniuses

Henry Wilson

The Credit Mobilier was not a textbook example of fraud and corruption, for too many people had to be involved. Because construction of the Union Pacific, which the Credit Mobilier controlled, had to be approved by government commissioners as mandated by law, it was imperative that no damaging legislation be introduced in Congress that might hamper building of the railroad or endanger the huge profits the syndicate was realizing. Representative Oakes Ames, therefore, was delegated to smooth the way with a number of his more susceptible colleagues, about a dozen altogether.

One congressman, George F. Hoar of Massachusetts, was appalled at the extent of the official involvement.

"When the greatest railroad in the world, binding together the continent and uniting the two great seas which wash our shores, was finished, I have seen our national triumph and exultation turned to bitterness and shame by the unanimous reports of three committees of Congress that every step of that mighty enterprise had been taken in fraud."

He did not mention his fellow congressman from Massachusetts, Senator Henry Wilson. Nor was there any implication in Hoar's indictment that Wilson had knowingly accepted bribes. But incoming Vice-President Wilson had been given twenty shares of stock, a fact he could not deny. Wilson insisted, however, that he had sold his twenty shares back to Ames after thinking the matter over and deciding he didn't like association with the Credit Mobilier.

He did not, he said, receive a dollar's dividend from his original investment, "and if $10,000 from it were due him, he would not touch a cent of it." Further, his only speculation since coming to Congress had been in "a little lot of land in his native town."

Concluding his defense before the committee, Wilson stoutly said of himself:

"Conscious of my innocence, I feel outraged at the charges which have been made against me, and I believe no greater wrong was ever perpetrated than has been perpetrated on many honorable gentlemen, who could not be influenced by the Pacific Railroad, or all the railroads of the country."

A committee member responded to this significant observation with one of his own:

"Let me ask whether this odium which has been created in the public mind has not, to some extent, arisen from mistakes which some gentlemen have made in endeavoring to conceal their connection with it."

He may have been thinking of the money Wilson had used to purchase the tweny shares of Credit Mobilier stock. Wilson and his wife had celebrated their silver wedding anniversary in 1865. Among the many gifts they received was a sum of money, totaling $3,800, presented by a group of admirers. To avoid embarrassment for the senator, the gift was made out to Mrs. Wilson, not to both of them as it should have been. So it was *her* money, not his, that bought the stock.

Four weeks later, Wilson made another appearance before the committee, apparently to correct a false impression his previous testimony had left. He assured his fellow senators, and through them the people of the United States, that any blame for investing in Credit Mobilier must fall upon him, not upon Mrs. Wilson. He wanted the country to understand that. He had made the investment, not his wife (who had died some three years before the hearings).

Although the committee accepted Wilson's explanations and cleared him officially, there were many bad moments for him. One newspaper issued a preliminary box score, before final results were in:

". . . Total loss, one Senator; badly damaged and not serviceable to future political use, two Vice Presidents and eight Congressmen."

(The writer of this assessment proved to be a poor prophet, for Wilson did go on to serve in the new Grant administration, and one of the eight congressmen, James A. Garfield of Ohio, became a president of the United States in his own right eight years later.)

Nor was the press alone in its cry of havoc. Hamilton Fish, President Grant's secretary of state, wrote to the American minister in England:

" 'Tis sad and sickening to see reputations which one had loved to believe well-earned and pure knocked to pieces, and leave no chance for friends to say a word."

But Wilson's well-earned reputation remained so. The Credit Mobilier, one of the more notorious scandals of a scandal-rocked era, did not permanently damage him. To most of the public, he was still

the same man, pure in heart, who had struggled out of the bonds of indenture and poverty to reach the second highest office in the land.

Henry Wilson's beginnings gave little indication of the success he
was to achieve. He was, in fact, not even born as Henry Wilson. Originally, he was Jeremiah Jones Colbath, son of a day laborer in a New
Hampshire sawmill.

At the age of ten, Jeremiah was indentured to a farmer, and only
secured his freedom after eleven years of unrewarding labor, for he
received no pay during all that time. He had educated himself during
his servitude by reading every book he could borrow, including Plu-
tarch's Lives, a memoir of Napoleon, and a biography of a Henry Wilson,
not further identified but who may have been a prominent Massachusetts politician of that time.

When Jeremiah Jones Colbath reached his twenty-first birthday and
finally escaped from his indenture, he had his name legally changed by
an act of the New Hampshire state legislature, to Henry Wilson, the
name of the man whose biography he had so admired.

Of all our chief executive officers, Henry Wilson can surely lay
claim to the most difficult childhood and adolescence. The years immediately following were no easier, for he apprenticed himself to a
Natick, Massachusetts shoemaker. But once having learned the trade
of making shoes, he was on his way to a modest fortune. Within a few
years, by the time he was twenty-seven, Henry Wilson had his own shoe
factory, and eventually employed as many as one hundred people.

The making of shoes did not interest Wilson as a lifetime occupation; the making of a name for himself in politics did. In 1840, when he
could at last afford it, he ran for public office and was elected for the
first of many times to the Massachusetts House of Representatives and
later to the state senate, and finally, in 1855, to the United States Senate.

The guiding principle of Wilson's career was an intense hatred of
slavery. It led him to bolt the Whig Party, his first affiliation, when he
became convinced the Whigs were wavering on the slavery question.
He joined the Free Soilers, and when that group failed to make a permanent impression upon the electorate, he temporarily joined forces with
the misguided Know-Nothings. His Massachusetts associate and admirer,
Congressman George F. Hoar, gently chided Wilson for his association
with the ultraconservative Know-Nothings, which Hoar thought was
carrying "the arts and diplomacies of a partisan . . . sometimes farther,
in my judgment, than a scrupulous sense of honor would warrant."

Whether Whig, Free Soiler, Know-Nothing, or Republican, as he
eventually became, Wilson devoted his entire energy to the dissolution
of slavery. For him it submerged all other considerations, as he once said
in a speech in New York City:

"Resolve it, write it over your door-posts, engrave it on the lids of
your Bibles, proclaim it at the rising of the sun and at the going-down of
the same, and in the broad light of noon. . ."

Wilson's southern colleagues despised him for his active opposition to slavery, and in the summer of 1856, they planned to murder him. For many weeks after that, Wilson carried a pistol in his pocket, and arranged his affairs so that his family would be taken care of in the event of his death.

The cobbler from Natick had served for sixteen years in the United States Senate when the Republican convention of 1872, meeting in Philadelphia's Academy of Music, chose him to be Grant's second running mate. Whether he would have made a first-rate chief executive did not enter into the Republican strategy. One newspaper said of him:

". . . One and all agreed that Henry Wilson was a good business man, an excellent manufacturer, thoroughly honest, highly intelligent, and a wonderful speaker."

The newspaper hedged this praise by admitting, in the same story, that had Wilson "possessed more breadth of mind, had he been able to see more of a subject, he would unquestionably have ranked very highly as a statesman."

But as with Schuyler Colfax four years before, Wilson's attributes or lack of them didn't matter to the Republicans. They were once again certain of victory with Grant, though his first term, not quite over, had shown him to be thoroughly inept and incapable of administering the affairs of a powerful nation.

The Republican strategists guessed correctly. Not even the revelation of the Credit Mobilier scandal, which the New York *Sun* blatantly placed before the electorate only a few weeks before the election, hurt the incumbent President. Nor was Grant damaged at all by his running mate's involvement in the scandal and the spreading of his name over front pages. Wilson would not be cleared until several months *after* the election; nevertheless, he and Grant received a larger plurality in 1872 than the ticket of Grant and Colfax had in 1868.

Henry Wilson did not make a very good vice-president. Even the minimal duties of presiding over the Senate were beyond him. He frequently had to consult with the Senate clerks for the proper parliamentary procedure.

Part of this failing may have been the result of a stroke he suffered shortly after he took office. Since Congress was not in session at the time and he was in New York, he managed to conceal his illness. But talk of his poor health consistently circulated through Washington over the next two years, so that, at one point, he asked the Associated Press to report that he was in the best of health, when in fact he was not.

On the morning of November 10, 1875, Vice-President Henry Wilson suffered a second apoplectic stroke while taking a bath. Despite vigorous rubbings, hot irons, opiates, and various medications, including whiskey injected into his shoulder, the Vice-President died twelve days later, with no one to look after him except colleagues who occasionally dropped into his sparsely furnished room. Wilson's wife, who had also been ill for a long time, had died in 1870 at the age of fifty-four, and their only child died in military service in 1866.

Newspapers all across the country lavished high praise upon the dead Vice-President, with no mention made of his part in the Credit Mobilier affair. In its lengthy story, covering many columns, *The New-York Times* had these comments on his passing:

"When the undertaker had done his duty, and the face of the dead Vice-President was exposed to the gaze of the few friends who had speedily gathered, there was a deep, serene repose depicted upon it, such as no one had remembered to have seen for many years."

19th Vice-President   William   Almon   Wheeler—Republican, New
York, 1877–1881 (President Rutherford B. Hayes). Born: June 30,
1819, Malone, N. Y. Died: June 4, 1887, Malone, N. Y.

Madmen and Geniuses

William Almon Wheeler

The death of Henry Wilson at the age of sixty-three left the vice-presidency vacant for the fourth time. But neither the country at large nor its leaders seemed overly concerned that the second executive chair would now remain unfilled for the next sixteen months. President Grant enjoyed reasonable health, with no indication of a major disability. There was little reason to worry about the lack of a presidential successor.

Approach of the nominating conventions of 1876 focused attention upon the Republicans. A number of President Grant's admirers were pushing him for a third term. Though he publicly disavowed the idea, Grant was pleased at the suggestion.

The President's popularity, however, once so high and lustrous, had fallen to a depressing low. His two terms had been riddled with scandal and ineptitude. With the country weary of corruption and the Congress opposed to a third term for Grant, the Republicans knew they had to look elsewhere for their next standard bearer.

When they convened at Cincinnati on June 14, 1876, they selected the temperate and guileless Rutherford Birchard Hayes, fifty-four-year-old governor of Ohio. His principal opponents for the Republican presidential nomination were two political bosses, James G. Blaine of Maine and Roscoe Conkling of New York.

Since the New York votes (without the connivance of Roscoe Conkling) helped to clinch the nomination for Hayes on the seventh ballot, the Ohio delegation, now in the driver's seat, decided upon a New Yorker for the second spot. There then began an exercise in low comedy.

Roscoe Conkling wanted one of his own puppets, Stewart L. Woodford, nominated for the vice-presidency. But the convention, still savor-
ing its success over northeastern party bosses, pushed for an anti-Conkling
man and selected, by acclamation on the first ballot, a man almost no
one in the counrty had ever heard of, William Almon Wheeler of Malone,
New York.

Earlier in 1876, when there was talk of a possible Hayes-Wheeler
ticket, Hayes wrote to his wife:

"I am ashamed to say, Who is Wheeler?"

Who indeed was Wheeler?

And why was he, of all possibilities, the chosen man?

A Hayes biographer reports that much of the New York delegation,
when told they could have the vice-presidential nomination, made a
huge joke of it by saying, "Take it, Chet," and "You take it, Cornell."
The merriment ended when someone made an inspired suggestion:

"Let's give it to Wheeler."

Choice of W. A. Wheeler to be Hayes's running mate was the
signal for tremendous applause from the convention, as reported by
The New-York Times.

"The vote could hardly have been put for the cheering," said the
Times.

But the assembled Republicans may have had other matters in
mind, for the *Times* dispatch ended with this:

"The delegates did not wait to continue the applause, but rushed
off in every direction for the hasty dinner, the car tickets, and the out-
speeding trains."

Two weeks later, the Democrats selected Samuel Jones Tilden,
governor of New York, and Thomas Andrews Hendricks of Indiana.

The election that fall had an unexpected and unprecedented result—nobody won.

Tilden and Hendricks, the Democrats, received 4,300,000 popular
votes, while the Republicans, Hayes and Wheeler, had slightly more
than 4,000,000. With 185 electoral votes needed to win, Tilden ended
with 184 and Hayes had 166, while the remaining 19, from three different states, were claimed and disputed by both sides.

What followed this deadlock can only be described as a fight for
power, with the presidency the prize. Plotting, counterplotting, and
bribery were the weapons, aided and abetted by "murder, maiming,
mutilation and whipping," as an observer reported the scene in one of
the disputed states.

In each of the three contending states, Louisiana, Florida, and
South Carolina, rival slates of Democratic and Republican electors insisted only they were legitimate and should be so recognized. There was
strong evidence that intimidation, violence and corruption had been
used by both parties to secure their own votes or to discourage, in many
cases forcibly, the newly enfranchised black people from casting their
ballots.

With a rancorous stalemate continuing for weeks and the scheduled presidential inauguration only a month or two away, Congress finally agreed upon an electoral commission to determine just exactly who had been elected. The commission was as close to nonpartisan as it was possible to make it; in its final composition it consisted of seven Republicans, seven Democrats, and one man who was supposed to be independent, but was more Republican than Democrat. As could have been forecast, the majority of eight voted in favor of the Republicans, Hayes and Wheeler.

Thus, only hours before the inauguration of March 4, 1877, Rutherford B. Hayes of Ohio and William A. Wheeler of New York became the nineteenth president and nineteenth vice-president of the United States, respectively, by an electoral count of 185 to 184. Although the Republicans strongly resisted charges of fraud or theft, it must be evident that, from the nineteen contested electoral votes, Tilden and Hendricks certainly should have taken at least one. And one only would have been enough.

But the decision of the electoral commission prevailed, so the Democrats lost, even though they had amassed 300,000 more popular votes.

There is no hard evidence that the New York delegation actually offered William A. Wheeler to the Republican convention because of a joke, but lacking evidence of other possibilities, it makes as valid an explanation as any; no logical reason existed for nominating Wheeler. (The venerated but hardly venerable tradition of geography did not hold in his case, for the Republicans, in the election that fall, lost Wheeler's home state of New York, and two adjoining states, Connecticut and New Jersey. In the previous five elections New York went Republican four times.)

Wheeler had a brief moment of prominence in 1875 when he successfully arbitrated a governmental dispute in Louisiana with a settlement proposal that came to be known as the "Wheeler Compromise." But Wheeler had done nothing else in his ten years as a congressman to earn national attention. All that could be said on his behalf was that he was a modest man and enjoyed a spotless reputation, much like his presidential running mate, Rutherford Hayes.

Not even the Democrats could find anything in Wheeler to attack. They made a futile stab at condemnation by falsely accusing him of participating in the "Salary Grab" of 1873. In that imprudent piece of legislation, roundly condemned by public and press alike, Congress had voted itself an increase in pay from $5,000 a year to $7,500, with back pay of $5,000 covering the previous two years. It was this latter provision that aroused the most anger, not the raise itself.

Congressman Wheeler had voted against this measure. In fact, he so strongly opposed it that he even went to all the trouble of returning his entire back pay, which in his case came to $4,482.40 "after specified deduction." So that accusation bore no fruit at all, and the Democrats gave up trying to find anything in Wheeler's background to expose.

Wheeler's political career was composed of modest beginnings and modest accomplishments. Educated as a lawyer, he served in a public office for the first time while he was still in his teens. His friends and neighbors in Malone, New York, chose him to be their town clerk at an annual salary of $30. A few years later, at the age of twenty-seven, he advanced to district attorney of Franklin County. From there he went to the New York state legislature, and then in 1861, to the U. S. House of Representatives. At that time, he was forty-two and financially comfortable.

The vice-presidency had no appeal for Wheeler. He did not want it, and did not actively seek it. He often said that he agreed with Benjamin Franklin's appraisal of the vice-president, for Franklin had once remarked that "the officer in question ought to be termed 'His Superfluous Highness'."

Wheeler did his best to preside effectively at Senate sessions, which he found boring and frustrating, as he revealed in a newspaper interview:

"He thinks any man is foolish to want to be Vice-President, unless he cares nothing for active life, and is willing to be a nonentity in the great debates which go on in his very presence, without being able to express an opinion."

Vice-President Wheeler did not even have the pleasures of social activity to compensate for his political inadequacy. His wife of thirty-one years had died in March of 1876, only three months before his nomination to the vice-presidency. With no children and no immediate relatives (his only sister died a short time later), Wheeler was left virtually alone. The deaths of his wife and his sister seemed to have destroyed what little taste he had for the gay, partying rounds of Washington life. Except for sedate Sunday evenings at the White House, where he joined President and Mrs. Hayes in the singing of hymns, he stayed pretty much to himself.

The decision of Rutherford Hayes not to seek a second term came as a relief to Wheeler. Not yet sixty-two at the expiration of his term, he wanted only to return to the small town of Malone in northeastern New York, where he intended to " 'husband out the taper' . . . with a moderate competence of worldly goods, and secure in the regards of those who have for so many years given him generous and neighborly support. . . ."

He spent the final six years of his life in quiet retirement in his home town, where he died at the age of sixty-seven. Even his death was unspectacular, according to a newspaper account of his passing:

". . . Life went out so gradually and quietly that it was hard to mark the exact moment of its flight."

20th Vice-President   Chester Alan Arthur—Republican, New York, 1881 (President James A. Garfield). Born: October 5, 1830, Fairfield, Vt. Died: November 18, 1886, New York, N. Y.

Madmen and Geniuses

Chester Alan Arthur

At its halfway point, the vice-presidency had become the last stop on the road to oblivion. For the man who filled the office, his future depended upon a higher authority than the American electorate, as one influential newspaper noted in March of 1881:

"It is the simple fact that the Vice-President of the United States is a cipher, a man on the shelf waiting for another man's shoes. . . . He is merely a contingent who may develop into greatness in the case of a President's death."

As a cipher, the vice-president lacked both influence and authority. In the area of patronage, a sensitive necessity for any politician who hoped to remain in power, the vice-president in the 1880s had at his personal disposal exactly four appointments, all of them petty and meaningless in terms of preserving his party strength. He was permitted to choose his private secretary, a private messenger, a telegraph operator, and finally, restaurant keeper of the Senate.

In the light of such official impotence, no practical politician or realistic seeker of public office would deliberately go after the vice-presidency. It is therefore all the more astonishing that a man who had arrived at eminence and fortune via the system of spoils would actually want the second office, and more, would look upon it as an honor. But that was the case with the Republican nominee of 1880. His acceptance of the vice-presidential nomination foreshadowed a struggle that was to have tragic consequences the following year.

Roscoe Conkling's defeat in the Republican convention of 1876 did not discourage him. He did not participate in the convention of 1880 as a candidate, but his influence was evident throughout the entire proceedings, for he was determined to renominate Ulysses S. Grant.

The former President had regained much of his earlier popularity by way of a highly publicized trip around the world with his wife. He still had the third term bug, so he permitted Conkling to place his name in nomination for the presidency when the Republicans met in Chicago's huge Exposition Hall in June of 1880.

The Republican Party of that year was roughly divided into two factions—the Conkling group, calling themselves the Stalwarts, and all others who opposed them, the Half-Breeds. Arrayed against Grant and the Conkling Stalwarts were two powerful candidates, Senator James G. Blaine of Maine and John Sherman of Ohio, secretary of the treasury in the cabinet of President Rutherford Hayes.

Throughout almost two days of voting and backstage maneuvering in the hot and stifling atmosphere of the Exposition Hall (where twelve thousand spectators had gathered to watch the action), the contest among the three leading contenders went on for ballot after ballot with no one gaining an advantage. By noon of the second day it was apparent that the three leaders would not crack.

Only a compromise candidate could break the deadlock. As if waiting in the wings for such a moment, John Sherman's floor manager, a fellow Ohioan, James A. Garfield, was thrust forward on the thirty-fourth ballot.

Two hours later, on the thirty-sixth ballot, the convention stampeded to Garfield and gave him the presidential nomination, with only 306 Stalwart votes for Grant refusing to yield.

Conkling was furious at his second consecutive defeat by the men from Ohio. He would not even accept, with the grace of a good loser, the second spot for any of his lackeys.

In an attempt to appease the angry Stalwarts, the Garfield forces approached Levi P. Morton of New York, a loyal Conkling follower, with an offer of the vice-presidency. Morton made the mistake of consulting his boss, Senator Roscoe Conkling, before giving his answer. Conkling curtly suggested he turn it down, and Morton dutifully complied.

The next man to be approached by the Half-Breeds was another New Yorker, Chester Alan Arthur, former collector of the Port of New York.

Arthur had never held an elective office. A tall, portly man of elegant bearing, fastidious dress, and worldly habits, he was the antithesis of the machine politician with whom he associated. He had graduated from Union College in Schenectady, New York, at the age of seventeen, after a comprehensive course in the Greek and Latin classics, and was honored, upon his graduation, with election to the local chapter of Phi Beta Kappa. He later studied law and was admitted to the bar, in New York City, when he was twenty-four. He made himself useful to the Republican organization in New York, and within a few years was one of Roscoe Conkling's trusted lieutenants.

In 1871, Arthur was appointed to the highly lucrative collectorship for the Port of New York by President Grant and remained there until July 11, 1878.

Although the salary was only a modest one, the post had enough side benefits, resulting from duties and levies placed upon shipping, so that Arthur's earnings averaged $40,000 a year. In addition to his princely income, the collector had the immense power of patronage, with many jobs at his disposal.

For Arthur, it was a position of great satisfaction, ruined at last by the crusading President Hayes, an avowed foe of spoils. In a prolonged battle, during which Arthur refused to resign, Hayes forced the New Yorker out in July of 1878, and Chester A. Arthur lost one of the most sought after posts in the country.

It was a matter of some irony that the very forces who had removed Arthur from the collectorship should now offer him the second executive office. To compound the contradiction, Arthur was eager to accept. In a scene reported by a newspaperman, who was the lone witness, Arthur found the still fuming Conkling in the almost deserted press room.

" 'I have been hunting everywhere for you, senator,' said Mr. Arthur.

" 'Well, sir,' replied Conkling.

". . . There was a moment of hesitation under the uncompromising attitude of the senator. Finally, Mr. Arthur said:

" 'The Ohio men have offered me the Vice-Presidency.'

"The senator's voice rang out in indignant tones:

" 'Well, sir, you should drop it as you would a red hot shoe from the forge. . . . This trickster of Mentor (James Garfield) will be defeated before the country.'

" 'There is something else to be said,' remarked Arthur.

" 'What, sir, you think of accepting?' fairly shouted Conkling.

"Arthur hesitated a moment and said slowly, but with emphasis:

" 'The office of the Vice-President is a greater honor than I ever dreamed of attaining. . . . I shall accept the nomination.' "

With those words, Chester Alan Arthur demonstrated a defiance of his boss that he had never before evidenced. How different our history may have been if Levi P. Morton, the first choice of the Ohioans, had shown the same spirit of independence.

The vice-presidential nomination went to Arthur on the first ballot, but not, by any means, with unanimous approval of the Republicans. John Sherman labeled the choice of Arthur as a "ridiculous burlesque" and a "scandalous proceeding." But E. L. Godkin, editor of *The Nation*, while admitting that it was now impossible to separate Arthur from the Republican ticket, had these words of assurance for his readers:

". . . There is no place in which his powers of mischief will be so small as in the Vice-Presidency, and it will remove him during a great part of the year from his own field of activity."

For most of the country Arthur's ties to the system of spoils, which the Republican platform had pledged to reform, didn't matter too much and they agreed that his performance in the collectorship of New York had "not been dishonest, just inefficient." When the results of the fall election were tallied, it was found that the Republican ticket of James A. Garfield and Chester Alan Arthur had defeated the Democrats, General Winfield Scott Hancock of Pennsylvania and William Hayden English of Indiana, by a bare 10,000 popular votes, and by an electoral count of 57.99 percent to 42.01 percent.

The people of America had chosen an executive team from Ohio and New York for the second consecutive time.

Arthur's tenure in the vice-presidency lasted exactly 199 days. He presided over a brief session of the Senate, and then spent much of his time running up to Albany, New York, to help the man he had deserted, Roscoe Conkling.

President Garfield had promised to consult Conkling on all New York appointments in return for the senator's support during the campaign. But once Garfield had safely reached the White House, he appointed an anti-Conkling man to the position previously held by the new Vice-President, the collectorship of the Port of New York.

Predictably, Conkling reacted with rage. The President had reneged on his campaign promises, and worse, was now threatening Conkling's control of New York State politics. Conkling decided to make a fight of it. He resigned his Senate seat, and then left it to the state legislature of New York to reappoint him. His position would thus be vindicated and strengthened, and he could resist the President with renewed power. Joining him in this questionable maneuver was New York's junior senator, forty-eight-year-old Thomas C. Platt.

Vice-President Arthur hurried back to support his former boss, Roscoe Conkling. His desertion of his president seemed to bear out the fears of those who had opposed his nomination the year before.

The sight of a vice-president prowling the legislative halls of Albany, New York, on behalf of a political chieftain aroused shock and hostility among the press. The cartoonist Thomas Nast pictured Arthur as a bootblack shining the shoes of Conkling and Platt.

The three Stalwarts all guessed wrong. The New York state legislature would no longer jump at the snap of Conkling's finger or meekly roll over and play dead. Not even the presence of the august Vice-President could move them, and they refused to reappoint either Conkling or Platt.

But news far more shocking and tragic than the decline and fall of Roscoe Conkling awaited the nation.

On the morning of Saturday, July 2, 1881, President Garfield was shot in the back by a demented religious fanatic, Charles J. Guiteau, who had waited for the President in a Washington railroad depot.

When the bullet struck him, the President gasped, "My God, what is this?" And Guiteau shouted, "Now Arthur is President of the United States. I am a Stalwart of the Stalwarts."

Although it would have been incredible to believe that the Vice-President had inspired the shooting of the President, the words of the crazed Guiteau spread the impression that Arthur and Conkling had in some way been responsible. Later testimony developed that Guiteau's act of madness had been at least partially stimulated by the interparty struggle between President Garfield on one side and Vice-President Arthur and Senator Conkling on the other.

Garfield did not immediately die. A horrified nation gripped with fear and dismay waited for bulletins on the condition of the wounded President. As Garfield lingered, the country learned that Guiteau, in the end, had been motivated as much by a religious "impression" that he must "remove" the President as by an entirely mistaken notion that Garfield had refused to appoint him to a consulship in Paris.

Arthur was in no way implicated. When it became evident Garfield could not possibly recover, the tone of the press toward the Vice-President turned conciliatory and faintly praising. He wasn't such a bad sort, after all. The New York *Sun*, particularly, had kind words:

"He is a gentleman in his manners, neither obsequious nor arrogant. His bearing is manly, and such as to prepossess in his favor all whom he meets."

After several weeks of suffering and useless torture by probing doctors, President Garfield succumbed at last to the assassin's bullet, which had never been removed. He died on September 19, 1881, at the age of forty-nine.

Chester Alan Arthur, as the tweny-first president, surprised his friends and enemies alike. He was a far better chief executive than anyone had expected him to be, and he served without the support or advice of Roscoe Conkling, who had, by then, completely lost all political power.

During the three and a half years he served as president, Arthur had a number of positive and far-reaching accomplishments to his credit. He modernized the navy and expanded the services of the post office, which cut its rate for letters to two cents. Even more surprising was the organization of the Civil Service Commission under his direction.

21st Vice-President   Thomas Andrews Hendricks—Democrat, Indiana, 1885 (President Grover Cleveland). Born: September 7, 1819, Muskingum County, Ohio. Died: November 25, 1885, Indianapolis, Ind.

Madmen and Geniuses

Thomas Andrews Hendricks

Failure of Chester Alan Arthur to pursue nomination for a full presidential term in 1884 puzzled his associates. Many of them were upset by his apparent indifference even though he was considered, along with Senator Blaine of Maine, to be the prime contender for the Republican nomination.

What his friends and associates did not know was that Arthur did not have much longer to live. Shortly after he became president, Arthur learned that he had a serious kidney ailment, Bright's disease.

President Arthur did not protest when a New York delegate placed his name in nomination at the Republican convention of June, 1884, held once again at Chicago's Exposition Hall. Yet he did not seem disappointed when the convention chose instead, on the fourth ballot, Senator Blaine who finally achieved the presidential nomination on his third try.

The Democrats convened at the same Exposition Hall a month later. There was talk of renominating Samuel J. Tilden, who had come so close to winning the presidency in 1876. But now, at the age of seventy, Tilden was a sick and feeble man; he had been debilitated by a stroke and by a general deterioration of health so that he walked with difficulty, in a tottering shuffle, and barely spoke above a whisper.

Tilden had his wits remaining to him, however, if little else. When it was reported to him that his running mate of 1876, Thomas A. Hendricks of Indiana, had expressed the hope that they might run again on the same ticket, Tilden commented, with a twinkle in his one good eye: ". . . I do not wonder, considering my weakness!"

The report was misleading, for Hendricks had always been bitterly disappointed that he himself had not been chosen for the presidency. In 1876 he had no desire to "play second fiddle to 'Shinplaster Sam,'" and the prospect of once again submerging his own ambitions in 1884 did not please him.

A month before the convention, Tilden announced that he would not be a candidate. The Democrats thus lost the one national figure they hoped would bring the country back to them. They were left with an array of uninspiring favorite sons.

The preconvention favorite was a governor whose career had been both pallid and brief. The three hundred pound Grover Cleveland had served for two years as sheriff of Erie County, one year as mayor of Buffalo, and was now in his second year as governor of New York. It was not a record to arouse exaltation, but Cleveland was Tilden's personal choice; besides, the Democrats were well aware that New York could prove decisive.

Nine other names besides Cleveland's were placed in nomination, including Hendricks's. On the first ballot Cleveland had 392 votes, far short of the 547 necessary under the Democrats' two-thirds rule.

Hendricks, with 45½ votes, had only the sixth highest total, but he made the most trouble for Cleveland. On the second ballot, his followers engineered an attempt to stampede the convention in his favor.

The Hendricks boom died aborning, even with his delegates shouting themselves hoarse and a band whooping it up for the usual parading in the aisles. At the end of the second ballot, Cleveland went over the top with 683 votes; Hendricks had the same 45½ votes.

With New York thus accounted for, attention shifted to another vital and always doubtful state, Indiana. In the previous election, New York and Indiana had gone Republican. If the Democrats were to win in 1884, both states were needed.

So the convention chose for vice-president the man who before then had been the irritant in the voting—sixty-five-year-old Thomas Andrews Hendricks of Indiana. He did not want the second spot and so instructed the Indiana delegation, who fought in vain to block his nomination.

Shouts went up all over the floor to redress the wrong that had been done Hendricks in the disputed election of 1876. The vice-presidency must be his. The Democrats would never forget that Tilden and Hendricks had won the popular vote in 1876 by 300,000, but had the election taken away from them by a partisan Republican majority on the electoral commission.

One delegate raised a cry that almost became a slogan for the Hendricks partisans:

"He deserves it; give it to him for God's sake!"

The vice-presidential nomination went to Hendricks by acclamation, in spite of his unwillingness. Cleveland, too, was unhappy with the choice of Hendricks, but he was practical enough to realize that the Democrats could lose the entire Midwest, as they had in 1880. With Hendricks on the ticket, they might at least salvage Indiana.

Nomination of Thomas Hendricks proved to be a wise move, for the Democrats did win Indiana, by a margin of 5,000 votes out of 475,000. They won New York as well, by exactly 1,500 votes out of 1,125,000. These two states were enough to provide the margin of victory. Cleveland and Hendricks defeated the Republicans with an electoral count of 54.61 percent. The Democrats were back in the White House for the first time in twenty-five years.

Despite an unimpressive record, Hendricks was quite acceptable to a sizeable segment of the electorate. His dismal opposition to civil rights, heartily applauded in the South (which voted solidly to support both him and Cleveland), found sympathy in much of the North as well, including his own state of Indiana. America, in the 1880s, was no shining citadel of enlightenment.

A lifetime Democrat, Hendricks achieved prominence at an early age when he began practicing law in Indianapolis. In 1848, when he was twenty-nine, he won election to the lower house of the Indiana Assembly. Over the next twenty-five years, he ran for public office at least a half-dozen more times, and was defeated as often as he was elected. He served as a congressman, United States senator, and one term as governor of Indiana. Of this last position, he said that "any man competent to be a notary public could be Governor of Indiana."

His law practice, in the meantime, flourished; his firm represented a number of railroads and large corporations. His fortune grew, as did his local fame. One sensational case, in 1871, brought him national attention.

A fellow Indiana lawyer, Lambdin P. Milligan, had been arrested in October of 1864 during the third year of the Civil War, and charged with treason. Milligan and others had been members of a secret organization known as "Knights of the Golden Circle"; they used as a password "Nu-oh-lac," Calhoun spelled backwards. Ardently pro-South and antiblack, they preached what amounted to insurrection against both the federal government and the state government of Indiana.

Milligan was tried by a military tribunal, which argued that under the suspension of civil law then in effect, it had the right to try civilians. Milligan was found guilty of the charge of treason and sentenced to hang. He managed to stave off execution through various appeals until the Supreme Court, in 1866, ruled that the military tribunal did not have the jurisdiction it had claimed. Milligan was freed.

Two years later, Milligan filed suit against the members of the tribunal for "an alleged wrongful arrest and imprisonment." He asked damages of $100,000, and retained former Senator Thomas A. Hendricks as his counsel.

The entrance of Hendricks into the case immediately created countrywide interest, for he was the leading Democrat in Indiana. It also seemed to imply, as opponents of Hendricks had long insisted, that he had always been in sympathy with the objectives of the Knights of the Golden Circle and may even have been a member of that subversive group.

Hendricks would admit to membership in only one "secret society," the Odd Fellows, but his record as a congressional legislator spoke for itself. In 1854, as a representative, he voted for the Kansas-Nebraska Act and for repeal of the Missouri Compromise; during his single term as a senator, from 1863 to 1869, he opposed the draft, emancipation for the slaves, the Freedmen's Bureau, and the Fourteenth and Fifteenth Amendments (dealing with the citizenship and rights of former slaves). In his view, "the Negro was inferior and no good would come from his freedom."

With such an attitude, it was not surprising that Hendricks agreed to represent Milligan in his damage suit against the tribunal.

Hendricks won the case, although the jury reduced Milligan's claim from $100,000 to five dollars.

With all its residue of treason, conspiracy, and subversion, the Milligan case did no harm to Hendricks's political reputation, for some months later, in 1872, his fellow Indianans chose him to be their governor. In a Republican year, Democrat Hendricks won the governorship by 1,200 votes.

Loss of the disputed presidential election of 1876 was a bitter blow to Hendricks and he never forgave Tilden for his pliant submission to the ruling of the electoral commission.

Hendricks continued to hope that the presidency itself would one day be his, even though he held no other public office after leaving the governorship of Indiana in 1876. He suffered a serious illness in 1882, and that should have been enough to bring about his retirement at last from the conniving and trickery and stratagems of political life. But he could not retire, and two years after his illness, he permitted the Democratic convention of 1884 to believe that he was still in the best of health, and he accepted nomination for vice-president.

Thomas Hendricks was sixty-five when he was inaugurated the twenty-first vice-president of the United States on March 4, 1885. He presided at a special session of the Senate, which met for exactly 30 days to consider the new presidential appointments.

When the special session of the Senate adjourned on April 2, 1885, Vice-President Hendricks completed his final official duty. The Forty-Ninth Congress would not convene for its regular session until the following December. The Vice-President died exactly two weeks before then, on November 25, 1885.

For the nation, the death of the Vice-President was unexpected, but Hendricks and his wife had both known for some months that the end might come at any time. Only a week before his death, Hendricks had told an associate:

"All this talk about my being a candidate in 1888 is the veriest twaddle. I shall never be a candidate for that or any office again."

Hendricks died alone in the bedroom of his Indianapolis home, while his wife was downstairs spending a few moments with a visitor.

22nd Vice-President   Levi Parsons Morton—Republican, New York, 1889–1893 (President Benjamin Harrison). Born: May 16, 1824, Shoreham, Vt. Died: May 16, 1920, Rhinebeck, N. Y.

Madmen and Geniuses

Levi Parsons Morton

On the evening of November 25, 1885, Washington was abuzz with the news of Vice-President Hendricks's death. But more than his passing concerned the politicians and Congressional leaders. They were confronted with the sudden realization that the nation had no elected successor to the President.

The Forty-ninth Congress, scheduled to meet for the first time on December 7, slightly less than two weeks away, still had to choose a Speaker of the House and a president *pro tempore* of the Senate. It was often the custom of the incoming vice-president to preside over the Senate for a few days after his inauguration, usually during a special session called for the express purpose of confirming nominations made by the new president, and then to leave the federal capitol to return home. The Senate would elect a president *pro tem* to occupy the chair in the absence of the vice-president.

Thomas A. Hendricks had fooled everyone. He had reported to the Senate chambers for each day of its thirty-day special session in March. No one expected him to be so persevering. It may be, as was reported, that he had nothing else to do; or perhaps he had a premonition and feared this might be his only chance to officiate. Whatever his motives, he gave the Senate no opportunity to choose a president *pro tem.*

Now, on the evening of Hendricks's death, alarmed Washington began to wonder about President Cleveland's health. Under the provisions of the Constitution then in effect, a successor to the duties of the presidency would be named by the Congress until an election could be held. Under provisions of legislation passed in 1792, the president *pro tem* of the Senate would be the first successor, and after him the Speaker of the House.

Since neither branch of the Congress had as yet chosen its presiding officer, it was imperative that Cleveland survive at least until December 7, for it was unthinkable that the nation be without someone to lead it. Fortunately for America's peace of mind, President Cleveland sailed through the next two weeks in perfect health. In fact, he was fine for the rest of his term, so actually the question of a successor was never put to the test.

It would be reasonable to suppose that the country's leaders would have been chastened by the death of their elderly Vice-President, and would then have made certain that their next candidates for the second chair would be young and vigorous men in the prime of life. But no, not so.

The Democrats, who met first, in the early part of June, 1888, renominated incumbent President Grover Cleveland for a second term, and, as his running mate, they chose Allen Granberry Thurman of Ohio, seventy-five years old. Not to be outdone, the Republicans, who convened two weeks later, nominated a ticket that was just as geographically balanced as the Democrats', and almost, but not quite, as elderly.

The Republicans chose for president a lawyer from Indiana, fifty-four-year-old Benjamin Harrison, and for vice-president, a wealthy banker from New York, sixty-four-year-old Levi Parsons Morton.

Nomination of Indiana's Benjamin Harrison deeply disappointed the New York delegation, who had expected the call to go once more to James G. Blaine of Maine. Now they would accept no less than second place. Eight years before, the New York machine, headed by Roscoe Conkling, had contemptuously rejected the vice-presidency. This time, with Thomas C. Platt to lead them, they were not about to make the same mistake.

Nor would Levi Morton allow the main chance to elude him again. He remembered all too keenly that the vice-presidency, which he tossed away in 1880, would have made him the president a year later. If it were possible for lightning to strike twice, he wanted to be there when it happened.

He accepted the Republican nomination gladly. He did no campaigning, but concentrated his efforts on fund raising, where he could do the most good. As always, he was strikingly successful.

Along with John Wanamaker of Philadelphia, who used the direct approach, a circular that simply said, "We want money and we want it quick!", Morton raised enough funds to help win the White House back for the Republicans. Although the ticket of Harrison and Morton lost the popular vote by 10,000, they won easily in the electoral totals. They even won New York, a tribute to Morton and a slap in the face to New York's other candidate, President Cleveland.

The Republicans and Benjamin Harrison had ample reason to be grateful to their new Vice-President.

Levi P. Morton came to politics at a late age. With little formal education beyond a few years in a Vermont seminary, he devoted the first half of a very long life to the business and financial worlds. At the age of fourteen, he took a job as a clerk in a general store at an annual salary of $50. Two years later, he moved to a bigger store and a larger salary, $200 per year. By the time he was twenty-one, in 1845, he owned a dry goods establishment in Hanover, New Hampshire, doing an annual volume of $100,000 a year.

From Hanover he moved to Boston and New York, growing more successful and wealthier with each move. In 1863, helped along by an old friend, Junius Spencer Morgan (whose son was to achieve worldwide fame as J. Pierpont Morgan), Levi Morton expanded into international banking. Within a few years, L . P. Morton & Co., with branches on both sides of the Atlantic, was one of the giants in international banking, and Morton counted himself one of the richest men in the country.

His first entry into the political arena came in 1876, when he was fifty-two. He ran unsuccessfully for Congress as the Republican candidate in Manhattan's Eleventh District, which had the city's most fashionable residences and contained more wealth within its confined boundaries than many states.

Two years later, Morton ran for Congress once again, this time successfully; he served exactly two years. Unlike many of his colleagues, he did little orating, for he was totally unaccomplished as a speechmaker. He preferred to stick to financial matters, particularly in the international area, a field he knew intimately.

When the Ohio delegation, in 1880, informally offered him the vice-presidency, it did so with the full knowledge that he did not deserve it based upon his political record alone. But the Ohioans also knew that he was one of their more influential money men, a supremely successful fund raiser, a generous contributor to the Republican cause, and a trusted Conkling associate.

From later developments, it would appear that Morton was not disappointed when he was ordered by Conkling to reject the vice-presidency. They both had something far more important in mind.

After the Republican convention of June 1880, Morton took on the task of fund raising as financial chairman of the Republican National Committee. But it was not the welfare of the Republican Party that concerned him and Conkling. They wanted presidential nominee James Garfield to guarantee that he would appoint Morton the secretary of the treasury in his cabinet. For Conkling, the treasury would mean unlimited control of federal patronage, since it was the cabinet position with the most jobs. For Morton, it would mean supervision of $700 million in government bonds that were about to come due and would thus have to be refunded. On either account, it was a juicy plum for any banker.

But Garfield evidenced a streak of stubbornness that surprised and shocked the Conkling-Morton faction. At the advice of Midwestern newspaper friends, who warned him against the corrupting influence of

Wall Street, he appointed William Windom of Minnesota to be his secretary of the treasury.

Levi Morton consoled himself with an ambassadorship, the ministry to France. Such a reward for a wealthy contributor had already become a time-honored custom, and would be a common and accepted procedure in future administrations.

Ambassador Morton was established in his palatial summer residence, the Château Champ Fleuri, near the French forest of St. Germain, when he received the news of the shooting of Garfield on July 2, 1881. A few weeks later, after Garfield had died, Morton was getting ready to go back to his mission. His biographer tells us what happened:

"As Mr. Morton prepared to return to Paris, to occupy his new Legation, he could not avoid the reflection that, had he consented to be nominated Vice President in 1880, he might have been moving into the White House. But if he felt any regrets, the fact was hidden even from his closest friends. His sorrow was not for lost honors, but for the loss of a cherished friend."

For a man who barely knew the departed President, this was deep sorrow indeed. But Morton's grief was shortlived. He entertained lavishly in Paris, where he lived for four years. He returned to the United States in 1885 to make a futile try for the United States Senate. He tried again two years later, once more without success. And with this record of political failure, the Republican convention of 1888 nominated him to run for vice-president, with Benjamin Harrison for president.

One of the richest men ever to occupy the second chair, Levi Morton brought something new to the vice-presidency. He bought a house on Washington's Scott Circle, and after extensive repairs and alterations, embarked on a program of lavish entertainment that had not been seen outside of the White House since the days of Dolley Madison some eighty years before. One of the Morton children described a typical Wednesday:

"In those days hordes of people went from one official house to another. . . (Mother) used to have as many as two thousand people pass through her rooms of an afternoon."

Vice-President Morton fulfilled his duties in the Senate's presiding chair more conscientiously than most of his predecessors. At one point, in late 1890 and early 1891, he opposed legislation offered by his own Republican majority, and therefore permitted southern Democratic opposition to carry on a protracted filibuster against the measure. His frustrated Republican colleagues tried every trick to get him either to cut off debate, or to absent himself from the chair long enough for someone else to do the job.

The Republicans even suggested "he make a trip to Florida for his health." He refused. And to make certain nothing was done behind his back, he gave up his lunches so that he could be on hand in the Senate at all times.

This incident, which eventually cost the Republicans their legislation, disenchanted many of Morton's associates and fellow northerners, who now began to talk of denying him a second term. In addition, New York labor did not want Morton back in the vice-presidency. Their choice was the much younger and far more personable editor of the New York *Tribune*, Whitelaw Reid.

So it was, when the Republican convention met in Cincinnati's Music Hall the first week of June, 1892, that incumbent President Benjamin Harrison was renominated, but his Vice-President was not. The vice-presidential nomination went to Whitelaw Reid by acclamation.

But perhaps the Republicans did Morton a favor. After the convention, a popular joke made the rounds.

Question: Why was Vice-President Morton not renominated?

Answer: Because God was good to him.

Rejection by the national convention of 1892 did not discourage Morton. He won the governorship of New York in 1894 at a personal cost to him of $19,790, including $16,000 contributed to the Republican State Committee.

He served for one term, and retired to his 1,000 acre farm in Rhinebeck, New York, where he died in 1920, on his ninety-sixth birthday.

23rd Vice-President Adlai Ewing Stevenson—Democrat, Illinois, 1893–1897 (President Grover Cleveland). Born: October 23, 1835, Christian County, Ky. Died: June 14, 1914. Chicago, Ill.

Madmen and Geniuses

Adlai Ewing Stevenson

The election of 1892 had little of the frenetic hullabaloo that had featured many a previous presidential campaign. Although there were a number of pressing issues, such as civil service reform, the regulation of monopoly, an excessively high tariff, and inflation, neither the Republicans nor the Democrats made more than a half-hearted attempt to resolve them. Basically conservative and basically alike in their approaches, the two major parties injected almost no controversy into the election so that what ensued after the nominating conventions of 1892 can only be classified as unexciting and stodgy.

Yet in its modestly dull way, 1892 had much to distinguish it. It had two presidents facing each other for the first time, incumbent President Benjamin Harrison on the Republican ticket and former President Grover Cleveland on the Democratic. Also, for the first time, the secret ballot was widely used. There were still numerous voting irregularities and fraud, but with the introduction of the secret vote, honesty was at last possible.

Finally, a third party had come on the scene, a genuine third party that created an authentic excitement among a substantial part of the electorate. Organized in Kansas by a group of disenchanted farmers who felt betrayed by the larger political organizations, the People's Party or the Populists as they came to be known, took on all the trappings of "a religious revival, a crusade, a pentecost of politics in which a flame sat upon every man." One of their insistent demands was the free coinage of silver at a ratio to gold of 16 to 1.

With prices high and their buying power badly restricted, many farmers and working people believed the cure for their ills was the circulation of more money, lots of it. (In 1875 the currency then circulating averaged $19 per person; by the end of World War II, it had risen to $200.) One way to achieve more money was to remove the country from the limiting hold of a gold standard and to augment it with silver. Thus the Populist demand.

The Republicans and the Democrats faced the silver question with obvious distaste. Characteristically, the Republicans did nothing about it. They met in the Industrial Exposition Building in Minneapolis during the days of June 7 to 10 of 1892, and took only one ballot each to choose their presidential candidate, Benjamin Harrison, and his vice-presidential running mate, Whitelaw Reid. Neither man was strongly in favor of silver.

The Democrats, meeting in Chicago two weeks later in a huge icehouse especially converted for their convention, went about their tasks with the same precision and lack of enthusiasm. They too consumed only one ballot for the nomination of Grover Cleveland as their presidential candidate. There was a brief flurry of opposition from the New York delegation, controlled this time by Tammany Hall, but nothing came of it. Cleveland was an easy victor.

With a tremendous rainstorm raging outside, and the massive convention hall full of leaks and puddles, with 16,000 unhappy spectators huddled miserably waiting for something to happen, the Democrats made just as fast a matter of it in the choice of their second man. To appease the new silverite states of the West and to reassure the grumbling electorate, the Democrats tipped their hats to the silver producers by choosing for vice-president, Adlai Ewing Stevenson of Illinois. Cleveland believed firmly in the gold standard; Stevenson did not.

On the face of it, the second half of the Democratic ticket seemed like a fortunate choice. Stevenson (grandfather of the more famous Adlai E. Stevenson II) was an amiable and friendly man, a popular Democrat in a Republican state. According to an observant journalist, Stevenson had "that quality which, lacking a better name, is called 'magnetism,' and the possession of which predisposes men in his favor."

Whether it was his magnetism or his tolerant position on the silver issue, Stevenson proved to be exactly the complement Cleveland needed. In the election that fall, Cleveland and Stevenson won enough support in the Western silver producing states to assure their election with 62.39 percent of the electoral count.

The Democratic triumph displayed at last the wisdom of a geographic and philosophical balance. In 1888, during Cleveland's unsuccessful try for a second term, the Democrats lost his home state of New York; in 1892, they took it back, and they even won Stevenson's Illinois, the first time that state had gone Democratic since 1856.

For another first, the Populists polled 1,041,028 votes, the first time a third party had gone over a million.

The new Vice-President favorably impressed both his fellow Democrats and his fellow citizens. Adlai E. Stevenson had a knack of making friends everywhere; most people liked him without reservation. His conversation sparkled with wit, to the delight of casual companions or political audiences. His outgoing, jovial personality and his ability to charm even those who disagreed with his views, helped him immensely as a lawyer and a politician.

Son of a small planter and slaveowner in Kentucky, Stevenson grew up and was educated in Illinois, where he made his home. He met Stephen A. Douglas in 1854, and from that day was an ardent Democrat, actively supporting Douglas in his campaigns for the Senate and the presidency.

After a short stay at Wesleyan University in Bloomington, Illinois, and two years at Centre College, Danville, Kentucky, Stevenson studied law and was admitted to the bar in 1858, when he was not quite twenty-three. A fortunate appointment two years later as a master in chancery (a court of equity or record) helped him to win his first try for public office; in 1864 he was elected states attorney for the Twenty-third Judicial District of Illinois. He served four years.

A thoroughgoing Democrat in a strongly Republican district, Stevenson was elected to the United States Congress in 1872. He quickly became known in Washington as a spokesman for bimetallism and fiscal reform. He served in Congress twice, the second time from 1879 to 1881.

Stevenson's tact, geniality, and friendliness undoubtedly influenced President Cleveland to appoint him first assistant postmaster in 1885. But Cleveland soon had cause to regret the appointment. Within a few months of his inauguration, President Cleveland found a pack of angry journalistic voices snapping at his heels. One of them was Joseph Pulitzer of the New York World.

Pulitzer did not approve of Cleveland's go-easy policy on patronage. Cleveland did not believe it proper to remove officeholders who happened to be Republicans so that they might be replaced by Democrats, who had, after all, worked so hard to elect him. Pulitzer publicly rebuked the President in the pages of the World.

"Cleveland must remember," Pulitzer wrote, "the obligations which an Administration elected by a great historical party owes to that party."

The first assistant postmaster agreed with Pulitzer. Stevenson issued a statement commending the World, while revealing his own position on patronage.

"Although it is daily asserted that hundreds of postmasters are being appointed," Stevenson declared, "yet the six months which have elapsed since Cleveland's accession finds only between ten and twelve percent of the offices occupied by Democrats."

Other faithful Democrats added their own stinging comments, so that before long it seemed as though the entire party were against the President. The senator from Louisiana denounced Cleveland as "a conspicuous and humiliating failure" and accused him of "treacherous conduct toward the party he claims to represent."

Under this combined attack from many quarters, Cleveland began to back down, and Stevenson was given the green light. As first assistant postmaster, he had a gigantic task facing him, one that had to be handled with tact. As a biographical sketch of him noted, he had to "serve his party's interests well and yet give as little offense as possible to the opposition."

Stevenson's job was to get rid of the country's fourth-class Republican postmasters; before he was through, he fired forty thousand of them and replaced them with people who presumably were more efficient and more deserving because they were Democrats.

"Naturally," went on the biographical sketch, "his course provoked scathing denunciation, although very little of the criticism came from the men actually removed from office."

For his remarkable display of pragmatic firing and hiring, Stevenson earned a not too flattering nickname—"The Headsman"—and an appointment by Cleveland to the Supreme Court. Cleveland made the appointment in early 1889, shortly before his first term was to end. But the Republican majority in the Senate was still smarting from the wounds inflicted by Stevenson's wholesale firings and refused to confirm him.

The Democrats, however, were eager to show their gratitude, and they rewarded him with the vice-presidential nomination in 1892. On the afternoon of June 23, after the previous session had kept the weary delegates at the icehouse convention hall until well past 2:00 A.M., the famous Hendricks Club of Indiana whipped up a momentary enthusiasm for their governor, Isaac P. Gray. But the New York Tammany delegation, which had been rebuffed by Indiana when it sought the aid of that state in rejecting Cleveland, now did the same to Indiana and refused to support Isaac Gray; their 72 votes went, instead, to Stevenson and helped to turn the tide in his favor.

It was by no means a united Democratic party that faced the Cleveland-Stevenson administration that began on March 4, 1893. Many Democrats voiced displeasure with their President, now serving his second term, while expressing admiration for Vice-President Stevenson. Six months later, although the country didn't know it, the admiration might well have turned to howls of dismay.

In an effort to reduce inflation and to blunt the damaging effects of a business panic that began to sweep the country in the spring of 1893, President Cleveland called a special session of Congress to meet on August 7. He and his associates were committed to gold, and were determined to remove silver as an adjunct. They wanted less money in circulation, not more. And they wanted the value of gold increased, to the detriment of its rival metal, silver.

But fate stepped in; a malignant cancer was discovered on the roof of Cleveland's mouth. The expert medical advice was immediate removal. But how to do it without alarming the country? How to do it without jeopardizing the special session of Congress? Support for Cleveland's position was by no means assured; the strength of his office and his actual presence in Washington were mandatory if his program were to succeed.

Hovering over this scene of uncertainty was the specter of Vice-President Adlai E. Stevenson, who would certainly scuttle Cleveland's gold program in favor of silver if he were to succeed to the presidency.

It was decided that the operation to remove the cancerous growth would be conducted in secret. Only a handful of people, including the Vice-President, knew of the operation, which took place on July 1, 1893, in the luxurious saloon of the private yacht *Oneida* as it slowly steamed up the East River of New York City's Manhattan Island.

Guided by a team of six specialists, the surgery involved removal of most of Cleveland's left upper jawbone; the excision was done from the inside of his mouth so that no external scar would show. The operation was a success, except that a second and precautionary operation was performed two weeks later, under the same secrecy, to remove an additional suspected malignancy. Cleveland was fitted with a vulcanized rubber jaw to replace the section that had been removed, and although the hard rubber was extremely painful against his raw, healing wound, his face at least looked normal.

With the return of the President to health and to activity, the Vice-President lost his chance for glory. The country was saved from the curse of silver, and Adlai E. Stevenson of Illinois served out the rest of his term in quiet and uneventful anonymity, rating no more than the usual footnotes devoted to surviving vice-presidents.

If history, however, has largely forgotten him, his fellow citizens did not. During the election of 1900 he received the unusual honor of being renominated for vice-president by three different parties: the Democrats, the Populists, and the Silver Republicans, who favored bimetallism and opposed the importation of Chinese labor.

Despite this tripartite support, Stevenson lost. Eight years later, he was again unsuccessful in a bid for the governorship of Illinois. He retired and died in Bloomington at the age of seventy-eight.

24th Vice-President Garret Augustus Hobart—Republican, New Jersey, 1897–1899 (President William McKinley). Born: June 3, 1844, Long Branch, N. J. Died: November 21, 1899, Paterson, N. J.

Madmen and Geniuses

Garret Augustus Hobart

The silver crusade took on new intensity with the approach of the 1896 presidential campaign. A series of disastrous economic crises contributed to a depression that brought bank failures by the score, unemployment, hunger, and crippling labor strikes (broken by bayonets and federal troops). The Democrats, not entirely the culprits, were blamed for the misery since they were the party in power.

The ebullient Republicans boasted that "a Republican rag doll" could be elected president. Under the guidance of their current boss, wealthy businessman Mark Hanna of Ohio, they used but one session at their convention of June, 1896, to choose both their presidential and vice-presidential candidates. The only item of interest in their colorless deliberations concerned the gold standard. They came out for it, thus clearly saying to the country's disadvantaged that "sound money" alone could provide the answer to the nation's anguish.

Republican silverites howled betrayal; their spokesman, Senator Henry Moore Teller of Colorado, displayed public emotion. One headline gave a graphic description:

"Twenty-one Silver Men Bolt the Convention, Led by Teller, Who Weeps Copiously as He Leaves the Hall."

It was now the turn of the Democrats to face the money issue. The silverites found popular opinion supporting their position; they seized their opportunity with the help of a thirty-six-year-old spellbinder from Nebraska.

At the Democratic convention meeting in Chicago's Coliseum, July

7 to 11, the delegates listened in rapt silence while the magnetic William Jennings Bryan, the "boy wonder from the West," mesmerized them with resounding voice, heroic posture, and hypnotic phrases. His theme was silver, silver to help the poor and the underprivileged.

Bryan had used this same speech before, but never with the response it was now receiving. He worked the convention to a fever pitch, so that by the end, twenty thousand people jamming the hall jumped to their feet with frenzied shouts of "Bryan, Bryan, Bryan!"

He pledged the Democrats would fight not upon the side of the "idle holders of idle capital," but upon the side of the "struggling masses." The Democracy, he vowed, would valiantly resist the Republican demand for a gold standard:

"You shall not press down upon the brow of labor this crown of thorns," he eloquently declared, "you shall not crucify mankind upon a cross of gold."

It was this stirring oration that helped to secure the Democratic presidential nomination for Bryan on the fifth ballot. Arthur Sewall, a wealthy shipbuilder from Maine and exactly the kind of "plutocratic businessman" the struggling masses did not want, was nominated for vice-president.

So the issue had been joined at last. Did the country want sound money, backed only by gold, or did it want soft money, lots of it, backed by silver as well?

The Republican position was exemplified by their two candidates chosen some three weeks before at the GOP convention held in a specially built auditorium in St. Louis. Each candidate was nominated by an overwhelming margin on the first ballot, with William McKinley of Ohio, the nominee for President, defeating six other contenders, while his running mate, Garret Augustus Hobart of New Jersey, easily won out over nine others. The gold platform, too, won as decisively, by a vote of 812½ to 110½. McKinley was perhaps less hawkish on gold than many of his colleagues would have liked. But he was astute enough to support his party's platform unhesitatingly; since the Republicans were against silver, so was he.

Hobart had no need to equivocate, for he was a gold man first and last. Almost unknown to the country itself, he had been the personal choice of Mark Hanna, who wanted an eastern candidate to balance McKinley of Ohio. The wealthy Hobart, influential in his own state, provided the answer. It didn't matter that few people outside of New Jersey knew of him; he was rich, and solid on the question of gold.

In reply to the official committee of notification, Hobart had this to say about the two metals:

"Gold is the one standard of value among all enlightened commercial nations. An honest dollar, worth 100 cents everywhere, cannot be coined out of 53 cents' worth of silver plus legislative fiat. Such a debasement of our currency would inevitably produce incalculable loss, appalling disaster, and National dishonor. The question admits of no compromise."

In spite of Hobart's dread of public speaking, an affliction that was no help to a candidate for national office, he proved to be an asset indeed to the Republicans. As a tribute to their native son, Hobart's state of New Jersey went Republican for the first time in twenty-four years.

The final results of the November election gave McKinley and Hobart a convincing win, in both the popular and electoral count. The nation had opted once again for the gold standard.

The extent of Vice-President Hobart's wealth was never revealed, but it must have been considerable by anyone's measurement. He was a director in at least sixty large corporations, and general counsel for many of them. He was president of the Passaic Water Company, the Paterson Railway Company, the Morris County Railroad, and several banks. One of his holdings may have indirectly affected William Jennings Bryan's bid for the presidency, as Bryan himself told Hobart one day.

"I have only one grudge against you," Bryan said.

"What is that?" asked the Vice-President.

"Well," Bryan replied, "you remember when I was stumping through New Jersey I stopped at your town of Paterson. Just as the crowd gathered to hear me all the electric lights went out and I was compelled to make my speech in absolute darkness. I wondered what the matter was, and subsequently I learned that you were the President of the electric light company."

The Vice-President and Bryan had a hearty laugh at that anecdote.

Hobart's wealth was self-earned. His father owned a country store and a small farm, and barely made enough to keep his family together. Hobart attended Rutgers College and graduated in 1863 at the age of nineteen. He later studied law under Socrates Tuttle, an old friend of his father's. Mr. Tuttle was his political mentor as well.

The commercial branch of law, which formed the basis for Hobart's vast wealth, was his immediate choice, and he quickly acquired both money and prominence. Judicious investments and directorships followed in rapid succession, with public office a natural result. He began his political career as Paterson city counsel, in 1871, when he was twenty-seven. He advanced to the New Jersey State Assembly, to the state senate, and to president of the state senate.

For a period of eleven years, he was chairman of the New Jersey state Republican committee. As such he wielded immense power both inside his state and within the national Republican Party. But almost no one else in the country had ever heard of him. He had never gone higher than the senate of his state, and had, in fact, been defeated for the United States Senate in his only try for that body.

When Mark Hanna chose Hobart for the vice-presidency in 1896, that canny Ohioan knew what he was doing. Hobart was a man of influence within the Republican Party and he had the riches to back up the task that Hanna had set for him. The Vice-President, for the first time in the uninspiring history of that office, was to work closely with the President, almost as the President's right hand. Officially, there was no more for Hobart to do than all other vice-presidents had done. But unofficially, behind the scenes, lay his real strength and his value to McKinley.

The first thing Hobart did was to rent the Tayloe Mansion on Lafayette Square, diagonally across the way from the White House. Here he and his wife embarked on a program of elaborate entertaining. More importantly for the administration, the Vice-President instituted a series of afternoon "smokers" to which Congressional leaders were invited for cards and drinks. McKinley himself often dropped in, and between them the two executives twisted many a recalcitrant arm during the course of these afternoon get-togethers.

In Hobart's estimation, the vice-presidency deserved far more respect than that strangely paradoxical office had been given in the past. He believed that the framers of the Constitution had intended the vice-presidency to be a position of power and influence. In actuality, it was nothing like that at all, but he insisted that others have the same high regard for the office as he did.

President McKinley, who knew the worth of Hobart's contributions to his administration, publicly acknowledged his Vice-President's contention of importance. At the President's first state dinner, which the ambassador from England was to attend, it was assumed that the British minister would have precedence in the seating over the Vice-President. But McKinley escorted Mrs. Hobart to dinner and permitted the Vice-President to escort Mrs. McKinley. To quote a newspaper report of the event:

". . . And that settled it."

The McKinley administration is remembered for little else than the Spanish-American War. Vice-President Hobart faithfully supported the President in pursuance of hostilities against Spain. When McKinley signed the formal declaration of war on April 25, 1898, he used Hobart's pen for his first name and a second pen for his last name.

Hobart was immensely useful to McKinley on another and equally significant occasion. At the end of the Spanish-American War, the United States found itself with the Philippine Islands on its hands. McKinley insisted he didn't want them, but he was troubled about what he called "the Philippine business." He asked for divine guidance, and one night it came to him, and he saw that there was "nothing left for us to do but to take them all, and to educate the Filipinos, and uplift them and civilize and Christianize them." Then he went to bed.

The following morning McKinley sent for the official map-maker, and instructed him "to put the Philippines on the map of the United States, and there they are, and there they will stay while I am President!"

Vice-President Hobart supported this position to the very last. A resolution to establish freedom for the Philippine Islands was brought to the floor of the Senate and resulted in a tie vote. Vice-President Hobart cast the deciding vote against the resolution and against freedom. He helped to launch the United States as a colonial power.

This was the last Senate session that Hobart attended. In the fall of 1898 he had become ill, with "symptoms of embarrassed respiration."

Although he seemed to recover, the strain of his duties as presiding officer of the Senate took a severe toll, so that by the time the session ended on March 3, 1899, he was a very sick man. He was taken home to Paterson, New Jersey, where his health declined alarmingly. By October 31, his family and physicians announced that he would not return to Washington and would never again take part in public life. His illness was described as "an affection of the heart."

On the evening of November 21, the fifty-five-year-old Vice-President suffered a sharp attack of angina pectoris. He rallied briefly, but the end was all too near. A sympathetic newsman described his final hours:

"He sank lower and lower, with full knowledge of his condition, until, as the clock at midnight sounded the passing of another day into the void of unrecallable time, the consciousness of things mundane faded forever from his mind. A few hours later, at 8:30 o'clock, he breathed his last. . ."

Among the many thousands who wept for the departed Vice-President was Mrs. Ida McKinley, invalid wife of the President. It was reported that she sobbed uncontrollably and convulsively when she heard the news.

25th Vice-President Theodore Roosevelt—Republican, New York, 1901 (President William McKinley). Born: October 27, 1858, New York, N. Y. Died: January 6, 1919, Oyster Bay, N. Y.

Madmen and Geniuses

Theodore Roosevelt

The approach of the twentieth century brought a growing awareness that the United States had become a world power, and as such
should be respected by other nations as equal if not superior. Many
American leaders openly rattled their sabers at every opportunity, although cooler heads generally prevailed so that the Spanish-American
War, which lasted less than eight months, was the only actual hostility.

With the expansion of the nation's influence, the presidency took
on new dimensions. The chief executive of the United States was now
regarded by other countries as the leader of 75,000,000 people, a formidable array of strength and a potential market of inspirational proportions. A country that was already importing $2 billion worth of goods
was to be treated as a neighbor worthy of consideration.

A natural development should have been the parallel growth of
the vice-presidency. There were those who believed that Garret Augustus Hobart exemplified such a growth in importance of the second office.
Perhaps he did, and perhaps, had he lived, he might even have made
more of it during a second term. Yet he was valuable to McKinley not
as the second in command but rather as a toiler behind the scenes. But
McKinley's blessing invested the vice-presidency with an eminence it
did not really have.

Some seven weeks after the death of Garret A. Hobart, the Congress
of the United States offered a number of memorial addresses in tribute
to the late Vice-President. In one of these eulogies, Senator Henry
Cabot Lodge of Massachusetts commented on the vice-presidency. His

observations still have application for us today, for he touched the heart of the problem.

"The decline of the Vice-Presidency in political weight and popular estimation has been an unfortunate development of the last fifty years," said the senator. "In our regard for that office and in our treatment of it we have departed utterly from the wise conception of the founders of our Government. The framers of the Constitution intended that the Vice-President should be, in all respects, in ability, in reputation, in weight of character, and in his standing before the people, *on a plane of absolute equality with the President.*" (Author's italics.)

Was Lodge correct? Is that what the framers of the Constitution had really intended? There have been long and scholarly discussions on this point. Some authorities contend that the vice-presidency was almost an afterthought and was included in the governmental format as a last minute solace for those who insisted upon a presidential backup. It was even proposed that the vice-president be paid only on a *per diem* basis rather than annually. If that provision had passed, the vice-president would have fared badly indeed, for precious little of his time was spent in actual presiding. Thomas Jefferson echoed the prevailing sentiment when he described the vice-presidency:

"It will give me philosophical evenings in the winter and rural days in the summer. The second office of the government is honorable and easy."

After some debate, in September of 1789, the First Congress set the salary of the president at $25,000 a year and that for the vice-president at $5,000. The second chair was accepted as part of the executive team, although with limited privilege and authority. To use a modern day analogy, one that has become a favorite of a recent chief executive, the backup quarterback did no training, did not know the plays, and was not even shown how to call the signals. If he were suddenly called upon to replace the number one quarterback, both he and his team would be slaughtered.

Yet, as Senator Lodge pointed out, much more had been intended in "the original clause of the Constitution, amended so long ago that it is well-nigh forgotten.

"In that clause," he said, "it was provided that the electors in each State should vote for two persons from different States without naming the office voted for, and that the man receiving the highest vote in all the electoral colleges should be President and the one receiving the next highest should be Vice-President. *In other words, the electors were to vote for two men who were equally fit to be President.*" (Authors italics.)

Senator Lodge himself admitted there were some dangers in this method, as exemplified by the tie vote between Thomas Jefferson and Aaron Burr in 1800, and, as he phrased it, by "the dangerous intrigue in the House to supplant the former by the latter." The constitutional amendment that followed calling for separate votes for the president and vice-president, he agreed had been necessary; yet it did not "touch in any way the original conception of the makers of the Constitution, nor should it ever have been allowed to affect it."

If, in the senator's view, the vice-president should always have been a man qualified to succeed to the presidency itself in case of death or disability, and "marked out by his position as the natural successor," the principle was abrogated more often than followed.

At the time of Lodge's eulogy, which was delivered on January 10, 1900, the United States had been served by twenty-four vice-presidents.

Of these, only three succeeded to the presidency "as the natural successor," John Adams, Thomas Jefferson, and Martin Van Buren.

Four succeeded to the presidency through "death or disability," John Tyler, Millard Fillmore, Andrew Johnson, and Chester Alan Arthur, with none of this quartet leaving more than a faint impression upon the historical consciousness of the nation.

Of the remaining seventeen, Aaron Burr and John C. Calhoun alone are remembered. The others disappeared into the mists of oblivion, honored perhaps only by their home towns and local historical societies.

As a further illustration of the deviation from the original intent, nine vice-presidents were refused renomination by their respective parties.

"The conception of the framers (of the Constitution)," said Senator Lodge, "has faded and grown dim. The Vice-Presidency has been treated too often by party conventions either as a convenient and honorable shelf upon which an eminent man might quietly close his career, or as a consolation prize to be awarded to the faction in the party which had failed to win the highest place."

In either case, the odds ran against the country, for the vice-president might be too old or prove to be totally incapable of sustaining the responsibilities of the presidency. As for the man who accepted his party's nomination to the second office, the vice-presidency "is almost universally looked upon as certain political extinction for any man with a career before him."

With all his misgivings and his recognition of vice-presidential impotence, Senator Lodge nevertheless regarded the vice-presidency as a "great office," one to be sought by worthy men. He therefore urged his friend, Theodore Roosevelt of New York, to accept nomination for the second office in 1900.

Lodge was not the only one who had that idea. Thomas C. Platt, Republican boss of New York, wanted very much for Roosevelt to be vice-president, for personal reasons that had nothing to do with the needs of the country. He was aided in his plan by his good friend, Pennsylvania boss Matthew Quay. And, in spite of what the bosses wanted or did not want (Mark Hanna was passionately opposed to Roosevelt), a spontaneous grass roots movement for the young New Yorker began to develop in advance of the Republican convention.

It was a curious coalition of political forces that brought Theodore Roosevelt to the second chair and ultimately to the White House.

Roosevelt's rise to national prominence was as flamboyant and spectacular as he was. Sick and feeble when he was a child, he developed a regimen of exercise and physical activity that became his hallmark. His early service as a New York state assemblyman, followed by two years as commissioner of police in New York City, gave him a taste for politics.

In 1897, largely through the intervention of his good friend Senator Henry Cabot Lodge, Roosevelt was appointed by President McKinley as assistant secretary of the Navy. It was in this position that Roosevelt bedeviled the McKinley administration to enlarge its fleet and to prepare for a war with Spain that Roosevelt considered inevitable. Roosevelt reveled in militarism with a zestful abandon; to him, warfare was a legitimate instrument of power. The United States was about to control two oceans, the Atlantic and the Pacific. If Spain had to be blown out of the seas and her island possessions taken away from her to bring about the rise of the United States, so be it. But a strong and invincible navy was needed to accomplish this goal that was now a Roosevelt passion.

To the impatient Roosevelt, the administration moved too slowly and carefully on the question of possible war with Spain. Finally, in February of 1898, an opportunity presented itself to the overzealous assistant secretary to take matters into his own hands.

On the evening of February 15, the American battleship *Maine* exploded in Havana harbor with a loss of 250 American lives. Although guilt for this catastrophe could not be placed upon Spain, the jingoistic press hysterically screamed for revenge against that country. Many citizens, from low to high, joined the clamor. Theodore Roosevelt was one of them, for he claimed that the *Maine* had been sunk "by an act of dirty treachery on the part of the Spaniards."

Two weeks later, the exhausted Secretary of the Navy, John Davis Long of Massachusetts, left Washington for a short and well-earned rest. Responsibility for the Navy was temporarily entrusted to the assistant secretary, Theodore Roosevelt.

Roosevelt wasted no time. With Long safely out of the way, he immediately sent a cable to the commander of the Pacific fleet, Commodore George Dewey.

"Order the squadron, except the Monacacy, to Hong Kong. Keep full of coal. In the event of declaration of war Spain, your duty will be to see that the Spanish squadron does not leave the Asiatic coast, and then offensive operations in the Philippine Islands. Keep Olympia until further orders."

Both Secretary Long and President McKinley were dismayed when they heard what Roosevelt had done without explicit instructions from them. But they did not rescind his order. Two months later, war against Spain was officially declared, and the Pacific fleet, under Dewey, gave the Spanish squadrons a terrific pounding.

The opening of hostilities was exactly what Roosevelt wanted. He resigned his cabinet post and wangled an appointment as a lieutenant-colonel of a new regiment of mounted cavalry. He and his Rough Riders were to fight in Cuba.

Roosevelt threw himself into combat with the same zest and enthusiasm that characterized all his activities. Faithfully reported by an adulatory press, Roosevelt became an overnight symbol of America's fighting spirit. With a wide grin, flashing teeth, a campaign hat jauntily cocked upon his head, Teddy Roosevelt led his fearless Rough Riders up San Juan Hill and destroyed the enemy with élan and eagerness.

"By this time," Roosevelt wrote, "we were all in the spirit of the thing, and greatly excited by the charge, the men cheering and running forward between shots. . . ."

To a chorus of acclaim, the cocky colonel came home from his "bully war" to find himself a hero. A half-million people lined the streets of New York City to shout their bravos.

"Never," reported the *Tribune*, "has this city given such an ecstatic welcome to one of her illustrious sons."

Within a few weeks, Roosevelt was running for governor of New York state. He won convincingly.

Governor Roosevelt did not endear himself to Boss Platt and other leaders of the New York Republican machine. He took reform too literally, particularly as it applied to the large corporations; he wanted to bring them under public regulation. They resisted, and brought their complaints to Platt, who decided that Roosevelt had to go.

But how to get rid of a man who was so popular? He would certainly not resign, and not even Platt could deny him renomination at the next gubernatorial election. The only way, as Platt saw it, was to "kick Roosevelt upstairs," into the vice-presidency, and thus make him helpless in New York matters.

Platt's announced motives gave a different picture.

"I firmly believed," wrote Mr. Platt, "that the virile personality of Mr. Roosevelt, supported by his war record in Cuba and by his administrative record as Governor of New York, would add great strength to the national ticket."

When Platt made the suggestion of the vice-presidency to Roosevelt, he found the young governor willing to listen although not ready to commit himself. Roosevelt's friend, Senator Lodge, had been making the same suggestion for some weeks. But Roosevelt had reservations about the office. He considered the vice-presidency "a most honorable office," although "for a young man there is not much to do."

It was this lack of work that disturbed him, as he wrote on a number of occasions.

"I can see nothing whatever in the Vice-Presidency for me. It would be an irksome, wearisome place where I could do nothing."

"There would be nothing in the world for me to do when once I became Vice-President. I could work at my historical studies, but after all I could do that better if I were professor of history in some college. . . ."

He was concerned as well by the social aspects of the office. He thought himself too poor to carry on the traditions of entertaining established by two recent vice-presidents, Levi Morton and Garret Hobart, both of whom had been extremely wealthy. Roosevelt himself was well off, for he had a comfortable income, a large house, and many servants. But he always looked upon his life as a comparative struggle to remain solvent.

It was not until Roosevelt discovered Platt's real motives, "to get me out of the state," that he finally decided he did not want the vice-presidency; he preferred to run once again for the New York governorship, despite Platt's opposition.

A three-way struggle developed. Platt and his Pennsylvania friend, Matthew Quay, formed one contingent, Roosevelt another, and Mark Hanna, who wanted no part of Teddy, the third.

Hanna did everything he could to block Roosevelt's nomination. He tried to have McKinley announce his own preference, which of course would not be Roosevelt. But President McKinley sensed a growing grass roots movement for Roosevelt. It would harm his image if he opposed the New Yorker, only to have his own convention overrule him. On the other hand, if he came out in formal support of Roosevelt, it might appear as if he were working in league with Platt and Quay and he wanted at all costs to avoid the taint of boss control. He therefore let it be known that the administration had no preference for the vice-presidency.

A frustrated Mark Hanna needed more than neutrality. He saw his carefully contrived control of the national Republican machine slipping away. No longer could he bend McKinley to his will. Beyond that, he saw Roosevelt as a menace to the country; to him, Roosevelt was "a madman."

"There is only one life," Hanna fumed, "between the Vice-President and the Chief Magistracy of the Nation. . . ."

It was this one nagging apprehension, that something might happen to McKinley, that became Hanna's guiding principle. Because of it, he summarily rejected Timothy Woodruff, lieutenant-governor of New York; Woodruff openly wanted the vice-presidency, and was rich enough to do justice to the office's social demands. But, as Hanna put it, Woodruff "would not be big enough to be President."

In recording this incident, Hanna's biographer had a trenchant comment.

"The nomination of politicians for the Vice-Presidency who were not fit to be President was one of the most ancient and best established of American political traditions . . . from any such point of view (Woodruff's) qualifications were unimpeachable."

In the end, it was Tom Platt who won, although not in the way he had planned.

Roosevelt announced to his fellow Republicans that he preferred to be governor of New York, but he phrased his statement in a way to leave the door open for the vice-presidency. When he arrived in Philadelphia, where the Republican convention of 1900 was to be held during the days of June 19 to 21, he found himself the number one candidate for the second spot. The Roosevelt boom was sparked by the western states, which openly admired him for his vitality, his charisma, and his love of the outdoors.

Despite Hanna's frantic efforts to stop the rush of sentiment toward Roosevelt, the Republican convention nominated the forty-one-year-old governor unanimously—except for one member of the New York delegation, presumably Roosevelt himself, who refused to vote.

The Democrats met in Chicago, July 4 through 6, and, as expected, nominated William Jennings Bryan for the second time. To run with him, they chose Adlai E. Stevenson of Illinois to be vice-president, also for the second time.

The election campaign that followed was exciting only because Roosevelt made it so. McKinley stayed at home, preferring to leave the strenuous part to his running mate.

Unlike previous vice-presidential candidates, Roosevelt campaigned hard and eagerly. He traveled from one end of the country to the other, flashing his toothy grin, waving his arms like bayonets, his clipped Harvard accent streaming out in a crackling fusillade of intensity and charm. The crowds loved him.

In all, Roosevelt traveled 21,209 miles and gave a total of 673 speeches to audiences that numbered well over three million. He visited twenty-four states, and 567 cities and towns. It was a performance to inspire awe.

When all the votes were counted in November, the results disclosed that McKinley and Roosevelt defeated their Democratic opponents by a greater margin than had McKinley and Hobart four years before. The Republicans even took Bryan's home state of Nebraska and Stevenson's home state of Illinois.

Theodore Roosevelt's tenure as vice-president was one of the shortest on record. He presided over a special session of the Senate for exactly five days, from March 4 to March 9, and then embarked on an extensive speaking tour. Organizations and groups all over the country were eager to have him address them; he accepted many of these invitations and further endeared himself to the country. There were some cynics who saw these appearances as his opening salvos for the presidency in 1904.

Roosevelt was spending a holiday in New York's Adirondack Mountains when he received word, in early September of 1901, that the President had been shot in Buffalo by an anarchist. Roosevelt hurried to Buffalo to be at the side of his wounded chief; assured that McKinley would recover, the Vice-President returned to the mountains, where his family and friends were waiting.

But the doctors were wrong. McKinley did not recover. On the afternoon of September 13, an urgent message was sent to Vice-President

Roosevelt, who was then hiking on Mount Marcy, that the President was sinking. With the use of a buckboard, one driver, and three separate sets of horses, Roosevelt made a headlong dash down the mountains that night, over precipitous trails, forty miles through the darkness to the nearest railroad station where a special train was waiting to take him to Buffalo. When he arrived at the station shortly after six in the morning, he learned that McKinley had died four hours before.

Roosevelt took the oath of office as the twenty-sixth president in the Buffalo home of a friend. He departed slightly from the ceremony to reassure those who were crowded into the room.

"It shall be my aim," said the forty-two-year-old President, the youngest man ever to serve in that office, "to continue absolutely unbroken the policy of President McKinley for the peace and prosperity and honor of our beloved country."

The crushed and bereaved Mark Hanna was not so sure. His assessment of Roosevelt gave graphic testimony to his bitterness.

"Now look," said Hanna, "that damned cowboy is President of the United States."

26th Vice-President Charles W. Fairbanks—Republican, Indiana, 1905–1909 (President Theodore Roosevelt). Born: May 11, 1852, Unionville Center, Ohio. Died: June 4, 1918, Indianapolis, Ind.

Madmen and Geniuses

Charles W. Fairbanks

Within a few weeks of McKinley's assassination, an enterprising publisher issued a book in honor of the dead President. Hastily put together by the *Memorial Publishing Company*, with a florid title and many subtitles equally grandiloquent, the book gave no insight to McKinley but concentrated rather on surface details and eulogies.

The title page told an entire story in itself:

OUR MARTYRED PRESIDENT, As a Man, the Noblest and Purest of his Times. As a Citizen, the Grandest of his Nation. As a Statesman, the Idol of Millions of People. MEMORIAL LIFE OF WILLIAM McKINLEY—with other subtitles giving the reader more of the same, and ending finally with a proud boast—*Profusely Embellished with Superb Engravings.*

In one of the later chapters, the book described the scene in the Buffalo home of Ansley Wilcox where Theodore Roosevelt took the oath of office as the new president. Shortly after the ceremony, the first man to enter the Wilcox house was Mark Hanna. Leaning heavily on a stout cane, Hanna was obviously ill and deeply shaken by the tragedy. Although McKinley had more and more become his own man, there nevertheless existed a strong bond of friendship between him and Hanna. The death of the President had a searing and lasting effect upon the aging politician.

The first meeting between Hanna and the new President was graphically described by the author of *Our Martyred President*.

"President Roosevelt descried Mr. Hanna before he had mounted

175

the steps of the house. He came alertly and expectantly through the crowd of well wishers surrounding him and held out both hands. 'How do you do, Senator, I am glad to see you,' he said, in tones rather modified from his usual resonant enunciation.

"The lifelong friend of the dead President had his soft gray slouch hat in his right hand. He transferred it to his left, which held his cane, and holding out his right hand, he looked steadily at the new national chieftain. 'Mr. President,' he said, and those who were standing within a few feet thought they detected a quaver in his voice. 'Mr. President, I wish you success and a prosperous administration; I trust that you will command me if I can be of service.'

"The two men, easily the two most interesting figures in the great tragedy, clasped hands for nearly a minute, but did not exchange another word."

Perhaps this version of the meeting was essentially correct. In any event, Hanna slowly began to change his mind about Roosevelt. He learned, as did the rest of the world, that Theodore Roosevelt was a dynamic, vital leader, a president with vision, and the daring to initiate and execute his views.

By 1904, there was no question that Roosevelt had earned his own term as president. Mark Hanna, who had never given up the thought of the White House for himself, died in February of that year. No other possible obstacle stood in Roosevelt's way. When the Republicans convened in Chicago, June 21 to 23, President Roosevelt was unanimously nominated on the first ballot to seek election in his own right.

Exactly forty-seven minutes later, Senator Charles Warren Fairbanks of Indiana was nominated for the vice-presidency. His selection, too, came unanimously on the first ballot.

To oppose Roosevelt and Fairbanks, the Democrats chose Judge Alton Brooks Parker of New York and former Senator Henry Gassaway Davis. Again, as had the Republicans, the Democrats took only one ballot for each of their candidates.

On either side, the vice-presidential nominations followed an established pattern, but for differing reasons. The Democratic choice, Henry Gassaway Davis, was eighty years old; he was the oldest man ever nominated for the office by a major party, and unfit for the presidency by virtue of age alone. But he was also very rich, and the Democrats needed a financial angel to combat the healthy war chest the Republicans always raised with a minimum of effort.

As for the Republican, Charles Warren Fairbanks, at fifty-two he was far younger, and though he was at least just as wealthy as his Democratic opponent, he was not chosen to finance the Republican campaign. Rather, his nomination was the result of in-party fighting and struggle for leadership.

In neither case was the vice-presidential selection made on the basis of qualifications alone.

Charles Warren Fairbanks could honestly say that he had gone from a log cabin to the vice-presidency, for he had been born in 1852 in the one story log house that stood on his father's farm. As a young man, Fairbanks worked briefly for the infant Associated Press, studied law, and started his practice in Indianapolis when he was twenty-two. Through an influential uncle, he began to work for the trustees of bankrupt railroads, and eventually found himself general counsel, director, or president of a number of rail lines, including the Terre Haute & Peoria, the Ohio Southern, the Danville & Ohio, and the Cincinnati, Hamilton & Dayton. Through these holdings and other investments, he became extremely wealthy; it was estimated that his fortune totaled $5 million at his death.

His wealth helped to smooth the way for him into Indiana politics. By the time he had reached his middle thirties, Fairbanks was widely acknowledged to be one of the top Republicans in his state. His method of operation was reminiscent of Martin Van Buren in his own early days some sixty years before. As did Van Buren, Fairbanks chose his affiliations carefully; if he had to flip-flop from one candidate to another, he did so with no compunction.

In 1888, he enthusiastically worked to swing the Republican presidential nomination to his good friend, Judge Walter Q. Gresham of Indiana. Then when it became apparent that Benjamin Harrison was to be the convention choice, Fairbanks, as enthusiastically, switched his allegiance from Gresham to Harrison. Four years later, he flip-flopped once again; he prematurely supported William McKinley for the Republican nomination in opposition to the incumbent President Harrison, and then just as easily dropped McKinley to work for Harrison. His sliding about from one man to another did not endear him to the Harrison forces, but it raised him high in the McKinley circle, for the Ohio people liked his early support of their presidential hopeful.

This support carried over to 1896, when McKinley did at last win nomination. As McKinley's personal choice for temporary chairman of the convention and keynote speaker, Fairbanks became a figure of influence within the national circles of his party, although he had not to that point ever held an elective office. The following March, Indiana rewarded him by electing him to the United States Senate.

By then, Fairbanks had become convinced that he himself was presidential material, and he made meticulous plans for the 1904 convention; McKinley, of course, would run again and win a second term in 1900. He would naturally not seek a third term. Fairbanks confidently expected the McKinley group to push him for the presidency in 1904, in the same way that he had diligently worked for McKinley. Fairbanks did not look upon Vice-President Roosevelt as a threat to his White House ambitions.

The McKinley assassination and the surprising emergence of Theodore Roosevelt as a strong and decisive president forced Senator Fairbanks to change his thinking and to look beyond 1904 to 1908. In the meantime, he would content himself with the vice-presidency under Roosevelt for that would be a step closer to his goal.

The junior senator from Indiana, Albert J. Beveridge, heartily endorsed his colleague's aspirations. The two men had been at political loggerheads for some years, with each doing his best to undercut the other in Indiana. The wealthy Fairbanks, unlimited funds at his disposal, had far the better of it. Whenever he needed supporters in a hurry, he arranged free railway passes for them through his many-faceted railroad affiliations. And Fairbanks's control of several Indiana newpapers did not help the frustrated junior senator, who had neither the money nor the resources to do proper battle.

When Fairbanks let it be known that he wanted the second chair behind Roosevelt, Beveridge was delighted; nothing would suit him more than to have Fairbanks sitting helplessly in the vice-presidency and out of Indiana politics.

Both men received a boost for their hopes by an unexpected Roosevelt maneuver. The President insisted that his friend and trusted associate, George B. Cortelyou, be appointed chairman of the Republican national committee. Roosevelt of course had his way, but at a cost.

The party's professional politicos were not keen on a nonprofessional such as Cortelyou leading them for the next four years. If they could not thwart the President on that matter, they would deny Roosevelt his vice-presidential preference. They wanted one of their own, a member of the Old Guard for vice-president, someone who could be trusted to support the orthodox Republican line, as opposed to the more enlightened Roosevelt policies. The name they came up with was Senator Fairbanks of Indiana.

Roosevelt would rather have had someone else, but as long as he had beaten the GOP chieftains with Cortelyou, he was willing to give in on the second chair, for he knew that the vice-presidency was an office of impotence and isolation. One man therefore was as good as another to be his running mate, even an Old Guard conservative like Fairbanks. When Roosevelt realized that the Republican pros meant to push the Indianan for the second spot, he wisely permitted them to go ahead with their plans.

The nominating and seconding speeches for Charles W. Fairbanks were made in the early afternoon of June 23, 1904, between 1:20 P.M. and 2:07 P.M. They were full of the usual clichés and elicited the usual applause. In the initial seconding speech, Senator Chauncey Depew of New York alluded to former vice-presidents.

"Let us remember that Thomas Jefferson, let us remember that old John Adams, let us remember that John C. Calhoun and George Clinton and Martin Van Buren were Vice-Presidents of the United States."

If Clinton and Van Buren were not exactly in the same class with Jefferson, Adams and Calhoun, Depew can be forgiven his oratory, for they were both from his home state of New York. Nor could Fairbanks, by any stretch of the imagination, be placed in the company of Jefferson and Adams. But Depew insisted, and the convention dutifully applauded, and dutifully nominated Fairbanks by acclaim after all favorite sons gracefully withdrew. One of those cheering the loudest was the junior senator from Indiana, Albert Beveridge.

During the campaign that followed, President Roosevelt stayed aloof, as McKinley had done; he permitted his vice-presidential running mate to do all the electioneering. In 1904, Fairbanks repeated the high-voltage, transcontinental stumping that Roosevelt had done four years earlier. Roosevelt comfortably stayed behind, and wherever he directed, Fairbanks went.

When Roosevelt heard that the Methodists of New York were lukewarm toward him, he wrote to Cortelyou:

"Cannot they be got at? Cannot Fairbanks be used in this way? He belongs to that church, and ought to be able to do us good among them."

Fairbanks' efforts may not specifically have won over the balky Methodist vote, but New York did go for the Republicans by a substantial margin. So, too, did Indiana, and so did West Virginia, home state of the other vice-presidential candidate, eighty-year-old Henry G. Davis. So, too, did most of the country, for Roosevelt and Fairbanks coasted to an easy win over their Democratic rivals.

Roosevelt's use of Fairbanks for the election campaign was the last time he paid much attention to his vice-president. In 1896, Roosevelt had declared that the vice-president should be given a seat in the cabinet and a vote in the Senate. Safely reelected, Roosevelt forgot all about these declarations and behaved as if Fairbanks did not exist. Because of Roosevelt's refusal to make use of him, Fairbanks became one of the more notable of the vice-presidential failures.

Fairbanks did not give up hoping for the main prize. He tried for the Republican presidential nomination in 1908, but Roosevelt, who considered his vice-president a "reactionary machine politician," wanted no further part of him. Instead, he chose William Howard Taft to be his successor.

But Fairbanks was not one to abandon his goal without a determined last effort. In 1916, believing the elusive presidency might yet be his, the sixty-four-year-old Indianan accepted the vice-presidential nomination as a running mate to Charles Evans Hughes. They were to oppose the Democratic incumbents, Woodrow Wilson and Thomas R. Marshall.

The election that fall, which took place on Tuesday, November 7, was a classic cliffhanger. By that evening, it seemed as if Hughes and Fairbanks were the winners. Many major newspapers, including the usually reliable New York *World* and *New York Times* excitedly flashed the news that the Republicans had defeated Wilson and Marshall. Fairbanks himself, awaiting the election results in Indianapolis, believed for a few heady hours that he was the new vice-president, for he wired a message of congratulations to Hughes, who was spending election night at New York's Astor Hotel.

Hughes did not return the compliment, probably because he wasn't that certain he and Fairbanks had actually been elected. There is a story, however, that he went to bed convinced he had won. In the morning, a reporter came to his hotel room to interview him, only to be told that "the President was asleep and could not be disturbed." The reporter answered, "When he wakes up, tell him he's no longer the President."

On the morning of November 8, it wasn't even certain that Wilson was the president, for two important states, Minnesota and California, kept swinging back and forth between the candidates as results were being tallied. It was not until 11:25 P.M. on Thursday, two days after the election, that the Republican chairman in California wearily conceded that Wilson had finally won that state by some 4400 out of 875,000. And that swung the election to Wilson and Marshall, for California's thirteen electoral votes gave the victory to the Democrats by exactly eleven. If Hughes and Fairbanks had taken California, *they* would have won by two electoral votes.

Strangely, Fairbanks did not congratulate the victorious vice-presidential candidate, Thomas R. Marshall, until two weeks later. Perhaps he brooded all that time over the closeness of the vote, and wondered how his last chance for glory had been snatched from him by a mere 4400 votes, when a total of 18,500,000 had been cast nationwide.

If Fairbanks had been reelected to the vice-presidency, he would have served exactly fifteen months, for he died on June 4, 1918, of a chronic "intestinal nephritis."

27th Vice-President James Schoolcraft Sherman—Republican, New York, 1909–1912 (President William Howard Taft). Born: October 24, 1855, Utica, N. Y. Died: October 30, 1912, Utica, N. Y.

Madmen and Geniuses

James Schoolcraft Sherman

Toward the close of his second term, Theodore Roosevelt began to behave as if he knew that future historians would rate him one of the great presidents. Admittedly the only chief executive since Abraham Lincoln to deserve superlatives, Roosevelt put himself into an exclusive grouping with Thomas Jefferson and Andrew Jackson. Those two presidents, at the height of their influence and popularity, personally selected their successors; Jefferson chose James Madison to succeed him, and Andrew Jackson chose Martin Van Buren.

No other presidents had dictated choice of their successors. Not until Theodore Roosevelt.

His first preference was his secretary of state, sixty-three-year-old Elihu Root of New York. But Root's ties to Wall Street as a former corporation lawyer, and to the large trusts that Roosevelt himself had assiduously tried to destroy, left him vulnerable to Democratic attack. Roosevelt therefore turned to another member of his cabinet, his secretary of war, fifty-year-old William Howard Taft of Ohio.

The huge, genial Taft would have rather served on the Supreme Court, but Roosevelt was a persuasive man. He wanted Taft in the presidency; so, too, did Mrs. Taft. Between them, they made a powerful combination Taft found impossible to refuse.

The Chicago Coliseum was once again the setting for the Republican's quadrennial get-together; this year of 1908 they were to meet from June 16 to 19. Roosevelt had some time before declared that he would not seek a third term, but nevertheless there was a determined effort to

183

draft him. The draft movement did not get very far, for the party bosses had been specifically instructed by their chief, T.R. himself, that the presidential nominee was to be William Howard Taft.

With their number one candidate thus selected in advance, the Republicans had nothing of interest to look forward to except their vice-presidential nominee. For days in advance of the balloting, many names were tossed about, including two from Indiana, Senator Beveridge and incumbent Vice-President Fairbanks (who really wanted the presidency), two from Iowa, Senator Jonathan P. Dolliver and Governor Albert B. Cummins, and finally, Congressman James Schoolcraft Sherman of New York.

Taft would have liked "some western senator who has shown himself conservative and at the same time represents the progressive movement." Since it was apparent that the Democrats, who were to convene the following month, would nominate William Jennings Bryan for the third time, there were other Republicans who shared Taft's concern. The publisher of the Kansas City *Star* was particularly anxious that the Grand Old Party choose "a running mate to help lick Bryan, not one to please reactionaries."

Perhaps geography presented the final and telling argument. Of the early front-runners, the one to emerge as the convention favorite, with the grudging approval of Taft and Roosevelt, was James S. Sherman of New York. He was the one least qualified to claim the progressive label, but geography was certainly on his side, since the presidential standard bearer, Taft, came from Ohio.

Once word was leaked to the press that Sherman was acceptable to Taft and to the White House, the Sherman boom erupted in a cacophony of noisy parades through hotel lobbies, with loud huzzahing and the singing over and over of a ditty set to a popular tune of the day.

> Hurrah for Sherman, he is a dandy,
> He is a blamed fine man.
> He's the whole blamed candy.
> He is a daisy, he drives us crazy.
> Eins, zwei, drei, vier,
> Sherman is the winner here,
> He is a blamed fine man.

All through the early morning hours of June 19 the noise for Sherman went on. "Eins, zwei, drei, vier, Sherman is the winner here." And so he was. When the weary delegates convened on Friday morning, they needed only one hour and nineteen minutes to complete their business and to rush through the nomination of James S. Sherman on the first ballot. By then, the hall was half empty, most of the delegates were dressed in their "going-away clothes," and no demonstration followed the formal announcement from the convention chair that Sherman was now the official choice for the vice-presidency. Almost everyone, in fact, hurried out as soon as the voting was over.

But one thing could be said in favor of Sherman's nomination. The Democrats would no longer be able to claim that *both* Republican candidates had been handpicked by the White House.

The 1908 election campaign was a dull, draggy affair. Not even the golden-voiced orator from Nebraska, William Jennings Bryan, could inject any life into the stodgy proceedings. He was no longer the boy wonder of the West; now he was just a middle-aged politician, still looking for the big victory.

It was the conservative Sherman who provided the only note of interest. A California attorney, one Edmund Burke, accused Sherman of improperly using his congressional influence when he was chairman of the House Committee on Indian Affairs.

As Burke told the story, he and Sherman were partners in 1901 in the New Mexico Lumber and Development Company, a $3-million concern incorporated in the Territory of Arizona. Through the strategic payment of a few hundred dollars each to certain gentlemen, including the governor of New Mexico and the federal superintendent of lands, Messrs. Burke and Sherman secured for themselves at a tenth of real value, 150,000 acres of choice timber land, to be sold in 160 acre lots to individuals. To legalize this obvious land grab, Representative Sherman, in his capacity as chairman of the Committee on Indian Affairs, prepared House Bill 11,062; the bill actually passed the House, but was killed by a more discerning and suspicious Senate.

Sherman made no response to Burke's allegations, although supporters and friends denounced the story as a "campaign libel." The Democrats chose not to make a big issue out of it and the charges did not in the end hurt the Republicans, for Taft and Sherman amassed 1,270,000 more votes than did the Democrats, and won easily in the electoral count. As they had hoped, Sherman's presence on the ticket did win New York for them.

The congressman's climb to the vice-presidency paralleled a familiar route. He studied law, entered practice in Utica, New York, when he was twenty-four, and five years later won election as mayor of Utica on the Republican ticket. He had deserted his family's principles, for they had always been Democratic, and an older brother had previously served as a Democratic mayor of Utica. Sherman worked closely with the New York Republican machines, and was allied with the Platt organization among others. In 1886, he won his first election to the United States Congress and served many terms in that body.

Sherman's twenty years as a congressman brought him into the national leadership of his party, even though he proposed little legislation and contributed almost nothing to the country's welfare. But he was an intimate friend and a favorite of two of the most influential men in the lower house, Thomas B. Reed of Maine and wily "Uncle Joe" Cannon of Illinois.

Both Reed and Cannon served many years as Speakers of the House. Cannon frequently permitted Sherman to take the chair as temporary

Speaker, for the New Yorker was a skilled parliamentarian, and had learned his lessons well from Uncle Joe. One newspaper referred to Sherman as a "perfect steamroller" in the chair.

"When he feels the handle of the gavel in his fist," wrote the reporter, "he has a knack of simulating total blindness when members of the minority demand recognition."

Congressman Sherman made friends easily; almost everyone called him "Smiling Jim," for he was perpetually optimistic and greeted friends and enemies alike with a cordial smile and an innocently disarming geniality. He was well practised in political strategy and tactics.

The Sherman boom for the vice-presidential nomination in June, 1908, was largely managed by Joe Cannon, along with other Congressional leaders. Cannon did not particularly care for President Roosevelt, nor did T.R. like him very much. Cannon's industrious efforts on behalf of his fellow conservative were expended as much to thwart Roosevelt as to nominate Sherman.

By this time, health had become an important factor to Sherman. Four years earlier, when he was not yet fifty, he suffered the first symptoms of a serious kidney ailment and his doctors had suggested he cut down on his work. But inactivity did not suit Sherman. Instead, he stuck to a careful diet and managed to avoid any more serious attacks until 1908. In the spring of that year he became gravely ill, and for awhile it was feared he might not survive. But he recovered soon enough to present himself to the Republican convention in June as a healthy man ready to assume his responsibilities.

The vice-presidency brought only empty honors to Sherman. President Taft looked to others for comfort and advice rather than to his Vice-President. From the beginning of his administration, the new President found himself surrounded by advisers, yet alone. His friendship with Theodore Roosevelt was rapidly crumbling. The former President did not like Taft's desertion of his appointees, nor was he happy with his successor's slow and fumbling approach to the program he had inherited. Taft could have used a Henry Cabot Lodge to advise him, but he had no one. He did not approve of Vice-President Sherman's machine politics, and therefore ignored him.

A year after assuming office, Vice-President Sherman made a move that ultimately proved to be a major blunder, and may well have been instrumental in reshaping the future course of the nation's history.

Former President Roosevelt, still at the height of his popularity, was offered the temporary chairmanship of a New York state convention, to be held in Saratoga toward the end to September, 1910. At this point, Sherman and his companions in the Old Guard decided to frustrate Roosevelt by giving the temporary chairmanship to the Vice-President. A victory for Sherman would boost his stock and push T.R. out of the limelight. To lend respectability to the project, word was leaked that Taft favored this plan.

The Old Guard and Sherman won—for a few weeks. The committee that met in August to arrange the agenda for the approaching convention selected Sherman. Roosevelt, smarting from the insult, carried the fight to the general delegate body.

Roosevelt's efforts were successful.

When the convention met on September 27, it rejected the proposal of its committee and chose Roosevelt instead of Sherman. Characteristically, T.R. had turned defeat into victory. But the entire episode had soured him even more on Taft, despite the President's assertion that he had never been part of the plot. Roosevelt believed he was, and that's what did the damage.

In some ways, Roosevelt was a petty man. He was not one to forget a grudge or an insult, and he had been wounded by the obvious slap in the face handed to him by the Sherman forces. There were other reasons why Roosevelt finally felt compelled to seek reelection in 1912, thus helping to defeat Taft by splitting the Republican vote. The affair of the temporary chairmanship of a state convention seemed small in itself, but in Roosevelt's mind it had been inspired by Taft. It gave the former President one more reason to run again, helping to strengthen his conviction that Taft had abandoned both him and his policies.

The Republican convention of 1912 renominated Taft for a second term, and prevailed upon Sherman to run once more even though he had again become ill with his recurring kidney ailment. With Roosevelt now an avowed candidate of a third party scheduled to nominate him in August, the Republicans desperately needed help in New York, home state both of Roosevelt and Vice-President Sherman. Sherman reluctantly accepted renomination, but could not campaign because he was too sick.

Within a few weeks, the end was evident for Sherman. At 9:42 P.M. on October 30, 1912, he died in his Utica home of uremic poisoning, brought on by Bright's disease. The years of illness had finally taken their toll. He was fifty-seven.

Since the presidential election was to take place within a few days, no successor could be chosen in time to place another name on the ballot. But it didn't really matter, said the Republican National Committee, since the people were voting for *electors* and not for candidates.

So the voters went to the polls on the following Tuesday and 3,484,980 of them voted for a dead man.

28th Vice-President Thomas Riley Marshall—Democrat, Indiana, 1913–1921 (President Woodrow Wilson). Born: March 14, 1854, North Manchester, Ind. Died: June 1, 1925, Washington, D. C.

Madmen and Geniuses

Thomas Riley Marshall

In sharp contrast to the lifeless campaign of 1908, the presidential election of 1912 was filled with high drama and excitement. The certain renomination of President Taft to be the Republican standard-bearer galvanized the supporters of Theodore Roosevelt into anguished action. When T.R. had won his own term in 1904, he immediately announced he would not run for the presidency again. He lived to regret that impulsive statement, for now, in 1912, he decided he did want to be in the White House once more. But the party regulars were committed to Taft, and bound to him by tradition. They could not very well dump their incumbent President in favor of a former chief executive who, it seemed to many of them, was running for spite as well as ambition.

Roosevelt would not be swerved; conservatives and reactionaries had taken over his reform program, and he was determined to replace his former protégé, William H. Taft. The struggle between the Roosevelt progressives and the old-line machine politicians brought joy to the Democrats, for they saw at last, in the bitter factionalism gripping the Republicans, an opportunity to regain the presidency they had not held for sixteen years.

The Democrats in one sense were right, for the family dispute temporarily destroyed the Republican Party as a dynamic entity, much as the Democrats themselves had been split by the disastrous schism in 1860, when the Southerners and Northerners ran separate candidates against Abraham Lincoln. But in 1912 the voters may well have turned against the incumbent party anyway, whether or not Roosevelt entered the race. The electorate wanted change. Reform was in the air.

As happened in later conventions, the Republican gathering of 1912 featured an angry and public squabble over the seating of some 250 delegates. The Roosevelt faction put up a spirited fight to seat their own people, but lost out to the Taft forces, who were backed all the way by the machine. It was evident that the rank and file, shouting themselves hoarse for Teddy, were not to have their way.

Two days later, Taft was renominated on the first ballot, with 344 delegates, most of them for Roosevelt, not voting. A statement by Roosevelt, read to the press before the convention had gotten underway, served notice upon the Republican bosses that no longer would they rule as self-appointed tribunes.

It was a statement filled with typical Rooseveltian fervor and passion, and underlined the almost religious emotion that would grip T.R.'s followers in the coming months.

". . . We fight in honorable fashion for the good of mankind; unheeding of our individual fates; with unflinching hearts and undimmed eyes; we stand at Armageddon, and we battle for the Lord!"

So Roosevelt's third party, its religious fervor unabated, met in Chicago, August 5 to 7, to complete the destruction of Taft's hopes for reelection. Without a single dissent, the Progressives nominated Theodore Roosevelt of New York to run for the presidency. As an indication of its fresh approach to politics, the new party reached clear across the country for its vice-presidential candidate and chose Senator Hiram W. Johnson of California to be Roosevelt's running mate. Geography was being served with a vengeance.

The Democrats, in the meantime, had their own problems but managed to resolve them to the ultimate benefit of the entire country. It took them five long days and weary nights to find their own presidential candidate. Like Roosevelt, there were many Democrats, William Jennings Bryan and others, who sensed the rising tide of progressivism. They held out for a man with enlightened ideas, someone who would help realize the hopes of the common man, without going too far to the left, as Eugene Debs and his Socialist Party were advocating.

Fortunately for the Democrats they had Governor Woodrow Wilson of New Jersey. Wilson firmly believed it was the function of the government to serve the people, not the other way around. A gifted political scholar, the intellectual Wilson was exactly the kind of candidate the Democrats needed. Finally, late on the night of July 2, 1912, the old guard Democrats gave up, and Woodrow Wilson was nominated on the forty-sixth ballot.

The liberal and visionary Wilson, astonished perhaps that the Democrats had in fact chosen him, asked a conservative congressman from Iowa, Oscar W. Underwood, to be his vice-presidential running mate. The influential Underwood, majority leader in the House, did not want to be buried in the second spot, and he refused. The convention choice was another governor, Thomas Riley Marshall of Indiana.

Wilson protested. "He is a small-calibre man," he said of Marshall.

But Wilson accepted the inevitable when it was pointed out to him that Marshall "was well located geographically," and an extremely capable politician.

At 1:56 A.M. in the early morning of Wednesday, July 3, 1912, Thomas Riley Marshall was nominated by acclamation at the end of the second ballot, and one of the longest and most decisive conventions in history finally adjourned.

It is possible that Marshall's geographical location played a critical role in the election, as did Wilson's, for the Democrats won the home states of their candidates for the first time since Grover Cleveland. It should be pointed out, however, that the combined votes in each of these states for Roosevelt and Taft totaled more than the votes for Wilson. The same was true in many other states that went for Wilson, as for example in Illinois, Massachusetts, New York, and Ohio. In the previous election, all of these key states voted Republican; this time, with two Republicans to split the vote, all four gave a plurality to the Democrats.

The results of the 1912 election have been debated and discussed endlessly with no definite conclusions. Wilson's popular vote was far less than a majority, only 6,300,000 against 8,800,000 for all the other candidates (including the splinter parties). But his electoral vote of 81.92 percent gave him an easy victory.

Did Wilson win because the normally Republican vote split between Roosevelt and Taft? The Roosevelt and Taft total of 7,600,000 was exactly the same as the entire vote cast for Taft alone four years before. But would many of these Republican votes have gone to Wilson if Roosevelt had not been in the race? Probably. The tide of reform was turning away from the conservative Taft. He might very well have lost in a two-man race, without Roosevelt to take votes away.

On the other hand, what would have happened if the two-man race had been between Wilson and Roosevelt? It's a provocative question, but one that cannot be answered. How many of the disenchanted would have stuck with Roosevelt, or have gone over to Wilson?

No one knows. Perhaps a two-man contest between Roosevelt and Wilson would have hinged, in the final analysis, upon the "Undecided." These voters, who refuse to be categorized, have been unsung. But history should pay them greater homage, for their very indecision often controls the balance of power.

The twenty-eighth Vice-President of the United States may have been a man of "small-calibre," but he brought a refreshing change to the federal capital. Thomas Riley Marshall, fifty-eight at the time of his inauguration, viewed himself and his fellows with a wry humor. He had no illusions about politics, his own capabilities, or the limitations of his office.

A slight man with a pixie smile and a twinkle in his eye, Marshall looked upon the vice-presidency with an amused detachment.

"Since the days of John Adams," Marshall wrote, "there has been a dread and fear that some vice-president of the United States would break loose and raise hell and Maria with the administration. Everything that can be done, therefore, is done to furnish him with some innocuous occupation. They seek to put him where he can do no harm."

One of "the nameless, unremembered" tasks assigned to the vice-president was to work as a regent of the Smithsonian Institute, where, as Marshall said, "he has an opportunity to compare his fossilized life with the fossils of all ages."

On another occasion, Marshall described a visit he made to Denver while he was vice-president.

". . . A big husky policeman kept following me around, until I asked him what he was doing. He said he was guarding my person. I said: 'Your labor is in vain. Nobody was ever crazy enough to shoot at a vice-president. If you will go away and find somebody to shoot at me, I'll go down in history as being the first vice-president who ever attracted enough attention even to have a crank shoot at him."

But Marshall did not go down in history, at least not for his vice-presidential labors. Although he was the first vice-president in almost one hundred years to serve two complete terms, he is largely unknown to most people. (Daniel Tompkins, James Monroe's second-in-command, was the last vice-president before Marshall to serve two complete terms. Actually, John Calhoun was elected for two vice-presidential terms following Tompkins. Calhoun served from 1825 to 1829 under John Quincy Adams, and was chosen for a second term under Andrew Jackson, from 1829 to 1833, but he resigned in December of 1832, and therefore did not complete his second term.)

Marshall's career prior to the vice-presidency was neither spectacular nor meteoric. He became a lawyer at the age of twenty-one, and gradually acquired a modest local fame in Columbia City, Indiana, as well as some standing in state Democratic circles. In 1908, when he was fifty-four, it was suggested that he run for Congress. Characteristically, he declined with the comment that he was afraid he might be elected. He did consent, however, to stand for the governorship of Indiana, for he admitted this was the one office he'd like to hold.

He did not expect to be elected, but he astonished the country by defeating his Republican opponent by more than 10,000 votes while the Republican presidential ticket of Taft and Sherman easily carried the state with a plurality of 15,000 votes.

Described as "a progressive with the brakes set," or as "a conservative in motion," an assessment Wilson preferred, Governor Marshall attracted national attention by advocating legislation far more humanitarian than most other states were ready to undertake. At the same time, he declared himself in favor of traditional American values and political institutions.

Marshall's humanitarianism carried over into his treatment of Indiana state prisoners, for he believed in "the conscientious administration of the law for the reformation of unfortunate criminals." To some of his opponents, his readiness to issue pardons and paroles was too soft-hearted, as he later wrote:

"Critics made a good deal of sport of me, as they called me the 'Pardoning Governor.' They even cartooned me, having a man jostling me in a crowd, saying: 'Pardon me, Governor,' and my response being: 'Certainly! What crime have you committed?' "

The vice-presidency did not change his behavior or his unassuming appraisal of himself, for he liked to think that he was "a plain, every-day average American citizen." In Washington, he was "Tom" Marshall, as he still was in Columbia City, Indiana.

One of the most popular men ever to sit in the second chair, Vice-President Marshall was in constant demand as a lecturer, for his dry wit and endless fund of humorous stories delighted audiences all over the country. He didn't at all mind traveling the lecture trail, for unlike a number of his immediate predecessors he was not a wealthy man, and he made good use of the healthy fees he commanded as a speaker.

In 1916, both Marshall and Wilson were renominated by the Democrats without opposition, and won re-election in a close race. Their Republican opponents were Charles Evans Hughes of New York and Charles Warren Fairbanks of Indiana. With Marshall and Fairbanks both from Indiana, this election marked the first and only time that the two major vice-presidential candidates came from the same state.

Wilson's second term, during which the United States entered and helped win World War I, was marked by events of magnitude. In one of them, Vice-President Marshall might very well have precipitated a crucial development for the country and as a result, elevated himself to a more exalted place in history. Instead, he preferred the quiet refuge of anonymity; he refused to permit crisis and another man's misfortune to thrust him beyond the vice-presidency.

When President Wilson returned from France in 1919 with the blueprint for the League of Nations, he found a hostile Senate blocking his cherished dream to join a worldwide concord for peace. Weary and depleted almost to the point of collapse, the President insisted upon taking his fight for the League to the people, in spite of warnings from his doctor.

On September 3, 1919, President Wilson and his party started a cross-country tour by train. The President was planning to make dozens of speeches, including many from the rear platform of the train. It was a grueling schedule, even for a healthy man, and Wilson was obviously ill and tired—very tired. On September 26, in Pueblo, Colorado, he suffered a breakdown, and was hurried back to Washington. Within a week, he was paralyzed, and seriously ill.

Without consulting the Vice-President or the cabinet or congressional leaders, Mrs. Wilson, the President's doctor and the President's secretary took it upon themselves to conceal the extent of Wilson's illness. They refused to allow anyone to see him, and they carefully screened everything and anything that was to be brought to his attention. The affairs of the administration came to a standstill, for there was no one to administer them. A bitter Congress began to accuse Mrs. Wilson of being the "Presidentress"; she had changed her title, it was said, from "First Lady" to "Acting First Man."

When it became evident that Wilson was not functioning in his role as president, Vice-President Marshall was urged to take over the duties of the chief executive. Even Mrs. Wilson, whose primary concern was her husband's health, discussed the possibility of having Wilson resign, so that Marshall might succeed to the presidency and relieve Wilson of the stresses that had almost cost him his life.

But one of the President's doctors, an eminent nerve specialist from Philadelphia, Dr. Francis X. Dercum, did not agree with Mrs. Wilson.

"For Mr. Wilson to resign," said Dr. Dercum, "would have a bad effect on the country, and a serious effect on our patient. He has staked his life and made his promise to the world to do all in his power to get the Treaty ratified and make the League of Nations complete. If he resigns, the greatest incentive to recovery is gone; and as his mind is clear as crystal he can still do more with even a maimed body than any one else."

The loyal Vice-President felt the same, for he refused to give in to the advice and suggestions pouring in upon him from friends, colleagues, and party leaders. The President was obviously disabled, they all told him. Under the terms of the Constitution, the same paragraph John Tyler had used in 1840 to assume the presidency upon the death of William Henry Harrison, Marshall had the right to replace the ailing Wilson.

But Marshall would not take advantage of this stipulation, for he was afraid of the consequences, as he confided to his wife: "I could throw this country into civil war, but I won't." And to the urgings of his secretary that he appropriate control of the administration, Marshall replied:

"I am not going to seize the place, and then have Wilson, recovered, come around and say, 'Get off, you usurper!'"

So Marshall remained as he had been, a vice-president lost in the shadow of his chief. Wilson ultimately regained a measure of his health, and some months later he once again picked up the routine of the presidency, although not with his previous vigor and vitality. Faced by a solid phalanx of "irreconcilable" senators, notably Henry Cabot Lodge of Massachusetts, William E. Borah of Idaho, and Hiram Johnson of California, the still ailing and feeble Wilson at last saw his dream for a League of Nations go down to defeat.

Inevitably, Wilson's long illness and Marshall's failure to take control of the presidency lead to an intriguing speculation. Would the course of the world's history have been different if Marshall *had* assumed the presidency?

When Zachary Taylor died in 1850, his successor, Millard Fillmore, immediately signed the omnibus legislation that came to be known as the Compromise of 1850. Taylor had vowed he would never accept it; Fillmore did, and probably delayed the start of the Civil War.

Might something similar have happened in 1919? Lodge and his fellow "irreconcilables" were willing to compromise on the League of Nations; Wilson was not. Marshall had said he was in favor of compromise. Had he become acting president, would he have salvaged Wilson's dream by making concessions Wilson would never have made? And what might have happened in Europe during the 1920s and 1930s, and after that the 1940s, if the United States had indeed become part of the League of Nations?

We cannot even guess. Nor can anyone say what Marshall might have done as chief executive. If he himself had any idea what path he may have followed, he never said.

Thomas Riley Marshall might have become a memorable name; instead, he is now simply one more of our country's forgotten leaders. Still, he did make one lasting contribution to our lore.

During a long and boring debate in the Senate, Senator Bristow of Kansas intoned his weary way through a dull speech on a subject dear to his heart, "What This Country Needs." The presiding officer, Vice-President Marshall, unable to contain himself, leaned over to an aide and said, in a stage whisper loud enough to be heard in every corner of the Senate chamber, and ultimately in every corner of the land:

"What this country needs is a really good five-cent cigar."

29th Vice-President Calvin Coolidge—Republican, Massachusetts, 1921–1923 (President Warren G. Harding). Born: July 4, 1872, Plymouth, Vt. Died: January 5, 1933, Northampton, Mass.

Madmen and Geniuses

Calvin Coolidge

As if by prearrangement, both presidential slates in 1920 presented a study in contrasts. On the Republican side, the presidential candidate was a handsome, friendly and outgoing man, while his running mate seemed chiseled from the chill, unbending granite of his native New England. For the Democrats, the order was reversed; it was their vice-presidential candidate who exuded charm and smiling warmth, while their number one man faced his task with solemnity.

Personalities aside, there were some rather startling similarities between the two presidential candidates. Both were from Ohio, both were newspapermen as well as politicians and, in the finest American tradition, both were self-made. In age they were four years apart.

But the two men running for the vice-presidency could not have been more dissimilar. The Democrat had been born to wealth, raised in luxury, and exposed to the finest aristocratic ideals, yet he was a liberal. His Republican opponent, reared in the uncompromising frugality of a Vermont farm and only moderately well-to-do, clung to conservatism and old-fashioned concepts. The Yankee was the older by ten years.

The Republicans were the first to make their choices, although not without trauma and surprises. On Friday morning, June 11, 1920, in Chicago's Coliseum, fifteen names were placed in nomination for the presidency. While many of them were obviously favorite sons, there were three who were genuine possibilities—General Leonard Wood of Massachusetts, Governor Frank Lowden of Illinois and Senator Hiram Johnson of California. Senator Warren Harding of Ohio and Governor

197

Calvin Coolidge of Massachusetts were also among the nominees, but were not given much of a chance.

At least so it seemed through the first four ballots, with none of the leading candidates able to muster a majority. That Friday evening when the convention adjourned, a group of party leaders, most of them from the Senate, gathered in a suite at the Blackstone Hotel. It was here that the notorious "smoke-filled room" so dear to politicos was born. And though it may have been neither as smoky nor as cut-and-dried as tradition would have us believe, it was nevertheless there that the decision was made to give the nomination to Senator Warren Gamaliel Harding of Ohio.

Word went out to the convention and to key delegations on the following morning, and eight hours and six ballots later, the edict from the Blackstone Hotel was obeyed. Senator Harding received the Republican nomination for the presidency. A more disastrous choice than the easy-going, inadequate senator from Ohio could not have been made, yet he was now the Republican candidate. It had been so decreed the night before. One delegate, editor and biographer William Allen White, protested vigorously:

"If you nominate Harding you will disgrace the Republican party. You will bring shame to the country."

But to others the selection was eminently practical, as another delegate phrased it:

"We got a lot of second-raters and Warren Harding is the best of the second-raters."

Besides that, to quote Teddy Roosevelt's outspoken daughter, Alice Roosevelt Longworth, "Harding could be counted on to 'go along'. In other words, he could be controlled."

With the handsome, gregarious Harding now the GOP's number one candidate, the Republican convention finally turned to its last remaining bit of business—nomination of his running mate. Again the leaders decided, and again word went out to rapidly dwindling delegations. To balance the conservative Harding, a progressive senator from Wisconsin, Irvine Lenroot, was to be the number two man. Dutifully, another senator placed Lenroot's name in nomination and the convention prepared to vote.

But then, with hundreds of delegates already gone, and most of the party bosses on their way home, the convention astonishingly erupted into revolt. A delegate from Oregon, a Mr. Wallace McCamant, jumped to his feet and demanded the floor. The convention chairman, Senator Henry Cabot Lodge, had just relinquished the dais to someone else, for, to all intents and purposes, the main business of the convention had been completed. His compliant replacement recognized Mr. McCamant. The steely-eyed Lodge, who had chaired the convention with a firm gavel and a good sense of deferring to the needs of the party leaders, might have declared McCamant out of order or disregarded him altogether while proceeding to the roll call. If that had been the case, our history would be different, for Lenroot's name would have been rushed through to a formal vote.

Mr. McCamant, however, did have the floor. In a squeaky voice that could not be clearly heard above the sound of chairs being pushed aside and feet departing and hundreds of delegates clattering their farewells, he made a short nominating speech that ended with these words:

". . . On behalf of the Oregon delegation I name for the exalted office of vice-president, Governor Calvin Coolidge, of Massachusetts."

The mention of Coolidge's name received "an outburst of applause of short duration but of great power," the convention stenographer recorded.

It was a dramatic and unexpected development, one that the bosses were powerless to halt. One delegation after another, all of them supposedly "controlled," hurriedly rose to second Coolidge's nomination. Like wildfire, the idea caught on to the consternation of the party leaders.

Only one ballot was necessary. Laconic "Silent Cal" Coolidge received 674 votes, while Lenroot supporters could muster but 146. For once, the rank and file had the final say.

When Vice-President Marshall received the news, he sent Coolidge a telegram that was more commiseration than congratulation: "Please accept my sincere sympathy."

The Democratic convention of 1920, meeting for the first time in San Francisco, was almost a repeat of 1912. The delegates labored through forty-four ballots before settling upon James M. Cox, wealthy publisher-politician from Ohio. His personal choice for running mate was the attractive and likeable Franklin D. Roosevelt of New York. It was said of Roosevelt that he had "a million vote smile."

But the women of America, who were to vote in a national election for the first time, preferred the masculine, middle-aged charisma of the Republicans' number one candidate, Warren G. Harding. Roosevelt's "million vote smile" could not overcome the huge popularity of the voluble and jovial Harding, who advocated a "return to normalcy," away from the visionary progressivism of Woodrow Wilson and the Democratic candidate, James Cox.

The results of the election showed a landslide victory for Harding and Coolidge, who received 16,000,000 popular votes to only 9,000,000 for Cox and Roosevelt.

Many myths and legends have developed around the silent image of Calvin Coolidge. He spoke so little it was said that whenever he opened his mouth, a moth flew out. Or when he finally smiled, "the effect was like ice breaking in a New England river."

A schoolmate and friend gave a description of Coolidge that was similarly picturesque:

"In appearance he was splendidly null, apparently deficient in red corpuscles, with a peaked, wire-drawn expression. You felt that he was always about to turn up his coat against a chilling east wind."

Once, Coolidge asked an associate to visit him in his office. The associate stayed well over half an hour. Not a word passed between the two. Finally, when the other man rose to go, Coolidge said: "Thank you for coming. I wanted to think."

It is surprising that a man of such taciturnity should have gone so far in American politics, with a string of elective victories virtually unbroken. (He had one minor defeat early in his career.) But the traditional maxim that "the office seeks the man" may have applied to Coolidge. He was also helped along the way by three men who saw in him a genuine honesty and a refreshing respect for economy. All of them—Frank Stearns, Boston merchant, Dwight Morrow, a Coolidge classmate and financier, and Senator Winthrop Murray Crane, Republican boss of western Massachusetts—worked to push him to the top.

Coolidge's appeal to the voters, during his various campaigns, lay in his incarnation of the traditional American ideals of frugality, plainness, and hard work. And he was undoubtedly one of the luckiest politicians of his era, for he always managed to be where good fortune could fall upon him. In 1898, at the age of twenty-six, he was elected to the city council of Northampton, Massachusetts, where he was practicing law. He later became city solicitor, clerk of the courts, mayor, member of the Massachusetts House of Representatives, member of the state senate, president of the state senate, lieutenant-governor of Massachusetts, and finally governor of his state. All of this took him a total of twenty years.

In early September of 1919, while he was governor of Massachusetts, fate played directly into Coolidge's hands. The Boston police, who had long been underpaid and underappreciated, decided to improve their lot by joining with the American Federation of Labor, then under the guidance of Samuel Gompers. The Commissioner of Police promptly suspended nineteen of the policemen's leaders for violating his orders against joining the AFL.

Just as promptly, the police went on strike, at 5:45 in the afternoon of Tuesday, September 9; the strike vote was 1134 for, 2 against.

With no police to guard the city, Boston mobs and criminals went on a rampage, looting and rioting through Tuesday night, Wednesday, and Wednesday night. The mayor of Boston was helpless. In the meantime, Governor Coolidge stoically sat on the sidelines, waiting for the proper moment to step in. By noon on Thursday, he made his move. He ordered out the state militia and expressed the fullest confidence in Boston's Commissioner of Police, who had contributed to the crisis by refusing to allow his men to organize for their betterment. In effect, Governor Coolidge supported this view and helped to break the strike. Years later, his "Autobiography" explained why:

". . . Police should not affiliate with any outside body whether of wage earners or of wage payers but should remain unattached, impartial officers of the law with sole allegiance to the public."

To an angry Samuel Gompers who accused the governor of improper actions, Coolidge sent a wire that brought him instantaneous and country-wide fame:

"There is no right to strike against the public safety by anybody, any time, anywhere."

It was a sentiment that delighted millions of Americans who were beginning to rebel against Woodrow Wilson's "New Freedom" and longed for a return of the good old days. Coolidge was an overnight hero.

When the Republican convention met in Chicago some months later, the rank and file delegates vividly remembered the unobtrusive Massachusetts governor who had broken a calamitous strike and restored peace to a troubled city. Despite the agonized opposition of the patrician Henry Cabot Lodge, who spluttered that it was unthinkable to choose a man who lived in a two-family house, Coolidge received the Republican nomination for vice-president largely because of his role in the Boston police strike.

The thrifty Calvin Coolidge did not appreciably change his ways once he moved from Boston to Washington. As lieutenant-governor of Massachusetts, he had lived in one room of the Adams Hotel in Boston; when he became governor, he and Mrs. Coolidge moved into two rooms of the Adams Hotel. In Washington, he decided that his vice-presidential salary of $12,000 a year could not support a house, so once again he and his wife took up quarters in a hotel, this time in the Willard.

The social rounds that faced the Vice-President and his wife did not overly appeal to Coolidge. He participated as little as possible in the chatter, kept his thoughts and opinions to himself, and promptly left every gathering at 10:00 P.M. But he never turned down an invitation, and when asked why, he snapped:

"Got to eat somewhere."

Within a short time, the Vice-President had become an appealing oddity in the capital; the man described by Alice Roosevelt Longworth as having been "weaned on a pickle" found himself the subject of story and legend. In a city of protocol and fraternal intrigue, Silent Cal was a prime character.

He took to his professional routine easily and naturally, for his long years of presiding in the Massachusetts state senate gave him a firm grasp of parliamentary procedure. His service as presiding officer of the United States Senate did not dismay or annoy him. He even claimed the Senate proceedings greatly interested him, but there is evidence that he was frequently bored.

President Harding invited Coolidge to sit in on cabinet meetings, but here, too, the Vice-President remained a passive onlooker. He sat but did not join the discussions.

The Harding administration was a troubled one. The President's cronies, infamously celebrated as the "Ohio gang," systematically indulged in fraud, graft, bribery and dissipation. The full extent of their wheelings and dealings and carousals only came out some years later, but there were excited buzzings in many a Washington salon. Coolidge certainly must have had some idea of what the Ohio gang was up to; if so, he kept his counsel. He went quietly about his own affairs while the Harding administration hurtled toward disaster.

By the spring of 1923, an agitated Harding began to be aware of the illicit schemes and intrigues of his friends. The good-natured and trusting President, himself no model of propriety for he had had at least two long-lived extramarital affairs, had always looked the other way. His poker playing, hard drinking cronies, he thought, were simply taking a commonly practiced advantage of their top level connections.

But it was far more than that, as he learned. If the truth came out, a major scandal could develop and destroy him along with the others. He himself had not been a party to the fraud and the graft, but these were his close friends and associates. Whatever threatened them threatened him.

In an effort to bolster his crumbling image, Harding planned a cross-country tour by train. He wanted the people to see him and to renew their confidence in his administration, for he intended to seek a second term, without Coolidge. He had his eye on someone else, as he confided to a friend:

"We are not worried about that little fellow in Massachusetts."

Harding was far more concerned about his own future when he and his party left Washington on June 20, 1923, on the first leg of a scheduled 15,000 mile journey. But the trip was not to bring him the reassurance he needed. In late July he suffered a collapse in Seattle and was moved to San Francisco, where he died in a few days, apparently of a heart attack. The date was August 2, 1923; Harding was fifty-five.

The Vice-President, in the meantime, had taken his family to his birthplace in Plymouth Notch, Vermont, for a summer vacation. They were staying at his father's farmhouse, which had neither electricity nor a telephone.

It was not until midnight, when the Coolidges had already been asleep for some hours, that an excited messenger came chugging up in an ancient automobile with the news that the President was dead. While oil lamps were lit, and reporters and neighbors gathered, the Vice-President calmly dressed in a dark suit, came downstairs, and prepared to take the oath of office as the thirtieth president of the United States.

In a room with faded wallpaper, a threadbare rug, and an oil lamp for illumination, the elderly Coolidge, who was a notary public, became the first and only father ever to swear in his own son as president.

When the last phrase of the oath was spoken, the new President solemnly placed his hand on the Bible and spoke the final words with fitting sincerity:

"So help me God."

A few minutes later, he returned upstairs, went back to bed, and fell asleep almost at once.

30th Vice-President   Charles G. Dawes—Republican, Illinois, 1925–
1929 (President Calvin Coolidge). Born: August 27, 1865, Marietta,
Ohio. Died: April 23, 1951, Evanston, Ill.

Madmen and Geniuses

Charles G. Dawes

After serving in the presidency for only ten months, it was evident that Calvin Coolidge had captured the confidence of the country. By handling the balance of the Harding administration with calm and dignity, he established himself as the Republicans' number one candidate for the presidency. Even those who were none too sure of him admitted that he would have little opposition at their upcoming convention.

The Republicans were scheduled to meet in Cleveland, Ohio, from June 10 to June 12 of 1924. Many of the delegates arrived a few days early and one group of influential Republicans came together at a Cleveland hotel the Saturday before the convention.

With Coolidge's nomination assured, most likely on the first ballot, these party leaders recognized that the only problem to face the assemblage the following week would be the vice-presidential candidate. They decided informally to make their own choice of Coolidge's running mate.

For most of them, the obvious man was former Governor Frank Lowden of Illinois. In 1920, Lowden had been one of the three early favorites, but lost out in the end to Harding. Lowden still wanted the presidency, but with Coolidge an avowed candidate, he could not possibly win the nomination for the top spot.

Would Lowden take second place? He had said he would not, and he had been definite on this point. The informal Republican caucus, therefore, began to examine other possibilities.

All through that Saturday, into Sunday, and Monday, the group

offered names, discussed them, tore them apart, rejected, and suggested
new names. For each prospect, there was always at least one serious
objection. But the search went on, hour after hour. Finally, at 4:00 A.M.
on Tuesday, the day the convention was to begin, one bone weary
member of the caucus got up and said he was leaving.

"I am going to bed," he announced. "The kind of man you are looking for as Vice-President was crucified nineteen hundred years ago."

President Coolidge himself had no specific choice, although it was
rumored he had asked Senator William E. Borah of Idaho to run on the
ticket.

Borah replied: "At which end?"

Whether this story was true or not, Borah was seriously considered
for the vice-presidential nomination until he demanded that his name
be withdrawn from consideration.

On the morning of Thursday, June 12, Calvin Coolidge was nominated on the first ballot to seek a full term. His selection was not unanimous, for thirty-four votes went to Senator Robert La Follette of Wisconsin and ten votes were cast for Senator Hiram Johnson of California.

The delegates reconvened after lunch to choose the President's running mate. The convention favorite was Governor Lowden. The names
of many other prominent Republicans were placed before the convention along with his, but he easily received a majority on the second ballot.
Now the question arose as to whether he would accept.

The only way to find out was to ask him. It was therefore decided
to adjourn the convention until that evening without declaring a candidate for the vice-presidency.

When the delegates reconvened at eight o'clock, they received
definite word that Lowden would not accept. For only the second time
in American history, a nominee for the vice-presidency declined the
nomination. The first time happened in 1844, when Senator Silas Wright
of New York telegraphed his refusal, and the nomination then went to
George Mifflin Dallas of Pennsylvania.

Now, in 1924, with Lowden unequivocally out, the Republican
convention turned to a man who had never held an elective office, yet
was undeniably one of the most powerful Republicans of his time. The
weary delegates, anxious to go home at last, gladly gave their votes to
wealthy financier Charles G. Dawes of Illinois.

Admittedly popular, Dawes undoubtedly helped the Republican
ticket. But it was the Democrats themselves who handed the 1924 election over to the Republicans almost as a gift.

In the longest convention on record, and certainly one of the most
discordant, the Democrats wrangled through ten feverish days and 104
ballots before reluctantly deciding on John W. Davis, a New York professor of law, as a compromise candidate. In the meantime, Senator La
Follette bolted the Republican Party, and accepted nomination by a
rejuvenated Progressive Party.

The self-lacerated Democrats, who had torn themselves apart during their quarrelsome convention struggle, were no match for "Cautious Cal Coolidge" and "Charging Charlie Dawes." Not even the presence of a potent third party made any appreciable difference, for Coolidge and Dawes, with a total of 15,725,000, outpolled the combined opposing tickets, which could muster only 13,200,000 votes between them: 8,400,000 for the Democrats and 4,800,000 for the Progressives.

Choice of the fifty-nine-year-old Dawes to be the vice-president had some justification, despite his lack of experience in elective office. As a wealthy industrialist and banker who had given up law for the world of investments and finance, he was a forceful executive and administrator. A strong believer in the status quo and a constant exponent of law and order, he conducted his affairs with a firm, no nonsense approach.

Charles Dawes drifted into politics as naturally as he had turned to the amassing of wealth. In 1896, he managed William McKinley's campaign in Illinois; his efforts gave McKinley the largest plurality any winning candidate had ever received in that state. President McKinley rewarded Dawes, who was then thirty-three, with an appointment as federal comptroller of the currency. Dawes resigned from this position in 1902, to make an unsuccessful try for the Senate.

His loss elicited a comment that may have inspired future defeated candidates. Dawes declared that he was "out of politics for good and all."

He kept his vow for twenty-two years.

By the time the United States entered World War I, Dawes was a multimillionaire and a power in the affairs of the Republican Party and the country as well. In 1908, Senator La Follette had denounced "the one hundred men who are running the country." Along with such prominent and financially formidable names as John D. Rockefeller, J. Pierpont Morgan, Andrew Carnegie, Levi P. Morton, Henry Frick, and others, La Follette included the young Chicago banker, Charles G. Dawes.

Dawes had one other qualification that set him apart from most politicians; he was a talented composer. He had taken almost no musical training, yet he had a natural ear. One of his compositions, "Melody in A Major," was published in 1911, and was subsequently arranged for almost every possible instrument, including the violin. In 1923 the eminent violinist, Fritz Kreisler, added the composition to his repertoire without being aware that its composer was a world famous financier.

When the United States entered World War I, Dawes was itching for military action. Through his good friend, General John J. Pershing, he received a commission as a major in the Seventeenth Engineers, U. S. Army. A few months later Pershing, who was head of the American Expeditionary Forces in Europe, appointed Dawes to be his chief purchasing agent. In this capacity the energetic Dawes was responsible for the buying and transportation of millions of tons of supplies and hundreds of thousands of horses and mules. He completed his army service with the rank of a brigadier general.

While the war was being fought, Dawes had only one goal in mind—to find his supplies and get them where they were needed as quickly as possible. Red tape or the niceties of meticulous records had to be dispensed with if they stood in his way. Get the job done and worry about it later, he always reasoned. He did have to worry about it later, in 1921, but it was his acccusers who came out on the short end.

A headline-hunting congressional committee, which had been dragging out its investigations for almost two years, was looking into the matter of United States expenditures during the war. They summoned Dawes in February of 1921 to testify about the unusual methods he had employed to make his purchases. The committee was particularly interested in some of the high prices he had paid for mules.

Dawes jumped to his feet.

"Hell 'n' Maria," he exploded, "I'd have paid horse prices for sheep if the sheep could have hauled artillery. We were fighting a war. . . . We didn't have time for duplicate vouchers and double-entry bookkeeping. It is a hell-fired shame for everybody to be trying to pick flyspecks on the greatest army the world ever knew. . . . We went to France to win the war and we did it."

His outspoken profanity reverberated around the country; many people reacted with shock, but there was far more smiling admiration for his courage in talking back to the publicity minded congressmen. Within a few months the committee and its investigation quietly expired. Nothing had been accomplished except to make the Chicago banker, with his underslung pipe jammed defiantly between his teeth, a national personality. "Hell 'n' Maria" became a byword.

In the area of civil rights, Dawes operated with a peculiar inconsistency. He was against lawlessness, particularly as exemplified by secret societies such as the Ku Klux Klan. Yet he saw nothing wrong with organizing his own private militia, a paramilitary group of vigilantes he called the "Minute Men of the Constitution." At the height of their influence, when they flourished in Illinois during 1923, the Minute Men numbered 42,786 members in 154 companies. Dawes underwrote the expenses.

The avowed aim of the organziation was "clean politics" and the "support of law enforcement." In the end, however, its real goal was shown to be antiunionism, and the membership gradually drifted away. At the same time, Dawes shifted his own interest to a broader canvas when he was selected to head an international committee to study the question of German reparations to be paid to the victorious wartime Allies.

The suggestions of the committee came to be known as the "Dawes Plan," and helped to stabilize the slumping German economy. For his formulation of this plan, Dawes was awarded the 1925 Nobel Peace Prize, which he shared with England's Sir Austen Chamberlain.

Dawes did not seek the vice-presidency, but when the Republican convention of 1924 named him as their second choice for the number two spot, he accepted without objection. The office itself did not terrify him; he approached it with the same sure confidence he had always exhibited in the business world.

Like many of his predecessors, Vice-President Dawes is little known today to most Americans, but the Senate of his time and Washington society had ample reason to remember him, one with animosity and the other with laughter.

Dawes got off on the wrong foot from the very beginning. It was expected that, as incoming vice-president, Dawes would make the usual innocuous short remarks for his inaugural speech and leave the real center of interest to the president. But Dawes was not a man to be intimidated either by custom or protocol. He had things to say to the Senate, over which he was to preside for the next four years, and he spoke out.

On March 4, 1925, promptly at noon, Dawes took the oath of office in the Senate chamber as the thirtieth vice-president and the new presiding officer of the Senate. He then proceeded to his speech.

After a few moments, the Senate began seething with collective fury, for the new Vice-President had the gall to tell them that their hallowed Rule XXII, which allowed one man or a small group of men to force their will on the majority by way of a filibuster, was undemocratic and not in the best interests of the country. He suggested, none too tactfully, that this long-established senatorial tradition had to be scrapped.

His speech created an uproar and crowded off the front pages the far more important inaugural address that was delivered shortly after by President Coolidge. Basically of course, Dawes was correct, but he went about it in the wrong way. The senators, standing guard over their domain like jealous gods, resented his public rebuke. He would have accomplished far more working behind the scenes. But he knew little of that technique; finesse was not for him.

Five days later the Senate had its revenge, and Washington had a hearty laugh at his expense. On March 9, the Senate was voting to confirm President Coolidge's cabinet appointments. Charles Beecher Warren of Michigan, appointed to be the new attorney general, was resisted because of his ties to the sugar monopoly.

A number of senators were scheduled to speak that afternoon on the Warren appointment. When the drowsy Vice-President was assured by both the majority and minority leaders that no vote could possibly be taken that day, he returned to his hotel for a nap. But the scheduled speakers decided not to continue the debate, so a vote unexpectedly was taken.

Republican leaders saw, to their horror, that a tie vote could easily develop. If that happened, they would need Dawes to break the tie. A frenzied call went out to wake him from his nap while the frantic Republican leaders did everything in their power to slow down the roll call. Dawes, still half asleep, dressing as he went, dashed out of his hotel, flagged a passing taxi, and careened through the streets of Washington to the Capitol, breaking the twenty mile speed limit by a considerable margin.

In the meantime, the roll call was completed, and it did end in a 40 to 40 tie. Dawes' taxi screeched up to the Capitol, where a group of younger Republicans were anxiously waiting for him. They carried him up the stairs and into the Senate chamber. Gasping for breath, the Vice-President ran down the aisle.

The heroic race was all in vain. Before Dawes arrived, one senator changed his mind and decided to vote against the Warren confirmation, so Coolidge's appointment lost by two votes, 41 to 39.

A prankster placed a sign near the entrance of the Willard Hotel: "Dawes Slept Here!"

Calvin Coolidge's terse announcement in August of 1927 that he did not "choose to run for President in nineteen twenty-eight" spelled the end to elective office for Charles G. Dawes. He continued active, however, in government service as ambassador to Great Britain and chairman of the Reconstruction Finance Corporation.

Charles G. Dawes died in 1951 at the age of eighty-five. With fitting irony, that same year there was a revival of his composition, "Melody in A Major." With lyrics and a new title, "It's All In The Game," it became one of the most popular songs of the year.

31st Vice-President   Charles Curtis—Republican, Kansas, 1929–1933
(President Herbert C. Hoover). Born: January 25, 1860, Topeka, Kansas. Died: February 8, 1936, Washington, D. C.

Madmen and Geniuses

Charles Curtis

In a bizarre display of obtuseness, the Republican convention of 1928 totally disregarded the warnings of the past. The Republicans paid no attention at all to the lesson they should have learned from the unexpected death of President Warren Harding a scant five years before. Perhaps because the country had survived this blow, and even prospered, the Grand Old Party was convinced that it could do no wrong. So it chose, as its candidate for vice-president in 1928, a sixty-eight-year-old senator who refused to admit that the United States, politically at least, had entered the twentieth century.

That such a man, at such a time, should have been selected for the second highest office, and would in fact be separated from the presidency itself by one fragile beat of another man's heart indicated the indifference most political leaders felt toward the vice-presidency. Yet in a curiously old-fashioned way, his nomination made sense, for he was the perfect balance for the Republican ticket.

The Republican delegates assembled in the Civic Auditorium of Kansas City, Missouri, June 12 through 15. On the evening of June 14, nine names were placed before the convention for the number one spot, but only one ballot was needed. Fifty-three-year-old Herbert Hoover of California, who would be running in a public election for the first time, easily won the nomination for president with 837 votes out of a total of 1,089.

To many of the delegates, the wealthy and stiffly sober Californian was a liberal who did not favor the agricultural policies that were neces-

213

sary for the vital midwestern vote. And there was also the question of
his inexperience as a campaigner. True, he was immensely popular as a
result of his widely heralded relief work during World War I, and his
long tenure as secretary of commerce under Presidents Harding and
Coolidge made him a leading national figure. Still, he had never before
run for public office.

What better way to bolster his candidacy than with a real pro, a
party regular from another part of the country, a man to attract the
farm vote? And perhaps even more satisfactory to the GOP masterminds,
a genuine reactionary, to counter Hoover's "liberalism"?

They found their perfect number two candidate in Charles Curtis
of Kansas, one-eighth Kaw Indian and seven-eighths incompetent. He
had served in Congress as a representative and senator since 1893.
He had assiduously played the political game according to its time-
honored rules, and had finally won for himself a place as a Harding
crony. In short, Curtis was a bumbling anachronism who was described
by one writer of the times as a "mediocrity who is as faithful to his party
as he is dull and dumb."

This was the man the Republicans selected to succeed to the presidency if that unhappy possibility ever same to pass. The Grand Old
Party was not yet ready to abandon tradition.

The Democrats met two weeks later in Houston, Texas, and managed to avoid the unfortunate experience of their previous convention.
They followed the Republican lead by taking only one ballot to choose
their candidate for president, Governor Alfred E. Smith of New York,
a Catholic and an opponent of Prohibition. To balance *him*, the Democrats chose for vice-president another governor, Joseph T. Robinson
of Arkansas, a Protestant and a dry.

But the electorate preferred the Republican balance. For the third
successive time, the Republican Party swept to a decisive victory. Herbert Hoover and Charles Curtis received 83.62 percent of the electoral
total with 21,390,000 votes to 15,000,000 votes for the Democrats.

It was an historic triumph, for this was the first and only time that
either of the two chief executive offices had ever been filled by a man
who had actually lived on an Indian reservation. The Republicans may
have taken unfair advantage of Curtis's ancestry, for immediately after
their convention, a laudatory campaign biography about Curtis was
rushed into print. Its title was *From Kaw Teepee To Capitol*, but its
subtitle was far more vivid:

"The Life Story of Charles Curtis, Indian, Who Has Risen to
High Estate."

Charley Curtis traced his Indian blood to Nom-pa-wa-rah, "White
Plume," head chief of the Kaws. Non-pa-wa-rah took as a wife Wy-he-
see, daughter of an Osage chieftain. These were the great-great-grand-
parents of the thirty-first vice-president. Their daughter married a
French trader, and her daughter, Julie, married another French trader,
Louis Pappan. The Pappans' daughter, Helen, became the wife of Oren

A. Curtis of Kansas. Their only son, Charles, was born in North Topeka on January 25, 1860.

Helen Curtis, one-fourth Kaw, remained rooted in her Indian heritage. When her son was little more than a year old, she gave him a pony named Kate and taught him to ride bareback fashion. Mrs. Curtis died two years later, when Charley was three. After that, he divided his time between his grandmothers; he lived with his grandmother Curtis in North Topeka between 1863 and 1866, and again from 1869 to 1876.

It was the three years between, from 1866 to 1869, he never forgot; it was then that he lived with his Indian grandmother, Julie Pappan, on the Kansas reservation of the dwindling Kaw tribe. There he became an expert at riding his pony, so expert in fact, that later as a teenager, he made a living as a jockey at county fairs.

In 1869 Charley moved back to North Topeka, to the home of his grandmother Curtis. He began attending public school, and even though at the age of nine he could not yet read, he quickly advanced and caught up with the other pupils. By 1876, he was ready for high school, and soon after, with the encouragement of a prominent Topeka attorney, he took up the study of law. To support himself during this period, he drove a hack; while waiting for fares, he sat in the back of his carriage and pored over his law books.

"If there had not been oil lamps on the side of the hack," he recalled some years later, "I never would have become a lawyer."

He was admitted to the bar in 1881, at the age of twenty-one. Within four years, Curtis had advanced far enough in his profession to win election as county attorney of Shawnee County. This was the first of a long string of electoral triumphs; in 1893 he was elected to the United States House of Representatives, where he served for fourteen years. Curtis then went into the Senate, and except for a brief interval of two years, 1913 to 1915, he stayed in that body until 1929.

From the beginning of his political career, Charles Curtis exploited his Indian blood. He did not seem to mind at all that some of his peers made constant reference to his ancestry. During his early service in the House, he inadvertently entered the office of Speaker Tom Reed of Maine to find he had interrupted a conference of Republican leaders. As Curtis started to back out, Speaker Reed roared at him:

"Come back in here, Indian, I want you to hear this!"

Others were not that friendly. When Curtis was serving as vice-president under Herbert Hoover, H. L. Mencken, in his usual acrimonious fashion, referred to the two heads of state as "Lord Hoover and the Injun."

Curtis's formula for success in politics rested upon one unbeatable factor, a comprehensive card index for his constituents. With the help of his half-sister, Dolly, who became his secretary, Curtis compiled an impressive file of the voters in his district. He and Dolly created dossier upon dossier, as she herself admitted in a book of memoirs she published in 1933:

"As a part of my duties as secretary, I began to keep systematic records for campaign use—books filled with the names of Kansas voters, the citizens of every county and town. All the names we could get. A short biography of each voter, with his achievements, sometimes with a description of his personality, all the facts we could gather about him."

Her efforts were not wasted, as her brother's many political victories attested. He knew how to make use of the information she had carefully gathered.

Curtis did not dazzle as a legislator; he seldom made speeches and offered almost no bills. But he hewed to the traditional party line, unswerving in his loyalty to the ideals of the past. One cynic said that for Curtis, "the trinity meant the Republican Party, the high protective tariff, and the Grand Army of the Republic."

By 1924 Senator Curtis and his still faithful associate, half-sister Dolly, had become convinced he was ready for higher office, the presidency itself. But with the nomination of Calvin Coolidge a certainty, they decided to settle for the vice-presidency. Unfortunately, Coolidge put an end to that plan, for Curtis had unwisely pushed a bill through the Senate that Coolidge had vetoed. Curtis, therefore, had to wait another four years for his chance at immortality.

As the Republican convention of June, 1928, opened, Dolly and other members of the Curtis family descended upon the convention hall to cheer brother Charles on to the top prize. To their obvious disappointment, he received only 64 votes for president, while Herbert Hoover was racking up his potent total of 837.

The next day, the vice-presidency was offered to Curtis as a consolation. Senator Borah of Idaho placed Curtis's name in nomination, to be seconded by Congressman Hamilton Fish, Jr., of New York; Fish described the Kansas senator as "that regular of regulars, that American of Americans."

Another seconding speech was made by Curtis's attractive daughter, Leona, who was there as a delegate from Rhode Island. While the band gallantly tootled, "Ain't she pretty, ain't she sweet?", the lovely young lady was escorted to the platform, where she seconded her father's nomination with a speech of exactly forty-three words.

It was a moment of happy triumph for the Curtis family, to be followed by an even greater triumph in the Republican landslide victory a few months later. Charles Curtis, Indian, and thirty-first vice-president of his country, had indeed "Risen to High Estate."

Vice-President Charles Curtis, who now refused to allow his cronies to address him as "Charley," but insisted upon "Mr. Vice-President," found the burdens of his office onerous and unproductive. But he thoroughly enjoyed one side benefit—the social rounds with their banquets, dinners, and parties. He covered them all, with the same gusto he had given to his political maneuvering.

As a widower, Curtis selected his half-sister, Dolly Gann, to be his official hostess, and insisted that she must take precedence over all other women in official Washington except for the First Lady, Lou Henry Hoover. This announcement brought on a storm of protest, led by the Speaker of the House, Nicholas Longworth, and his wife, Alice Roosevelt Longworth, the spirited daughter of T.R. Although Mrs. Longworth made light of the affair in her own memoirs, published in the same year as Dolly's, she was an active participant in the furor. The Dolly-Alice feud enlivened the Washington scene for months.

The Longworths, along with many others, refused to concede that a sister of the vice-president outranked all others except the First Lady. The only one who could rightfully claim this honor would be the *wife* of the vice-president. Dolly Gann, therefore, no matter what Vice-President Curtis may have insisted, would have to be placed far below most of the official wives, most particularly behind the wife of the Speaker of the House.

But Curtis and Dolly stuck to their guns. So too did the Longworths. In early October of 1929, President Hoover hosted a state dinner for the visiting Prime Minister of England, Ramsey MacDonald. Despite the obvious importance of the event, Speaker Longworth and his wife, who normally would have been high up on the "preference list," did not attend, for Washington knew in advance that Dolly Gann was to be seated on the President's left, while the wife of the British ambassador would be on his right. In that case, Dolly would have outranked Alice.

The Longworths stayed away, and Vice-President Curtis and Dolly Gann won their point.

A few days after this memorable episode, the stock market fell with a shattering crash, and the Great Depression was on its way. To the Vice-President and his sister, who happily continued on their merry rounds of socializing, the Depression was but a temporary inconvenience. At one point, in a speech she made on behalf of the Hoover-Curtis administration, Dolly announced that the Depression was over.

One newspaper headlined, "Dolly Calls It Off."

With hunger and misery and unemployment in full swing, many Republicans knew their party was in trouble. When they gathered in Chicago June 14 to 16 for their quadrennial convention, they faced their task with little enthusiasm. Hoover had no thought of stepping aside, even though it was apparent his former popularity had all but evaporated. Apathetically, with scant hope of success, the delegates did as they were expected to do and renominated their incumbent President. And because Hoover let it be known that he wanted Charles Curtis with him on the ticket once again, Curtis too was renominated.

The Democrats, meeting in the same Chicago Stadium two weeks later, countered with Governor Franklin Delano Roosevelt of New York, the man with "the million vote smile," and for his running mate, John Nance Garner of Texas.

The Republicans quickly learned how deeply in trouble they were to be. Thousands upon thousands of hungry Bonus Marchers, veterans of World War I, were assembling in Washington to plead for help for themselves and their families. On July 14, one month after the convention that nominated him for a second term, a terrified Vice-President Curtis personally ordered out two companies of marines to disperse a crowd of Bonus Marchers who were milling outside his window. Luckily, cooler heads recalled the marines and no damage was done, except to the Vice-President's reputation.

By July 28th, President Hoover had had enough of the pleading Bonus Marchers, who wanted only the same kind of help the administration was perfectly willing to hand out to big business. So Hoover directed General Douglas MacArthur to disperse the veterans. MacArthur did, with troops and tear gas, leaving a bitterness that would never die. It was not a day for the Republican Party to cherish.

But still the Vice-President seemed totally unaware of the larger issues. He went off to Los Angeles to open the tenth summer Olympics in the name of the President. He made frequent stops along the way, and just as frequently he was heckled by an unsympathetic citizenry. In Iowa he lost his temper and shouted that the voters were "too damn dumb" to understand what he and Hoover were trying to accomplish. At Las Vegas someone yelled at him:

"Why didn't you feed those ex-soldiers in Washington?"

The touchy Vice-President exploded. "I've fed more than you have, you dirty cowards! I'm not afraid of any of you!"

In answer, the crowd started chanting, "Hurray for Roosevelt!"

This disdainful treatment of the Vice-President was a prelude of the disaster that followed a few weeks later when the country went to the polls to elect a new president and vice-president. Roosevelt and Garner swamped Hoover and Curtis with 88.89 percent of the electoral vote; the Republicans won only six states.

For the Hoover–Curtis team that was the end of public office. Hoover lived on for thirty-two more years, until the age of ninety, and came to be respected as an eminent "elder statesman." Curtis died on February 8, 1936, three years after leaving office, without adding luster to his name. He was seventy-six at his death.

President Roosevelt issued a statement eulogizing the former Vice-President; the statement was full of the usual platitudes.

"I am deeply distressed to learn of the sudden passing of my old friend Charley Curtis," the President said. "Whether they knew him as a senator, as the Vice-President of the United States, or as the man he was in his own right, his legion of friends will remember him, always affectionately, and will mourn his passing."

32nd Vice-President   John Nance Garner—Democrat, Texas, 1933–
1941 (President Franklin Delano Roosevelt). Born: November 22,
1868, Detroit, Red River County, Tex. Died: November 7, 1967,
Uvalde, Tex.

Madmen and Geniuses

John Nance Garner

When Charles Curtis relinquished the vice-presidency in March of 1933, official Washington witnessed the end of a long era of lightweight incompetence. The bewildered, confused Throttlebottom had at last passed from the scene, to live only on the pages of "Of Thee I Sing." There would again be jokes at the expense of the vice-president, but unlike the fictional Throttlebottom, future occupants of the second chair would no longer have to search for two references so they could have a library card or to be ashamed to tell their mothers what office they were holding.

The vice-presidency now stood on the threshold of maturity, although it would still be treated as bait in the often complicated game of political wheeling and dealing. The Democratic convention of 1932 presented a classic example of backstage maneuvering, with frantic cross-country phone calls, last minute offers, and decisions arrived at by a small group of powerful men.

For the first time in sixteen years, the Democrats knew they had a real chance of winning the presidency. With Hoover and the Republicans helpless in their feeble attempts to reverse the Depression, the country clamored for a change at the top. Hoover's hopeful declarations that "prosperity was just around the corner" did not mollify the hungry and shabby millions of unemployed. Breadlines and soup lines grew longer, while the Republicans floundered and the Democrats plotted.

The man to beat for the Democratic presidential nomination was unquestionably Franklin Delano Roosevelt, fifty-year-old governor of

New York. He had the charm, the vote getting appeal, and the social aims that were desperately needed to pull the country out of despondency and starvation.

But three men stood in his way—Alfred E. Smith, badly beaten candidate of 1928, once Roosevelt's close friend; John Nance Garner, Speaker of the House and perennial congressman from Texas; and William Randolph Hearst, influential newspaper owner and molder of public opinion.

After his distressing defeat four years before, Smith had no desire to face the Catholic issue once again. But the lure of the presidency was too strong; he knew that 1932 was a Democratic year. As titular head of the party, he felt the nomination should be his by right of tradition and experience.

The road before him, however, was a rocky one, for the immensely wealthy and powerful William Randolph Hearst hated him. Some years before, on a New York matter, Smith had defeated Hearst; in the process he had been imprudent enough to describe Hearst as "this pestilence that walks in the darkness." He had even labeled Hearst's New York *American* the "Mud-Gutter Gazette."

Hearst never forgot and never forgave, and so would not support Smith under any circumstances. Nor did Hearst want any part of the liberal Roosevelt, whose views were too internationalist for the California-based publisher.

One candidate did have all the qualifications Hearst thought necessary. That man was the sixty-three-year-old Speaker of the House, John Nance Garner of Texas. Hearst bought time on the NBC radio network to tell the country why the salty Texan should be the next president.

"Unless we Americans are willing to go on laboring indefinitely merely to provide loot for Europe," Hearst told his listeners, "we should personally see to it that a man is elected to the presidency this year whose guiding motto is 'America First.'"

Such a man was Garner, who was, said Hearst, "a loyal American citizen, a plain man of the plain people, a sound and sincere Democrat."

As a result of Hearst's support, the Garner forces came to the Democratic convention, which met in Chicago, June 27 to July 2, with 90 pledged delegates, 44 from California and 46 from Texas. Smith had about twice that number. Roosevelt had considerably more, at least a majority, though not the two-thirds he would need to win.

After an afternoon and night of interminable nominating and seconding speeches, the Democratic delegates finally got around to voting for their presidential candidate at 4:28 in the early morning of Friday, July 1, 1932. At the end of the first ballot, the count stood 666 for Roosevelt, 201 for Smith, and 90 for Garner. After two more ballots, there was almost no change, and the Roosevelt camp showed a touch of panic. Their strength would last only for one or two more roll calls, and then there would be a rapid erosion.

The key lay with Garner, and behind him, William Randolph

Hearst. No deal was possible with Smith, who continued to hold out implacably against his former friend and protégé.

At 9:15 A.M., the convention adjourned, to allow the unshaven, unbathed, and weary delegates to go to their hotel rooms for a few hours of sleep. For the Roosevelt people, there was no rest.

A cross country phone call went out to Hearst in California. He agreed to advise Garner to release his California and Texas delegations provided Roosevelt make a public renunciation of his "internationalist" views. Reluctantly, the Roosevelt forces accepted Hearst's demands. Hearst then instructed his Washington man to visit Garner to tell him what had been decided.

Aware that his convention strength, particularly in California, was due only to Hearst's support, Garner now realized that his bid for the presidency was no longer realistic. He called his floor manager in Chicago, fellow Texan, Congressman Sam Rayburn, and authorized him to release the Texas and California delegations.

When the convention reassembled that afternoon, it was all over. On the fourth and final ballot, California and Texas formally gave their votes to Roosevelt, and he had enough for the nomination.

Was the "quid pro quo," as the *New York Times* phrased it, the vice-presidency for John Nance Garner? There were many, close to all the negotiations, who consistently denied a deal of that kind had been made. Yet the evidence strongly suggests that such had been the case. Only one ballot was required to nominate Garner for the vice-presidency.

For the ebullient and aristocratic Roosevelt, the rough-hewn "Cactus Jack" provided the traditional Southern balance, so he was more than acceptable on geographical terms. That he lacked the polish and sophistication of the Groton-educated New Yorker did not bother Roosevelt at all. Garner was a power in Washington, and that was good enough for the pragmatic FDR.

Yet a nagging question arises—why did Garner give up one of the most powerful offices in the country for the maligned and downgraded vice-presidency? Years later, he made some telling comments on his acceptance of the deal that gave the presidential nomination to Roosevelt.

"Worst damn-fool mistake I ever made was letting myself be elected Vice-President of the United States," he said. "Should have stuck with my old chores as Speaker of the House. I gave up the second most important job in the government for one that didn't amount to a hill of beans."

Why had he left the Speakership which he had finally achieved only the year before? Astute and knowledgeable in the twisting paths of politics, Garner knew his way around. He recognized that the vice-presidency had, until then, been pretty much of a dead end. But he did accept, and accepted with his eyes open. He had a reason, although as it turned out, a hopeless one.

Garner's influence in Washington was based on a career that covered thirty consecutive years of service in the House of Representatives. Texas born, Garner made his home in Uvalde, some sixty miles from the Mexico border. He had moved there as a young lawyer because of his health. Doctors thought they detected tuberculosis and suggested a hot, dry climate. Uvalde was certainly hot enough and dry enough, and propitiously for a young ambitious man, rich in opportunity. By the time Garner was twenty-five, he was a judge in Uvalde County. He then served two terms in the Texas House of Representatives, and in 1903, when he was thirty-four, he won the first of his fifteen congressional terms. In the meantime, Garner used his native shrewdness and his wife's money to become a millionaire.

The Fifteenth Texas District, which Garner represented, was huge and sprawling, almost as large as the entire state of New York. It was full of cacti, cattle, goats, and pecan groves. Garner quickly learned that the best way to win reelection was to do things for his constituency in Washington. So after his first couple of terms, he never again campaigned, never made speeches to the voters of his district, and, in fact, saw very little of the vast area he served. Yet the people of the Fifteenth District, without ever laying eyes upon him, sent him back to Washington year after year.

Nor did Garner waste time in speechmaking in the House or proposing legislation. He was a skillful strategist who did most of his work off the floor and in committee. From the beginning he fought against "the autocratic leaders" of the Democratic Party, who thought of him, as he once reminisced, as "just another cow thief from Texas," and buried him in minor assignments. Through persistence and the right contacts, he eventually worked his way into the inner circle both of the Democratic Party and the House.

One of the ways he used to promote himself was poker. He became part of a group that met regularly at the "Boar's Nest," a celebrated Washington hideaway at which the crafty Speaker of the House, Uncle Joe Cannon, presided. Garner made many valuable friends at these poker sessions, and a great deal of money. Always canny, often ruthless, he sometimes won in the course of a year more than his annual salary of $10,000. But he was not a careless or reckless bettor; he "played them close to the vest." When he bet a dime, one of his colleagues said, Garner was not betting ten cents, but the interest on two dollars.

As Garner's influence grew, so too, did his use of persuasion. Whenever a fellow congressman needed a little prodding or coercing, Garner invited him to his office to "strike a blow for liberty" by way of a few nips of choice bourbon and branch water. Here too, Garner created a "Board of Education," where, with the cooperation of his Republican counterpart, Nicholas Longworth, he helped balky representatives along the way to enlightenment.

During the 1920s Garner was considered the ranking House Democrat, but it was not until December, 1931, that his party once again gained a majority in the House, this time by a single vote. When the Seventy-second Congress convened, Garner was elected Speaker.

It had taken the man from Uvalde twenty-nine years of service in the House to reach the goal coveted by every congressman. His acceptance of the Democratic vice-presidential nomination the following year is therefore all the more surprising. He stated, publicly and to his associates as well, that he gave up the Speakership in the interests of party harmony. There was a more compelling motive, however, than Democratic unity.

In spite of his age—Garner was sixty-four when he was inaugurated vice-president in March of 1933—he still believed he could be the president. He knew he might have to wait until 1941, eight years later, when he would be seventy-two, but he had not the slightest doubt that he would be capable as ever and in full control of his faculties. At no time were his presidential ambitions given as his reason for accepting the vice-presidency, but his later actions strongly underscored this thesis.

Roosevelt's willing acceptance of the Texan as his second in command did not find universal agreement among his associates and aides. Rexford G. Tugwell, one of the original "Brain Trust," had little regard for Garner, as he described the Vice-President in a Roosevelt biography:

"He was a confused Texan who, as the most prominent congressional Democrat, had had the responsibility for shaping alternatives to the Hoover policies. He was, however, so conservative and so lacking in imagination that nothing had occurred to him that Hoover had not thought of first."

Others were not quite that harsh. FDR's secretary of the interior, Harold Ickes, spoke of the Vice-President with the greatest respect and admiration.

President Roosevelt invited Garner to sit in on cabinet meetings, and looked to the former congressman for help in pushing through his legislative program. Although Garner did not always agree with Roosevelt's objectives, he nevertheless did his best for the chief.

After a bit, the cabinet meetings became mere window dressing, "a delightful social occasion," to quote one cabinet member, "where nothing was ever settled." FDR preferred to make his own decisions, and he also suspected that his Vice-President was leaking half-developed information after cabinet sessions.

By 1936, a flood of New Deal reforms brought a measure of hope to a country still badgered by the effects of the Depression. To most people, Roosevelt represented salvation, and there was little doubt that he would be reelected. The Democratic convention of June, 1936, renominated him by acclamation without even bothering to take a vote. Garner, too, was renominated without opposition. Their victory a few months later in the November election was even more dramatic than their first triumph in 1932, for their Republican opponents, Alfred M. Landon of Kansas and Frank Knox of Illinois, won only two states— Maine and Vermont.

The Roosevelt-Garner rapport began to come apart shortly after their second inauguration on January 20, 1937 (the date had been changed from March 4 by the recently enacted Twentieth Amendment). Without prior warning to his cabinet or to his Vice-President, Roosevelt announced a plan to pack the Supreme Court with six more nominees. The nine justices of the Court had knocked down some of FDR's legislation, and he was determined to circumvent their strict constructionism by appointing enough liberal justices to help constitute a majority that would vote his way.

Garner was appalled by Roosevelt's audacious plan. When the President later asked for Garner's assessment, the Vice-President answered frankly.

"Do you want it with the bark on or off, Cap'n?" he asked.

"The rough way," said the President.

"All right, you are beat," Garner replied. "You haven't got the votes."

He was right; Roosevelt withdrew his proposal and backed away.

For Garner, this episode marked the end of his qualified support for the President and the New Deal. Their second term had little of the unity they had demonstrated between 1933 and 1937. Garner now started looking to 1940, when Roosevelt would retire from the presidency, and it would at last be his turn.

The Vice-President's plan hit a double snag in 1939. In March of that year, he harmed his image with the liberal and black vote by refusing to permit his name to be used as a sponsor for a Marian Anderson concert. Denied the use of Constitution Hall by the Daughters of the American Revolution, the renowned black contralto sang in the open, at the Lincoln Memorial in Washington, with 75,000 massed at the base of the monument. It was this outdoor concert, hastily arranged by the First Lady, Eleanor Roosevelt, that Garner refused to endorse.

Some four months later, disaster struck again. Garner ran into trouble with organized labor when he opposed changes in the Wages-Hours Act that would benefit the working man. A furious John L. Lewis, head of the CIO, lashed out at Garner as "a poker-playing, whiskey-drinking, labor-baiting, evil old man."

Garner's problems did not end there. Roosevelt did everything possible to embarrass him at cabinet meetings, and even the Vice-President's former defenders deserted him. Harold Ickes now called him "that political billy goat from Texas," with a "red, wizened face."

"I cannot understand," Ickes wrote, "how anyone looking at Garner could possibly ever think of him for President."

Despite these setbacks, Garner continued to believe that the 1940 nomination could be his. In December of 1939, he announced his candidacy for the presidency. Roosevelt's subsequent decision to run for a third term, or as he preferred it, to accept "a spontaneous draft," infuriated the Vice-President, who blasted FDR's third term candidacy as a cynical violation of a sacred tradition.

With Roosevelt's hat in the ring, Garner had reached the end of the line. At the 1940 Democratic convention, which met once again at the Chicago Stadium, he received 61 votes to Roosevelt's 946.

Garner went back to Texas, and sulkily refused to return to Washington to preside over the Senate, which was still in session. It was a most ignominious close to a long and fruitful career.

The ex-Vice-President outlived most of his colleagues, friends, and detractors. He retired to his large house in Uvalde, surrounded by live oaks and pecan trees. He was still an object of curiosity to visitors, even as he neared the end of his long life.

"People come by here to see me," he once said to an interviewer. "They want to see what a former Vice-President looks like. They expect to see some big imposing man, and it's me. I'm just a little old Democrat."

John Nance Garner died in Uvalde on November 7, 1967, two weeks short of his ninety-ninth birthday.

33rd Vice-President   Henry A. Wallace—Democrat, Iowa, 1941–1945 (President Franklin Delano Roosevelt). Born: October 7, 1888, Adair County, Iowa. Died: November 18, 1965, Danbury, Conn.

Madmen and Geniuses

Henry A. Wallace

Two emotional issues highlighted the Democratic convention of 1940—Roosevelt's dramatic break with the two-term precedent, and a raucous, bitter fight over the vice-presidential nomination. The bad war news from Europe made it certain that FDR would run again. Hitler's blitzkriegs against Denmark, Norway, The Netherlands, Belgium, and finally France, placed the Western world in danger of collapsing before the lightning tactics of the savage Wehrmacht.

This "hurricane of events," in Roosevelt's words, convinced him that a forceful leader concerned about the world was needed at home. Garner and others he dismissed as impossible and incapable of handling the pyramiding crises that would face the next president; FDR decided he would have to seek a third term.

But his renomination would have to be handled carefully. On the basis of old fashioned virtues alone, many Americans objected to the scrapping of the two term precedent, for it had existed through the entire life of the republic. And for many, the isolationism of "America First" transcended international needs.

FDR, therefore, had to be "drafted." The mechanism for a rank and file summons was skillfully arranged and set in motion on the evening of Tuesday, July, 16, 1940.

The Chicago Stadium was jammed with thousands of delegates and spectators. Senator Alben W. Barkley of Kentucky, as the convention's permanent chairman, addressed the assembled delegates at the evening session. Included in his speech was a message from FDR.

"The president has never had," Barkley told the attentive multitude, "and has not today, any desire or purpose to continue in the office of president, to be a candidate for that office, or to be nominated by the Convention for that office."

This of course was a deliberate ploy, but the silent delegates were not aware of it.

"He wishes in all earnestness and sincerity," Barkley went on, "to make it clear that all the delegates to this Convention are free to vote for any candidate."

For a moment, the dumbfounded spectators could not believe what they were hearing. Then suddenly, a single voice thundered over the loudspeakers:

"We want Roosevelt!"

As if prodded into action, a number of delegates burst into the aisles repeating the shout, while the organist swung into a popular song of the day, "Franklin D. Roosevelt Jones," and the mysterious microphone voice relentlessly continued to boom into every corner of the crowded hall:

"The country wants Roosevelt! The world wants Roosevelt!"

The convention went wild. Now the aisles were packed with hysterical Roosevelt supporters, while the music blared, and frenzied shouts of "Roosevelt! Roosevelt! Roosevelt!" poured out of the loudspeakers to be taken up by a surging, screaming mob. All across the nation, millions of electrified listeners sat glued to their radios and heard a demonstration that erupted without letup for fifty-seven minutes of uncontrolled bedlam.

Roosevelt had his "spontaneous draft."

What the convention and the country did not yet know was that the microphone voice was none other than Chicago's superintendent of sewers. Blessed with leather lungs, he had been strategically placed in the basement to bellow out his message at a prearranged signal.

FDR's renomination the following night was a mere formality, although it was hardly unanimous. There were still many who opposed a third term on principle alone or feared its effect on the electorate. On the first and only ballot, four other candidates received a total of 148 votes, but Roosevelt won easily with 946.

Next came the question of Roosevelt's running mate. When FDR let it be known that his choice was the secretary of agriculture, Henry A. Wallace of Iowa, he sent a shock wave through even his most ardent supporters. Shy, austere, often introverted to the point of unfriendliness, Wallace was an idealist whose views terrified the political pros. James Farley, national chairman of the Democratic Party, told Roosevelt that the people considered the Iowan "a wild-eyed fellow." A man who had studied Judaism, Buddhism, Zoroastrianism, Mohammedanism, and Christian Science, among other religions, Wallace was thought by some to be a dreamer, a mystic, "a person answering calls the rest of us don't hear."

Wallace was the wrong man on some additional counts as well, for he was a "renegade" Republican who had turned Democrat only a few years before. Worst of all, he was a liberal, and that, in the opinion of the pros, was too much shattering of precedent. The third-term try was bad enough, but not to balance the ticket with the traditional conservative Southerner was carrying innovation a bit far.

But Roosevelt insisted, and his aides fell in line. They scurried all over the convention hall, pleading with one delegation or another to get behind the chief.

It was not an easy task. When Wallace's name was placed in nomination, boos and cries of disgust exploded in an angry chorus of hostility, and each time the Iowan's name was repeated, so were the boos. For the millions listening to their radios, the Democratic convention became a shambles.

The President, himself one of the radio audience, reacted with rage. If the convention did not want Wallace, they could not have him, either, and he scribbled a message rejecting the presidential nomination in the event Wallace did not win. Fortunately, the message was never delivered.

The calm, dignified presence of Eleanor Roosevelt, who had made a special trip to Chicago at the urging of her husband, restored the convention to order. She had come to speak on behalf of Wallace and unity, and she told the assembled delegates that "the strain of a third term might be too much for any man." The next president would be given a "heavier responsibility, perhaps, than any man has ever faced before in this country."

The convention, so disorderly a short time before, now sat attentive and absorbed, as the First Lady simply and eloquently told the delegates what they must do.

"You will have to rise above considerations which are narrow and partisan," she said. "This is a time when it is the United States we fight for."

Her meaning was clear. It was possible the President would not survive the next four years; his successor must be someone both willing and able to carry on his program and his ideas.

Soon after, the roll call began. There was still much grumbling about Wallace, but he managed to squeak to victory on the first ballot with 627 votes out of 1,100. If not for the scrapping of the two-thirds requirement, which had been replaced by a simple majority at the previous convention, Wallace could not possibly have won. Nor could he have won without Mrs. Roosevelt.

President Roosevelt's choice of Henry A. Wallace to be his second running mate was fundamentally correct. It had long been the custom of both major parties to choose, as far as it was feasible, a ticket that was balanced philosophically as well as geographically.

If the presidential candidate were conservative, his running mate must therefore lean to the liberal, or at least be considered not quite as dogmatic in his support of entrenched interests.

If the presidential candidate lived in the North, or the Northeast, his running mate had to come from the South, or from a border state.

If the presidential candidate favored urban areas to the possible detriment of the rural, his running mate had to have a strong appeal to the farm bloc.

Henry A. Wallace, as the lower half of the 1940 Democratic ticket, totally violated the first principle, partially fulfilled the second, and only on the third did he answer the necessary condition.

It was Roosevelt's thinking that his vice-president, in the event he accidentally succeeded to the presidency, must bring a similar political ideology to the White House. If, for example, Roosevelt were to die halfway through his term, a conservative successor rather than a liberal might well destroy his program and bring the country and perhaps the world to chaos.

For years, the Democrats and Republicans both had ignored this basic need. In balancing their tickets, they had concentrated on the geographical and political and had disregarded the ideological.

That Roosevelt was now aware that a change in approach was mandatory indicated his grasp of the quickly moving flow of history. Future conventions followed the example of the 1940 Democrats, so that every ticket from then on, almost without exception, was either all liberal or all conservative, or a little more or less of one or the other.

Wallace differed from Roosevelt in personality, for the President was outgoing and vivid while the Vice-President was reserved and colorless. But their internationalist philosophies synchronized, and their hopes for the future were much the same.

Wallace was important to Roosevelt on another level as well. Wallace had long been a friend to the farmer, both in his private life during the 1920s and early '30s, and after that in his government service as Roosevelt's secretary of agriculture.

If the South should desert the Democrats in the November, 1940 election because the vice-presidency had been given to another section of the country, the farm vote could prove decisive. But the South stayed as solid as ever for the Democrats, while, paradoxically, some of the vital midwestern farm states, including Wallace's home state of Iowa, voted Republican.

The results of the election did not give Roosevelt the same sweeping mandate he had received in 1936, but he and Wallace nevertheless defeated their Republican rivals, Wendell Willkie of New York and Senator Charles McNary of Oregon, by a comfortable margin.

Henry Wallace devoted his life to agriculture. He had been raised in a family that had dedicated itself to improving the material and spiritual welfare of the farmer. His grandfather, the first Henry Wallace, had been educated as a minister and had given up the pulpit for a farm in Iowa. He founded *Wallaces' Farmer*, a weekly newspaper that crusaded on behalf of better farming. The second Henry Wallace, father of Henry A. Wallace, took up the burden and succeeded to the editorship of the family paper upon the death of the first Henry in 1916. Henry II served as Secretary of Agriculture in the cabinets of two presidents, Warren Harding and Calvin Coolidge, and died in 1924.

The third Henry Wallace was thirty-six at his father's death; he continued the family tradition by taking over the editorship of *Wallaces' Farmer*. Henry A. had by then achieved a modest fortune and some fame in agricultural circles by his work in the development of hybrid corn, which he marketed through his own organization, the Hi-Bred Corn Company.

When Wallace was in his twenties, he had been intrigued by statistics in the calculation of corn-hog price ratios. As a result of his interest, he had tackled "the problem of using multiple correlation coefficients to determine the relationships between summer rainfall and temperature, on the one hand, and corn yields on the other."

This was neither the language nor the concern of politicians. That such a man should find himself in the midst of American politics during the last twenty years of his life seems contradictory, yet Henry A. Wallace became one of the most influential and controversial men of his generation.

Wallace's constant attempts to better the lot of the farmer brought him to the attention of President-elect Franklin Roosevelt in 1932, and FDR then appointed him secretary of agriculture. It was a post that Wallace worked in for an unbroken stretch of eight years. During his tenure he encountered both praise and condemnation.

There were those like the famous Ohio author, Sherwood Anderson, who spoke of the Iowan in the most glowing terms.

"There is something in common between Will Rogers and Henry Wallace," Anderson wrote. "There is the same little smile. . . an inner rather than an outward smile. . . ."

A journalist on the *Baltimore Sun* had less complimentary things to say:

"(He) should have been born in the Middle Ages and set himself in the quiet of a cloister garden to commune with his soul and the Infinite while finding out the laws of hybridism. . . . Wallace, in short, is a queer duck."

Undoubtedly, Wallace preferred the study of agriculture to the bustle of government; free-lance genetic research and seed development fascinated him, the responsibility of a large scale organization did not. But he had come to Washington at the President's request to do a job, and he intended to do his best.

One of his first major accomplishments was the Triple A, the Agricultural Adjustment Agency, established in May of 1933 under the terms of the Farm Act, which Wallace spoke of as a "Declaration of Interdependence." The primary purpose of the Triple A was to raise depressed farm prices to a decent level by requiring farmers to control their production and, if necessary, plow under some of their crops. The government would pay them for crops not raised.

Part of Wallace's program necessitated the slaughter of six million

little pigs, which became 100 million pounds of pork to be distributed to
the poor. The pigs were slaughtered before their usual marketing age
so that the future price of full grown hogs could be increased, and, in
addition, to save 75 million bushels of corn the little pigs would have
eaten in the process of becoming hogs.

An outraged *Chicago Tribune* let loose a journalistic barrage at the
Secretary. The newspaper called him "The Greatest Butcher in Chris-
tendom."

The uproar puzzled Wallace. "To hear them talk," he said, "you'd
think that pigs were raised for pets." Or perhaps people preferred that
"farmers should run a sort of old-folks home for hogs." But the important
point was the price of hogs; within a year it went up by more than 50
percent.

The Roosevelt administration's continuing concern for the farmer
and for the working man translated itself into positive action; by the end
of Roosevelt's second term, the New Deal had slowly helped to point
the country in the direction of recovery.

When FDR decided that Wallace was to be his running mate in
1940, he overrode all objections.

"I've got to have a man I know can do the job," he insisted, and
the Iowan in his view was such a man.

Official Washington was not quite so sure, for Wallace was still a
puzzle, even after eight years. He did not drink, smoke, or play poker;
he despised small talk and ribald jokes. What was he, really? A politician, a scientist, a Christian mystic—or a little of each?

To FDR, Wallace was an extremely capable man. In July of 1941,
a few months after beginning his third term, Roosevelt demonstrated
his confidence in the new Vice-President by expanding Wallace's duties
far beyond those that any previous vice-president had ever handled.
Roosevelt established an Economic Defense Board composed of eight
cabinet members, with Wallace as chairman. When the United States
entered World War II in December of 1941, the Economic Defense
Board became an enlarged Board of Economic Warfare, with many more
responsibilities for Wallace. Never before had a vice-president been
given so much to do.

But Wallace and his board came into conflict with another important member of the Roosevelt team, Jesse Jones of the Reconstruction
Finance Corporation. Jones insisted that much of the BEW's work fell
into the province of the RFC. His angry opposition to Wallace and the
BEW finally prompted Roosevelt to dissolve the BEW and to curtail
much of Jones's authority on the RFC. In the process, Wallace became
only a vice-president once again.

Although Wallace did as much for the war effort as anyone in
Washington, he was more concerned about the peace that would come
after the hostilities. He saw the war itself as a life and death struggle
between freedom and darkness, and he cried out against evil with spiritual indignation. But it was the future he worked for; he wanted a new

world without war, without ignorance and disease and hunger. His world would belong to everyone, as he said in a speech he delivered in 1942:

"Some have spoken of the 'American Century.' I say that the century on which we are entering, the century which will come out of this war, can be and must be the century of the common man. . . The people's revolution is on the march, and the devil and all his angels cannot prevail against it. They cannot prevail, for on the side of the people is the Lord."

He praised America's wartime allies, the Russians, in speech after speech, and he warned against permitting "Fascist interests motivated largely by anti-Russians bias (to) get control of our government." Earl Browder, leader of the American Communist Party, commended the Vice-President's partiality toward the Russians, but then so did Wendell Willkie, Republican candidate for president in 1940.

But there were those who looked upon Wallace's praise of wartime allies as a form of treason. John W. Bricker, governor of Ohio, and shortly to become the Republican vice-presidential candidate for 1944, blasted Wallace as a "wild radical, a visionary idealist, and a merchant of globaloney."

Many Democrats were just as disturbed, most particularly the big city bosses. They transmitted their misgivings to President Roosevelt. By then, the strain of twelve years in the presidency and the immense pressures of fighting the costliest and the deadliest war in history had begun to take their inevitable toll; FDR was weary and ill. When he heard what the party bosses had to say about his Vice-President, he listened, for he was too tired to dismiss them, as he would have years before. Wallace's days in the vice-presidency were numbered.

When Wallace spoke out for civil rights for American blacks and denounced the poll tax, he lost any support he may have had in the South. Unlike Roosevelt, he did not know how to placate or play the game.

Roosevelt did not entirely desert Wallace. He told the Democratic convention of July, 1944, that if he were a delegate, he personally would vote for Wallace's renomination, but he did not want it to appear that he was dictating to the convention, and he therefore asked the delegates to do their own deciding.

For Wallace, this was the "Kiss of Death," as headlines later phrased it. Despite a Gallup Poll that showed 65 percent of Democratic voters preferred Wallace, he lost the 1944 vice-presidential nomination, and with it, ultimately, the presidency.

On that same poll, Alben Barkley of Kentucky had 17 percent, Sam Rayburn of Texas had 5 percent, and trailing far back with 2 percent was Senator Harry S Truman of Missouri.

34th Vice-President   Harry S Truman—Democrat, Missouri, 1945
(President Franklin Delano Roosevelt). Born: May 8, 1884, Lamar,
Mo. Died: December 26, 1972, Kansas City, Mo.

Madmen and Geniuses

Harry S Truman

For the first time in the history of the republic, a vice-presidential nomination became more important than the presidential. With the ailing FDR assured of renomination for a fourth term, the Democratic party bosses were painfully aware that he would probably not make it through another four years. Edwin Pauley of California bluntly summarized the dilemma facing Democratic leaders in 1944:

"You are not nominating a Vice-President of the United States, but a President."

Who was to be the next vice-president and the probable next chief executive?

Certainly not incumbent Henry Wallace, for no one wanted him except the rank and file Democrats and a majority of the people at large. The Democratic pros were determined that the idealistic and visionary Iowan would be retired back to the farm.

A group of party bosses, including Pauley, Bob Hannegan of St. Louis, Ed Flynn of New York, Frank Walker of Pennsylvania, and Mayor Ed Kelly of Chicago, met with President Roosevelt to sift through other possibilities. One by one, for various reasons, names were discarded.

Alben Barkley, sixty-six-year-old majority leader of the Senate, was too old; James Byrnes, an important Roosevelt official, could not muster labor support, and, as a former Catholic, would antagonize the Catholic vote; Supreme Court Justice William O. Douglas had no organization backing. As for Henry Wallace, he had a sizeable part of the population with him, most notably labor, liberals, and the blacks, but the South despised him, as did northern conservatives.

Only one man would be acceptable to all groups—Senator Harry S Truman of Missouri, with two percent of the vote the lowest man on the Gallup poll of Democratic preferences. Everyone at the high level conference agreed that his candidacy would stimulate little enthusiasm, but at least there would be no outward antagonism. FDR conceded that he could live with Truman.

To indicate his approval of the senator from Missouri as a prospective candidate, Roosevelt gave Hannegan a letter that over the years has precipitated dispute and controversy.

"You have written me about Bill Douglas and Harry Truman," Roosevelt wrote. "I should, of course, be very glad to run with either of them and believe that either of them would bring real strength to the ticket."

When this letter was later shown around, the names were reversed so that Truman was first, and it thus appeared that the man from Missouri was FDR's primary choice. Whether FDR himself authorized this change or whether Hannegan somehow engineered it has never been established. But the Hannegan version boomed Truman's candidacy, so that with the help of the bosses, Truman suddenly emerged as a real contender.

In the meantime, to compound the confusion, the exhausted President, in his twelfth grueling year as the country's chief executive, allowed both Wallace and James Byrnes to believe that each of them was his number one choice. To an anguished Byrnes, who telephoned Roosevelt at his Hyde Park country home after hearing of FDR's announced preference of Truman or Douglas, the President wearily responded:

"We have to be damn careful about words. They asked if I would object to Truman and Douglas and I said no. That is different from using the word 'prefer'."

Byrnes, however, angrily withdrew from the race when Hannegan convinced him that Truman was indeed FDR's first choice. But Wallace refused to pull out. He would not believe that his chief had dumped him, for FDR had said to him:

"I hope it's the same team again, Henry."

Yet, in reality, Roosevelt had no intention of retaining the same team. When his wife asked him to keep the Vice-President on the ticket, Roosevelt retorted:

"Wallace had his chance to make his mark and if he could not convince the Party leaders that he was the right person, I cannot dictate to them twice."

The 1944 Democratic convention again met in Chicago, this time for a period of three days, July 19 to July 21. As expected, Roosevelt easily won renomination on the first ballot.

Nominations for the vice-presidency were to begin on the evening of Thursday, July 20. When the name of incumbent Vice-President Henry A. Wallace was mentioned, an enthusiastic demonstration sparked by screaming Wallace supporters in the gallery brought the convention to a standstill. The organist, over and over again, played "Iowa, That's Where the Tall Corn Grows," until Pauley threatened to chop through the amplifier wires. From all parts of the hall, Wallace signs bobbed into view.

The permanent chairman, Senator Samuel D. Jackson of Indiana, finally managed to clear the aisles. It had originally been planned by Hannegan and Pauley that Truman would be nominated that evening, but the boisterous support for Wallace, and the continuing din, made it clear to them that the convention could easily be stampeded to the Iowan if a vote were taken that night.

There was only one solution—recess the convention and bring a halt to the highly charged Wallace bandwagon. Ed Kelly, Mayor of the host city, Chicago, came up with the way to do it. Because of the packed conditions of the gallery, Chicago fire laws were being violated. The hall would have to be cleared at once.

Chairman Jackson called for a vote to adjourn. There were a few scattered "Ayes" and a thundering chorus of "No! No!"

Ignoring the overwhelming sentiment against adjournment, Jackson calmly announced over the hullabaloo that the ayes had it, and the convention would stand adjourned until the following day. Hannegan, Pauley & Co. had effectively throttled the will of the assembled delegates.

All that night and into the next morning, the pro-Truman group worked feverishly to line up votes for the man from Missouri. Even with the ceaseless efforts of Hannegan, Pauley, and the others, the first roll call on the afternoon of Friday, July 21, was disappointing to them, for the count at the end of the ballot stood 429½ for Wallace, 319½ for Truman, 208½ for three favorite sons, and a scattering for eleven others.

But at least their tactics of arbitrarily adjourning on the evening before had stopped Wallace. Although he was comfortably in front, he was far short of the 589 he needed. Surprisingly, he had picked up 9 votes from Florida and 26 from Georgia. So not all of the South despised him as much as the bosses had convinced FDR it did.

The second ballot was even closer, but there was a definite shift to Truman, for he ended with 477½, while Wallace had 473. With the momentum now manifestly Truman's, a rush began to board the bandwagon. One after another, favorite sons released their delegations to Truman, and he was the winner at the end of a revised second ballot with a final count of 1031 to 105.

An uninspiring, rather ordinary man from Missouri had won the most consequential nomination of the twentieth century. Once again a combination of expedience and cynicism, tempered by shrewdness and hardheaded adaptability, had created a political miracle.

The principal objection to Truman's candidacy sprang from his long association with the Pendergast machine in Kansas City. The notorious Tom Pendergast had ruled the Democratic Party in Missouri for decades. He had plucked Harry Truman from obscurity to thrust him, virtually unknown, into the United States Senate. But Truman had never been corrupted by Pendergast or his henchmen. Even his detractors were forced to concede that Truman was scrupulously honest. Early in his career, boss Tom Pendergast grudgingly said about him, with a touch of admiration:

"He's the contrariest man on earth."

Unlike the overwhelming majority of his vice-presidential predecessors, Truman did not practice law nor did he have a college degree. After graduation from high school in Independence, Missouri, he worked at a variety of unimportant jobs, and then spent eleven years as a partner on his father's 600-acre farm at Grandview, not far from Independence. In 1917, despite thick glasses, which he had worn for years to correct a defect diagnosed as "flat eyeballs," Truman fought in World War I. He saw a great deal of action in France, and ended his military service in 1919 as captain of Battery D, 129th Field Artillery. He was then thirty-five.

Two of the boys in the 129th were to play decisive roles in Truman's life. One of them was Eddie Jacobson, a shirt salesman. When the war was over, Truman and Jacobson opened a haberdashery on West Twelfth Street in downtown Kansas City. In less than three years they were out of business, unable to pay their bills. Jacobson declared personal bankruptcy, but Truman would not accept that way out. He insisted that all his creditors must be paid in full. The last debt was finally paid many years later, when he was in the United States Senate.

It was the other man from the 129th whose friendship proved to be more providential. Jim Pendergast was the son of Mike Pendergast, who shared control of the Pendergast machine with brother Tom.

Truman's unfortunate experience as a haberdasher left him, at the age of thirty-seven, with no career and worse, no prospects. Since a number of his fellow officers and other veterans of World War I had successfully entered politics, Truman decided to take a crack at what seemed to him a promising field.

With the help of his army buddy Jim Pendergast, he won the sponsorship of Mike Pendergast, who immediately announced that Truman would be running for county judge of Jackson County (an administrative position, not judicial). Truman surprised many, including himself, by winning a three man race that fall. The year was 1922, and Truman was thirty-eight.

For his second elective office he again had the backing of the Pendergasts. This time they pushed him slightly higher, to the seat of presiding judge of Jackson County. By 1934 he was ready for still another step upward, but Tom Pendergast, who was then in control of the entire Democratic apparatus in Missouri, refused to consider him for county collector (a real plum at $25,000 a year), for congressman or governor. A disconsolate Truman thought that "retirement in some minor county office was all that was in store for me."

But suddenly, to quote a prestigious national weekly, Truman was "yanked out of obscurity so deep that few Missouri voters had ever heard of him." For his own personal reasons, Pendergast decided that Truman was to be the next Democratic candidate for the United States Senate. Why Pendergast made this decision was not clear. One man reported that Pendergast had told him:

"I want to put (Truman) in the Senate so I can get rid of him."

Yet someone else said that Pendergast finally realized that some senators represented oil, others represented railroads, steel, or utilities, and he wanted his own "office boy" in Washington.

Whatever Pendergast's motives, Truman was happy to accept his support, despite an Associated Press account that described a Kansas City municipal election in this way:

"Big Tom Pendergast's Democratic machine rode through to overwhelming victory today after a blood-stained election marked by four killings, scores of sluggings and machine gun terrorism."

The intensely loyal Truman saw only the good in his relationship with the Pendergasts. To his critics he replied:

"I owe my political life to the Pendergast organization. I never would have had an opportunity to have a career in politics without their support. They have been loyal friends."

In the midst of a New Deal year, the 1934 senatorial election in Missouri was no contest. The fifty-year-old Truman easily defeated his Republican opponent with a whopping plurality of 262,000 votes. From that moment, Truman would never again be Pendergast's "office boy," or anyone else's for that matter. The ornery, contrary former farmer, would-be haberdasher, and incorruptible county judge was his own man, although it would take a number of years to prove it.

Washington was interested in the junior senator from Missouri as an oddity only; too many of his senatorial colleagues, particularly the old-timers, believed that his entrance into the upper chamber was not entirely untainted. It was reliably reported that the only ones seen smiling at Senator Truman's swearing in ceremony were two Pendergast lieutenants who sat in the gallery broadly beaming.

In time, a few of the more influential senators, including Carl Hayden of Arizona, William Borah of Idaho, and Charles McNary of Oregon, gave Truman their blessing. But it was Vice-President Garner who did the most for him. Truman became one of his protégés and one of those privileged to join Garner in "striking a blow for liberty."

When Truman ran for reelection in 1940, he had to do it without the awesome Pendergast machine, for old Tom had finally been caught for bribery and fraud and was serving a fifteen-month prison term. What was left of his once powerful organization was now in the hands of his nephew Jim. But Truman had made many other friends and admirers during his first term in the Senate. With their help, aided by the remnants of the Pendergast machine, plus an intensive campaign, he gained a clearcut victory over his Republican opponent, 930,000 to 886,000.

This time, when Truman walked into the Senate after his exciting win, he received a standing ovation from his colleagues.

Truman's chairmanship during World War II of the Special Senate Committee to Investigate the National Defense Program made him a national figure, for everyone spoke of his group as the "Truman Committee." Over a space of three years his investigations saved the government an estimated fifteen billion dollars. By the time the 1944 Democratic convention gathered in Chicago, Truman had become prominent enough to be a serious contender for the vice-presidency, despite an inconspicuous personality and a flat, monotonous way of speaking.

In a biography of her father, Truman's daughter Margaret claimed that he did not seek the vice-presidency and did not want it.

"The Vice-President," he wrote to a friend, "simply presides over the Senate and sits around hoping for a funeral. It is a very high office which consists entirely of honor and I don't have any ambition to hold an office like that."

Nevertheless, when he won the nomination in place of the incumbent Vice-President, Henry A. Wallace, he made no objection. Because FDR's health was so obviously precarious, Truman did most of the campaigning for the Democratic ticket. The Republicans, with a young, vigorous team of governors, Thomas E. Dewey of New York and John Bricker of Ohio, were hopeful that the White House would finally be returned to them. But once again the Democrats were victorious, and Harry S Truman of Missouri became the thirty-fourth vice-president at the age of sixty.

Truman had one of the shortest and busiest vice-presidencies on record. Because of the war, Congress remained in continuous session, so he did a lot of presiding, a job he did not like. But the boredom of his new office was neutralized by the flood of invitations that poured in upon him and his wife. They were invited everywhere and they accepted all invitations. On some days they attended three cocktail parties and a dinner. One columnist said of the happily socializing Truman:

"He has guzzled at more feed troughs than Whirlaway."

Reality in its grimmest form, however, intruded. Exactly eighty-two days after beginning his fourth term, Franklin D. Roosevelt, thirty-second president of the United States, died of a cerebral hemorrhage. The date was April 12, 1945.

Harry S Truman, a simple, unsophisticated average man, characterized by Time magazine as "homespun and plain as an old shoe," had traveled, miraculously, from a haberdashery in Kansas City to the White House.

He described his emotions to some reporters the following day.

"I don't know whether you fellows ever had a load of hay fall on you, but when they told me yesterday what had happened, I felt like the moon, the stars, and all the planets had fallen on me."

The new President asked the reporters to pray for him.

For the United States, and much of the world, the succession of Truman to the presidency meant dread and apprehension; he had neither the training nor the experience for the job. During their brief service as a team, Roosevelt had told him nothing, had given him no briefings, had not taken Truman into his confidence. In the light of his rapidly failing health, it is incredible that FDR did not give the Vice-President an intensive crash course on the problems that would face him.

Even worse for the confidence of the country, Truman did not look like a president, or behave like one.

But Harry Truman had a combination of qualities going for him that astonished the world. He had toughness, integrity, shrewdness, a willingness to accept responsibility. His speech was often earthy and spiced with hells and damns and s.o.b.'s. But he made decisions unflinchingly, and stuck with them. Many of his decisions had far-reaching implications that affected the lives of hundreds of millions of people for decades beyond his own years in office.

During his administration, America saw the beginning of the cold war; witnessed the establishment of the Truman Doctrine, the Marshall Plan and NATO; and watched its government inexorably embark on a policy of containing the Soviet Union.

In view of the momentous Truman measures, historians inevitably wonder what Henry A. Wallace would have done if he had been the president. He had always fought for accommodation with the Soviet Union. And there are those today who insist that we would have had no cold war, no Korea, and no Vietnam if Wallace had succeeded to the presidency instead of Truman.

This argument overlooks one inescapable fact. Wallace would have been confronted by a hostile Congress, for in the election of 1946, the Republicans captured control of both Houses. Together with conservative Southern Democrats, and those of the North who despised everything Wallace stood for, Wallace might well have been the first president since Andrew Johnson to face impeachment proceedings.

Were the political pros correct, therefore, when they maneuvered the 1944 nomination for Truman? There is a prophetic ring to words expressed by Bob Hannegan when he appraised the results of his work in July of 1944:

"When I die, I would like to have one thing on my headstone— that I was the man who kept Henry Wallace from becoming President of the United States."

35th Vice-President　Alben W. Barkley—Democrat, Kentucky, 1949–1953 (President Harry S Truman). Born: November 24, 1877, Lowes, Graves County, Ky. Died: April 30, 1956, Lexington, Va.

Madmen and Geniuses

Alben W. Barkley

The death of Franklin Roosevelt in April of 1945 could not have been unexpected to his associates; but the passing of the thirty-second president was a sudden blow that left the American people in a state of shock. From all parts of the land there were expressions of despair and hopelessness. "Who will take care of us now?" became an oft-repeated lament, as if the government had been set adrift and leaderless, as if the new president, Harry S Truman, did not exist.

But Harry Truman did exist. He stepped into the void under conditions that would have destroyed a lesser man. His handling of the complex matters that Roosevelt had bequeathed him turned skepticism to admiration. In the first Gallup Poll taken after his succession to the presidency, Truman received a popularity rating of 87 percent, three points more than FDR's highest total.

By the fall of 1946, Truman's popularity skidded to a sickening 36 percent. There were many who were convinced that he was in way over his depth. He seemed powerless to handle the growing military-industrial complex and the arrogant career men in government service. Nor was he able to endear himself with labor; in the 1946 off year election, coal miners booed every mention of his name. One senator running for reelection, Harley Kilgore of West Virginia, tried to evoke some sympathy for the President.

". . . About the most you could do," said Kilgore, "was to defend him in a humorous fashion by using the old Western saloon refrain: 'Don't shoot the piano player. He's doing the best he can.'"

Truman's best was more than enough for a large segment of the country. Gradually, perhaps grudgingly, his popularity rose again, so that, as 1948 approached, his rating reached 56 percent. He was ready to make a run for his own full term in the presidency.

Party pros, however, viewed his candidacy with scant enthusiasm. In December of 1947, former Vice-President Henry Wallace announced that he was forming a third party, and one of his supporters won a special congressional election in New York City in February of 1948. Democratic leaders were clearly concerned; and labor's continuing refusal to endorse the President evidenced real trouble ahead. An official of the Teamsters gave a succinct appraisal of Truman:

"That squeaky-voice tinhorn. I want nothing to do with him."

There was even a serious attempt, headed by three of FDR's sons, to enlist General Dwight D. Eisenhower as the Democratic presidential candidate. The general firmly resisted with the declaration that "life-long professional soldiers (should) abstain from seeking high political office." With Eisenhower definitely out of the race, the Democrats knew it now had to be Truman, even though they were certain he could not win re-election. They assembled in Philadelphia's Convention Hall in July of 1948 exhibiting defeat and gloom. Signs were hung all over the hall: "We're Just Mild About Harry." And normally pro-Democratic newspapers exhorted the party to concede defeat to the Republicans and thereby save the wear and tear and the expense of campaigning. The Democrats, wallowing in despondency, had all but handed the coming election to their opponents.

But Harry Truman paid no attention to the faultfinders and pessimists. Convinced that he would be renominated without opposition, he set about to select a running mate. His first choice was Supreme Court Justice William O. Douglas, whose name had been included in FDR's famous letter of 1944. But Douglas, vacationing in Oregon, had no desire to be a number two man to a number two man, nor did he want to be part of a ticket that would go down to a crushing defeat.

A few other names were proposed. Clare Booth Luce, perhaps none too seriously, suggested FDR's widow, Eleanor Roosevelt. In the end, Truman selected a man he had not himself considered.

For twenty years, Senator Alben Barkley of Kentucky had been submitted to one Democratic convention after another as either a prospective president or vice-president. In all that time he had gotten nowhere. Now at the advanced age of seventy, when most people admitted they had passed their prime, Barkley set his sights on one of the offices that had so long eluded him. But, as he confided to friends, "it will have to come quick. I don't want it passed around so long it is like a cold biscuit."

Once again, Barkley was the convention's keynote speaker. He had performed the same duty twice before. This time he delivered what he modestly described as a "ripsnorter." He laced into the Republicans, most particularly their presidential candidate, Thomas E. Dewey, who had been nominated for the second time. The listless convention came to life and lustily shouted and applauded all the way through Barkley's speech. With the same modesty, he told of the crowd's reaction:

"When my speech was over—and these are facts which have been reported and interpreted by others—the hitherto apathetic delegates were on their hind legs and cheering."

A number of delegates urged him to run for the top spot, but he knew the best he could hope for was the vice-presidency. He telephoned Truman directly to ask for the job.

"Why didn't you tell me you wanted to be Vice-President?" Truman said. "If I had known you wanted it, I certainly would have been agreeable."

The word went out, "Barkley is willing." So was the President, and the vice-presidential nomination went to the Kentuckian by acclamation. Truman won his own nomination on the first ballot, although he had some opposition. Between them, the sixty-four-year-old Truman and the seventy-year-old Barkley comprised the oldest presidential ticket ever offered.

One of the most popular men in the national capital, and justly renowned as a story teller, Barkley had a fund of humorous anecdotes that he could pull out of his endless reservoir whenever he needed to make a point. One of his stories, which he related to the vice-presidency in 1944, may well have applied to him four years later.

It seems, said Mr. Barkley, that there was a hungry Republican who decided to go after a state job when Kentucky elected its first Republican governor in 1895. He rode his mule a distance of a hundred miles to the state captial of Frankfort, where he hung around for six months until his money ran out. When he finally decided to go back home, a friend asked him why he was in such a hurry to leave.

"Hurry!" the frustrated job-seeker exclaimed. "All my life I've heard that the office should seek the man. Well, I've been here six months and haven't seen an office seeking a man yet. If you happen to run across one after I've gone, will you please tell it that I'm a-ridin' out Somerset Pike, and ridin' damned slow!"

In Barkley's case, the office did at last find the man, but perilously late. Almost everyone, experts and average man alike, predicted an overwhelming victory for the Republicans in November. Truman now had two disaffected splinter groups to contend with, Henry Wallace's Progressive Party and Strom Thurmond of South Carolina and his Dixiecrats. The Thurmond group had bolted the Democratic convention in anger over a strong civil rights plank in the party platform.

But Truman and Barkley refused to give up. The President vigorously crossed the country going directly to the voter, to the common man who was so much like himself. In a slashing, attacking campaign, during which crowd after crowd shouted "Give 'em hell, Harry!", he told the people what they wanted to hear.

As for Barkley, that aging veteran of the political wars threw himself into the fight with an energy and enthusiasm that would have done honor to a man half his years. He covered twenty-six states by airplane, delivering as many as fifteen speeches in a day, his booming baritone regaling delighted listeners with back country wit, and speaking always without notes or text.

When the results of the November election were in, despite a gloating and premature headline in the *Chicago Tribune*, DEWEY DE-FEATS TRUMAN, Harry Truman and Alben Barkley had beaten all their opponents. The two splinter parties, between them, had received slightly more than 2,000,000 votes, not enough to keep victory from the underrated and underdog Truman and Barkley.

For two elderly gentlemen, it was an impressive and sweetly savored triumph.

Aside from his age, (at seventy-one the oldest of all vice-presidents), Alben W. Barkley had one other distinction. He was the last vice-president born in a log cabin. His birth took place, as he tells it, in Graves County, Kentucky, "on the twenty-fourth of November, 1877, at 3:30 o'clock in the morning." Actually, he was born in his grandfather's log house, for his paternal grandmother was the midwife at his birth.

Barkley's father was a poor tenant farmer in Kentucky. Alben's early years were filled with struggle and privation, but he was determined to acquire an education. When his family moved to Clinton, Kentucky, he enrolled in Marvin College at the age of fourteen. He paid for his schooling by being a janitor for the college. Marvin later proudly hung a sign on one of its buildings, "BARKLEY SWEPT HERE."

From Clinton, Alben Barkley moved to Paducah, where he studied law and ran for his first public office in 1905 astride a one-eyed horse named Dick. Barkley claimed that his entrance into politics was inevitable, for he was a Kentuckian and a lawyer, with "a natural inclination to stop whatever I was doing and start making a speech any time I saw as many as six persons assembled together."

He won that first race, and became prosecuting attorney of McCracken County at the age of twenty-eight. Four years later, as had Harry Truman, Barkley became a county judge, an administrative position only. In 1913, when he was thirty-six, he entered Congress, and stayed in the House of Representatives continuously until 1927, when he successfully ran for the United States Senate.

The Kentuckian's political attributes were many. Aside from his homespun charm, his geniality, and astuteness, he was hailed by some reporters as "the greatest hog-caller who ever came out of the Blue Grass State." One awestruck writer said that whenever Barkley spoke, "nature pauses in a kind of stunned silence." Barkley readily acknowledged this was so, for his father, he said, was the loudest "amener" in Graves County.

As a senator, Barkley was an ardent New Dealer and supporter of FDR; his election as Democratic majority leader of the Senate in 1937 placed him in the position of faithful wheelhorse for the White House.

Through Barkley's efforts, much of Roosevelt's cherished legislation saw the light of day.

When Barkley was inaugurated as the thirty-fifth vice-president on January 20, 1949, he had the best wishes and the good will of the entire country, but more importantly, he had the confidence of his chief, President Truman. Truman saw to it that Barkley became a working vice-president, for Truman remembered all too vividly his own unhappy experience when he had succeeded to the presidency not quite five years before totally unprepared for the job.

At Truman's request and approval, Congress passed an act making the vice-president a member of the National Security Council. In addition, Truman asked Barkley to represent the White House at numerous functions all over the country. Barkley estimated that he traveled, mostly by air, more than any other vice-president up to that time.

For awhile, Barkley was much in demand as a crowner of queens at various celebrations such as Apple Blossom Festivals or Cherry Blossom Festivals. Part of his duties at these affairs involved what he called "this osculatory business," kissing the queen. He always faced this task manfully and with obvious relish.

As a measure of the country's affection for its elderly Vice-President, it bestowed upon him the title of "Veep," a nickname concocted by Barkley's ten-year-old grandson, Stephen Pruitt. Stephen thought that since V. P. stands for vice-president, "why not stick in a couple of little *e's* and call it 'Veep'?" Although the term has more and more come to mean the holder of the second chair it is still distinctly Alben Barkley.

Vice-presidential exploits rarely, in previous years, rated total press coverage except for misdeeds, as in the Credit Mobilier case during the administration of Ulysses S. Grant. But in the fall of 1949, the seventy-one-year-old Veep, a widower since 1947, made excited headlines by falling in love with a thirty-eight year old widow from St. Louis, Jane Hadley. During many of the boring Senate debates, Barkley wrote love letters to Mrs. Hadley while he sat in the presiding chair.

Three months and twenty-two days after their first meeting, the Veep and Mrs. Hadley announced their engagement, to a battery of newspaper, radio, and television reporters, photographers, and cameramen. It was a press conference worthy of a major presidential announcement. Eighteen days later, on November 18, 1949, the Veep and Jane Hadley were married. One national radio show interrupted its regular schedule with a bulletin about the marriage.

Harry Truman decided he would not run again in 1952. For Barkley, this was his opportunity to achieve the one prize that had eluded him. He issued a statement advising that, although he was not actively seeking the presidential nomination, he would not decline if the forthcoming Democratic convention, which was to meet in Chicago July 21 to 26, were to draft him.

Kentucky immediately pledged its 28½ votes to him and by the time he and Mrs. Barkley arrived at the convention, he had picked up a few more, for a total of 31. But his advanced years, which had given a mellow glow to his reputation, now dimmed his hopes. A coalition of labor officials turned down his bid for their support because he was too old for the presidency at seventy-four.

Two days later, in a bitter attack upon "certain self-anointed political labor leaders," Barkley announced his withdrawal from the race. For once, his usual wry sense of humor had deserted him.

The Democrats did not entirely forget the old pro, even though they would not accept him as a contender for their presidential nomination. When he rose to address the convention on July 23, the delegates gave him a standing ovation that "all but tore the hall apart," as one newspaper reported the scene.

Alben William Barkley, the "man of oak and iron," was not yet finished with politics. In the off year election of 1954, he ran once more for the United States Senate. Despite a personal appearance by President Eisenhower on behalf of the Republican incumbent, John Sherman Cooper, the seventy-six year old Barkley won easily, and returned to Washington as the junior senator from Kentucky.

Barkley's new senatorial career lasted only sixteen months. On April 30, 1956, Barkley and his wife traveled to Lexington, Virginia, to attend a mock convention conducted by the student body of Washington and Lee University. The former Veep was to make the keynote address, as he had done many times at actual conventions.

At five in the afternoon, he arose to address the crowded hall. His wife sat in the first row. Barkley spoke for fifteen minutes. Following his usual pattern, he attacked the Republicans for their "stagnation" and praised the Democrats, who symbolized "progress." He then talked about his own career, and told the audience how he had served as a congressman, a junior senator, majority leader, and vice-president of the country.

"And now," he said, "I'm back again as a junior Senator. I am willing to be a junior. I'm glad to sit on the back row. I would rather be a servant in the House of the Lord than to sit in the seats of the mighty."

These were the last words he ever spoke. He collapsed to the floor. By the time his wife reached his side, he was dead.

36th Vice-President   Richard M. Nixon—Republican, California, 1953–1961 (President Dwight D. Eisenhower). Born: January 9, 1913, Yorba Linda, Calif.

Madmen and Geniuses

Richard M. Nixon

On March 29, 1952, at a Jefferson-Jackson Day dinner, President Truman announced to 5300 assembled Democrats that he would not be a candidate for reelection.

If the Democrats were shocked, the Republicans were relieved. They had endured a protracted Roosevelt-Truman drought of five terms and two decades, but now they confidently expected a return to greener pastures; the presidency would once again be theirs. They would achieve their long awaited goal with an unbeatable candidate, General Dwight D. Eisenhower, by all odds the most popular man in the country.

After years of not being sure which party he supported, Eisenhower had finally decided he must be a Republican. As an officer in uniform he had kept himself above politics, but once he left active duty in 1948 he got around to voting for the first time in his life, and he voted the Dewey-Warren ticket. It was at last apparent, to himself and to others, that he was indeed a Republican. From then on GOP leaders systematically applied pressure upon him to make a run for the presidency; in January of 1952 he gave in and announced that he would accept the Republican nomination if it were offered to him.

Selection of the GOP vice-presidential candidate was much simpler. Thomas E. Dewey, despite consecutive defeats in the last two presidential races, was still the titular head of the party. He now wanted a young, aggressive Westerner to balance the sixty-one-year-old Eisenhower. Although the general had been born in Texas and raised in Kansas, he was a resident of New York State and was considered to be the choice of the GOP's eastern wing.

One man had all the necessary qualifications to balance Eisenhower —Richard M. Nixon, thirty-nine-year-old junior senator from California. He was aggressive, hard-hitting, and not afraid to stretch a point if it served his purpose. The kindly, paternalistic Eisenhower could not be expected to assault the opposition with half-truths, unexplained insinuations, and convenient distortion of fact. Nixon could handle all of these with ease and competence, as he had demonstrated in his earlier campaigns. He would be a perfect counterweight to the Eisenhower father figure, who would condemn and accuse in a low key.

This was the program mapped out by Dewey and his fellow tacticians. When they asked Eisenhower for his own preference as to a running mate, he removed from his billfold an "eligible list" he had previously prepared. Of the eight names on the general's list, that of Senator Richard Milhous Nixon of California was first.

Since Nixon was their choice as well, Dewey and the other leaders enthusiastically approved, so the list was destroyed and the remaining names never published.

Voting for the presidential nomination took place on Friday, July 11, 1952, in Chicago's International Amphitheatre. By the end of the first ballot, Governor Earl Warren of California had 77 votes, Senator Robert Taft of Ohio had 500, and Eisenhower had 595, nine short of the 604 necessary for nomination. With the momentum so obviously Eisenhower's, and with a "Taft can't win" mood pervading much of the hall, a rush began for a switch to Eisenhower, and the first and only roll call was amended to declare him the winner unanimously.

Later that afternoon, Richard M. Nixon was chosen by acclamation to be the Republicans' candidate for vice-president. Few of his fellow Republicans understood him, or liked him. His was not the kind of personality to inspire warmth or adulation, yet he had climbed to within one step of the very top in the unbelievably brief span of six years.

Many of Nixon's contemporaries asked, "Who and what is Richard Nixon?" In the summer of 1952, that question did not have the puzzled relevance it assumed in later years, for he knew what he wanted and he went after his goal with a singlemindedness that his associates and opponents recognized. There were those who did not approve of his tactics, but in the turbulent, intricate world of politics, results become all important. Richard Nixon achieved results, with efficiency and expedition. His was a practical and realistic approach; find the other fellow's weakness and attack that weakness relentlessly.

The one issue that seemed to have the strongest appeal after the end of World War II was anti-Communism. The Truman administration embarked on the cold war and a policy of containment vis-à-vis the Soviet Union. At home, the government instituted a loyalty oath and began to root out subversives. Our former Russian allies were now the avowed enemy; anyone who harbored the least bit of sympathy for the Soviet Union, its people, or its aims, was immediately suspect. To be "soft on Communism" was to leave one's self open to accusations of possible treason or, at the very least, disloyalty.

When Richard Nixon first settled upon politics as his career in 1946, he chose anti-Communism as his major advocacy. It was a theme he was to repeat almost continuously throughout the following years.

Richard Nixon was always a loner, even through his childhood and adolescence. He worked hard and studied hard; after school he helped out in his father's service station and grocery store and then stayed up until early morning hours completing his homework. Raised in the Quaker faith, young Richard was diligent, disciplined, and sober; he carried these qualities with him into adulthood.

Nixon was born in Yorba Linda, California, a barren settlement some twenty-five miles south of Los Angeles, in January of 1913. (He was the first vice-president born in the twentieth century.) He went to school in Whittier, California, where his family moved in 1922. With a scholarship grant from Duke University in Durham, North Carolina, Nixon studied law and passed the bar in 1937, when he was twenty-four.

The years between 1937 and World War II were neither distinguished for Nixon nor marked with success. He practiced law in Whittier and did well enough to marry Pat Ryan in 1940. But he seemed to be waiting for something more eventful than a junior partnership in a Whittier law firm. When the United States entered World War II, he applied for a naval commission, despite his Quaker background, which could have exempted him from active service or acted as a self-disqualifier because of the Quaker precepts of peace and nonviolence. Nixon served as lieutenant, junior grade, for fifteen months with much of his tour of duty in the South Pacific.

Richard Nixon's incredible political career was given its initial impetus in late 1945 without any effort on his part. A group of wealthy Republican buinessmen, bankers, and party officials in Southern California's Twelfth District constituted themselves a "Committee of One Hundred" to find a "Congressman candidate with no previous experience to defeat a man who has represented the district in the House for ten years." They preferred a veteran.

The name of Richard M. Nixon was suggested to the Committee by a conservative Whittier banker who was himself a Quaker, and a friend and associate of Nixon's maternal grandfather.

The Committee found Nixon suitable in all respects. They then began their campaign to unseat incumbent Jerry Voorhis, a liberal congressman who had long been the object of their vendetta. One committee member engaged, for a $500 fee, a Beverly Hills lawyer experienced as a political publicity man. The lawyer, Murray Chotiner, was to serve Nixon on a part-time basis.

Chotiner had a simple, direct strategy—attack, and more attack. ". . . Fight the battle on the ground on which you are strongest; avoid the tactical error of fighting on your opponent's strongest ground."

Since Nixon, as a newcomer to politics, had no record to defend, he slashed away at Voorhis's. He linked Voorhis with the left-wing Political Action Committee (PAC) of the CIO. "A vote for Nixon," proclaimed one of his leaflets, "is a vote against the PAC, its Communist principles,

and its gigantic slush fund." There was more of the same, with jabs at
"lip-service Americans," and government officials "who front for un-
American elements."

Representative Voorhis, who had been selected by Washington
correspondents as the "best congressman west of the Mississippi," suddenly found himself on the defensive, replying to charges that were only
partially true. He could only defend, not accuse, for there was nothing
in Nixon to attack except his anti-Communism, and Voorhis agreed completely with this position. In the final analysis, the electorate of the
Twelfth District did not accept Voorhis's constant denials of Communist
sympathies. The veteran, liberal Voorhis was defeated by the conservative newcomer, and Richard M. Nixon won his first election by a vote
of 67,784, to 49,431.

Two years later, Nixon easily won reelection. It was during the
end of his first term that he became a figure of national and international
prominence with his persistent and astute prosecution of the Alger Hiss-
Whittaker Chambers episode. Whittaker Chambers, an admitted former
Communist, had placed before the House Un-American Activities Committee, of which Representative Nixon was a member, a list of government officials Chambers claimed had been Communists with him. One
of these was Alger Hiss, formerly of the State Department. At the time
of the House hearings, Hiss was president of the prestigious Carnegie
Endowment for International Peace.

Hiss denied all of Chambers's allegations. President Truman called
the affair a "red herring." Editorials in pro-Republican as well as in Democratic newspapers denounced the investigation. Embarrassed members
of the House Un-American Activities Committee wanted to forget the
whole thing and go on to other matters. But Nixon would not give up.
He uncovered discrepancies in Hiss's testimony, and Hiss eventually was
convicted of perjury and sent to prison.

One jubilant Nixon supporter suggested that Hiss's conviction
would propel Nixon into the presidency. Ralph de Toledano, Nixon's
first official biographer, agreed, with reservations:

"The Hiss Case," de Toledano wrote, "won for Richard Nixon the
Vice-Presidential nomination in 1952, the Presidential nomination in
1960. But in all other ways it cost him dear."

There was one more hurdle for Nixon to face before the vice-presidency. In 1950, he ran for the United States Senate, against a fellow
member of Congress, actress Helen Gahagan Douglas. With Murray
Chotiner now working full time on his behalf, Nixon again used the
issue of Communism against his opponent. The results were even more
telling than they had been in 1946.

One pro-Douglas newspaper angrily charged the Nixon camp with
attempting to defame Mrs. Douglas "by falsely accusing her through
infamous insinuations and whispered innuendo of being a Communist."
The newspaper labeled her opponent "Tricky Dick" Nixon.

The Nixon staff issued a "Pink Sheet," in which it listed 354 oc-

casions when Congress woman Helen Gahagan Douglas had voted the
same as Vito Marcantonio, "the notorious Communist party-line congressman from New York." Most conveniently, the Pink Sheet failed to
mention the numerous times Republicans had voted the same as Marcantonio, or the 112 times Nixon himself had voted with Marcantonio,
in two years less service than Mrs. Douglas.

The damage had been done. The "Douglas-Marcantonio Axis" was
firmly planted in the electorate's consciousness. Mrs. Douglas, as had
Jerry Voorhis, found herself on the defensive, but the opposition's onslaught was too formidable and overwhelming. The infamous Senator
Joe McCarthy of Wisconsin made a radio speech for Nixon over a statewide network. He warned Californians that the battle had been joined
"between the American people and the administration Commicrat Party
of Betrayal."

Mrs. Douglas went down to a humiliating defeat. The final totals
gave Nixon 2,183,454, and 1,502,507 for Mrs. Douglas—a plurality
of almost 700,000.

This smashing senatorial victory gave a tremendous boost to
Nixon's reputation in Washington. In May of 1951, four months after
taking his seat as the junior senator from California, he was selected
to join the United States delegation to the World Health Organization,
then meeting in Geneva. En route, he stopped off in Paris for a conference with General Eisenhower, NATO head. Both men consistently
denied that politics came up during their discussion. Yet it was soon
after that Eisenhower began to give serious consideration to the presidency, and it could not have been an idle gesture on his part to place
the eager young senator from California as the first name on his vice-
presidential list.

The Republican convention of 1952 was not conducted in complete unanimity, for there were those who did not agree with the choices
made by the Dewey combine. Senator Taft, particularly, was bitter over
the defection of Richard Nixon to the Eisenhower camp, for the right-
wing Taft had believed that the Californian's conservative ideology
matched his own. After the convention chose Eisenhower and Nixon,
Taft betrayed his resentment when he referred to Nixon as "a little man
in a big hurry," with a "mean and vindictive streak."

Traditionally, vice-presidential candidates attract peripheral attention only during the election period. In Nixon's case, he soon made it
apparent that he meant to be a visible and vocal personality; as the fall
campaign swung into action, he warned that he intended to make "Communist subversion and corruption the theme of every speech from now
until the election." The battle for the White House was not to be a
"nicey-nice little powder puff duel."

The Democrats accepted the challenge. On September 18, 1952,
the anti-Republican New York *Post* published a full page story headlined: SECRET NIXON FUND.

It was a shocker. During his term in the Senate, said the *Post*,

Nixon had accepted more than $18,000 from unpublicized admirers. The fund had gone to pay expenses that otherwise would have come out of his own pocket.

Candidate Eisenhower and the GOP brass were horrified. There were anguished demands that Nixon be dumped from the ticket. Eisenhower refused to take the initiative and insisted the decision to remain or withdraw be left to Nixon himself. But, Eisenhower made it clear, sternly and unequivocally, Nixon would have to prove himself innocent of wrongdoing and come out of the mess "clean as a hound's tooth."

The shaken Nixon refused to withdraw. Instead, at the general's suggestion and with the hasty, last-minute efforts of Murray Chotiner, Nixon appeared on a nationwide television and radio broadcast the night of Tuesday, September 23, to clarify his position.

At a cost of $75,000, which the Republican National Committee supplied, Nixon spoke to an estimated audience of 60 million people, the largest single group ever to hear a political speech. In a remarkable half-hour performance that bordered occasionally on the lachrymose, Nixon explained away the private donations as a necessary expense he needed to help him in his fight against Communism and corruption. Without such help he could never have gotten his message across to the people of California and to the nation. It was a rationale no one could fault.

He then skillfully bared the low state of his private finances. He admitted that he and Pat owned a 1950 Oldsmobile, but no stocks or bonds; "Pat doesn't have a mink coat, but she does have a respectable Republican cloth coat; and I always tell her," Nixon confided to his unseen listeners, "that she'd look good in anything."

He even spoke of a gift from a man in Texas, a little cocker spaniel dog that Nixon's six-year-old daughter, Tricia, had named "Checkers."

"I just want to say this right now," Nixon went on, "that regardless of what they say about it, we are going to keep him."

This most famous of all vice-presidential appearances came to be known as the "Checkers speech." At the end of it, hundreds of thousands of messages flooded network and radio stations and Republican headquarters in Washington pleading with Nixon to stay on the ticket. Almost in a matter of moments, Nixon became a national hero, for his candor and teary-eyed openness found a sentimental empathy that poured out of millions of hearts and millions of homes. No one seemed to care that he did not deny accepting the secret fund; he explained it, and that was enough.

Nixon had turned disaster into triumph. The next day, a beaming Eisenhower greeted Nixon with outstretched hand and gratified smile. "You're my boy," said the happy general.

The Republicans had reason to rejoice. The final results of the presidential election in November showed 33,800,000 votes for Eisenhower and Nixon against 27,300,000 for the Democrats, Adlai E. Stevenson II of Illinois and John Sparkman of Alabama. Perhaps as noteworthy was the California result, which found that state going Republican for the first time since Herbert Hoover.

The vice-presidency proved to be more than a dead end for Richard Nixon. He was not content to be a figurehead or a partygoer. President Eisenhower, following an already established custom, asked the Vice-President to sit in on cabinet meetings, and even requested Nixon to preside over cabinet sessions whenever he himself had to be absent from Washington. In the fall of 1953, Eisenhower sent Nixon and his wife on a highly publicized tour of Asia. The Nixons covered nineteen countries in ten weeks and traveled 45,539 miles.

In the 1954 off year election it was decided that President Eisenhower would remain aloof and gently detached, while the Vice-President would do the electioneering. Nixon was to be a "one man GOP task force." As it turned out, he was more of a hatchet man, for he continued with his favorite theme of Communism and corruption, and hammered away at the Democrats as "the party of treason," because of their failure to root out subversives in government. Former President Truman, the object of many Nixon accusations, dryly retorted:

"If I'm a traitor, the United States is in a helluva shape."

Once again Richard Nixon tried to rely upon innuendo and half-truths, but this time he failed, for control of Congress, which had gone to the Republicans in 1952, went back to the Democrats.

Suddenly Vice-President Nixon had become an embarrassing liability to the Republicans. There was a move, in 1956, to deny him renomination. Some GOP leaders had determined from private polls that he would cost President Eisenhower, who had announced he would seek reelection, up to 6 percent of the votes.

But Nixon was far more popular with the rank and file Republicans than some of his enemies realized. His calm and measured behavior during two Eisenhower illnesses, a severe heart attack in 1955 and ileitis the following year, had impressed the country with his sincerity. Nor did it hurt his image that he made no move to take over the reins of government while Eisenhower lay so seriously ill in 1955. What most of the people did not know was that those closest to the President, as when Woodrow Wilson was ill, took care of govenmental affairs themselves. It was Sherman Adams, the presidential assistant, who was the "Acting President." Nixon could only watch helplessly from the sidelines.

When the dump Nixon movement reached its peak in the summer of 1956, President Eisenhower again refused to make a firm commitment. He preferred, he said, to allow the convention to choose his running mate. In effect, he was no longer endorsing Nixon, although he allowed the faithful to believe that Nixon was more than acceptable to him.

As Eisenhower suspected, the 1956 Republican convention overwhelmingly supported Richard Nixon for renomination. In the campaign that followed, it was a different Nixon who stumped the country.

No longer did he shrill about the party of treason or indiscriminately shower guilt by association. He was subdued, a perfect gentleman, for he wanted to prove to the country that he was presidential material.

The second Eisenhower-Nixon victory was even more spectacular than the first; this time they won by a plurality of 10,000,000. The new Nixon was well on his way to his supreme goal.

As a fascinating look at the New Nixon, we have an incident that took place in January of 1957, when he was interviewed by British publisher David Astor. Astor was curious about the dirty campaign Nixon had waged in 1950 against Helen Gahagan Douglas. With an air of sadness, Nixon answered:

"I'm sorry about that episode. I was a very young man."

By the time the Republican nominating convention of 1960 rolled around, Nixon was no longer young or inexperienced. He had achieved worldwide fame as the result of two trips he had made with his wife. In 1958, during a swing through South America, Mr. and Mrs. Nixon were almost attacked by a hostile mob in Caracas, Venezuela. The following year the Nixons visited the Soviet Union. Nixon conducted a running debate with Russian Premier Nikita Khrushchev in the kitchen of a model home being exhibited by the United States at a trade fair. This "kitchen debate" attracted international headlines, and proved, to the delight of the Vice-President's supporters, that he had the courage to stand up to the contentious Soviet leader.

Nixon was now the compleat politician, the GOP's man of the hour, the only vice-president in 125 years to have a chance for the big prize, even though his chief, President Eisenhower, had few words of praise for him.

At a press conference, Eisenhower was asked, "What major decisions of your Administration has the Vice-President participated in?"

"If you give me a week," Eisenhower replied, "I might think of one."

But no matter. On the afternoon of Wednesday, July 27, 1960, Richard Milhous Nixon received the unanimous nomination for president from his fellow Republicans. The former fighter against corruption and Communism had reached the penultimate pinnacle.

37th Vice-President Lyndon Baines Johnson—Democrat, Texas, 1961–1963 (President John F. Kennedy). Born: August 27, 1908, Stonewall, Tex. Died: January 22, 1973, San Antonio, Tex.

Madmen and Geniuses

Lyndon Baines Johnson

The 1960 presidential scramble saw four Democratic senators actively seeking the nomination of their party. Two of them, Lyndon B. Johnson of Texas and Stuart Symington of Missouri, were willing to gamble on the upcoming Democratic convention, scheduled to meet in Los Angeles, July 11 to 15.

The other two contenders, John F. Kennedy of Massachusetts and Hubert H. Humphrey of Minnesota, had a different approach. They placed their futures directly in the hands of the electorate by participating in state primaries.

Lyndon Johnson, the Senate's majority leader, did not agree with this tactic. Somebody, he said, had to remain behind in Washington to take care of senatorial matters.

"I have simply got to stay here and mind the store," he proclaimed.

Johnson's displeasure with his two campaigning colleagues was simply a public posture, for he believed they were wasting their time. The power and majesty of his position as majority leader would sweep him into the presidency, and he would then magnanimously tap Kennedy for the second spot.

"I can see it all now," said one of his aides. "Johnson will be standing in the hotel room after he wins the nomination, and he'll say, 'We want Sonny Boy for Vice-President. Go fetch him for me.'"

It didn't work out quite that way. Johnson's failure to participate at least in the West Virginia primary cost him the nomination. Kennedy had won one primary contest after another, and he now had to show only that his Catholic religion would not turn off Protestant voters. West

Virginia, which was 97 percent Protestant, gave him the final boost he needed with an easy victory that astounded the nation.

On the night of Wednesday, July 13, 1960, in the Los Angeles Memorial Sports Arena, the Democrats took one ballot only to select forty-three-year-old John Fitzgerald Kennedy to be their presidential candidate. Of eleven other candidates, Johnson was the closet pursuer, hopelessly far behind with 409 votes.

Johnson had an explanation for his defeat and for Kennedy's triumph.

"Jack was out kissing babies while I was passing bills."

Kennedy now set about to choose his running mate. It was an agonizing decision, for he preferred a northern liberal, but he needed help in the Bible Belt South, which traditionally resented Catholics, and most particularly a northern Catholic. What he had to have was a man the South would respect and accept, and he had to be a degree or two to the left of center, or at least seem to be.

After hours of discussions with his brother Robert and with aides, Kennedy finally made a choice.

On the morning of Thursday, July 14, the vice-presidential nomination was offered to Lyndon Baines Johnson. Much to Kennedy's surprise, Johnson appeared interested, even though he had insisted, on the day before the convention, that he "would not trade a vote for a gavel." Kennedy later described Johnson's immediate reaction.

"I didn't offer the Vice-Presidency to him—I just held it out like this, and he grabbed at it."

But first the offer had to be cleared with Johnson's friends from Texas. LBJ telephoned John Nance Garner in Uvalde. The former Vice-President, who was then ninety-one, told Johnson:

"I'll tell you, Lyndon, the Vice-Presidency isn't worth a pitcher of warm spit."

Other influential Texans, including House Speaker Sam Rayburn, tried to dissuade Johnson from accepting. But in the end, by early afternoon, they all agreed he ought to go ahead.

At 4:00 P.M., Kennedy called a press conference to announce that Lyndon Johnson was to be his running mate. The announcement was greeted with gasps of surprise and, in some cases, shock and outrage. Liberals and labor threatened insurrection. But the Kennedy staff had calculated wisely. Neither northern liberals nor labor would support the Republicans, nor could they in good conscience desert the Democrats, in spite of Johnson's presence on the ticket; the cries of anguish would eventually die down.

But, just in case revolt was still planned, precautions were taken. After Johnson's name was placed in nomination that evening, convention chairman Leroy Collins, governor of Florida, quickly recognized House Majority Leader John McCormack of Massachusetts. McCormack moved that the convention dispense with the roll call and nominate Johnson by acclamation.

This motion required a two-thirds vote in favor. Despite repeated shouts for a state-by-state ballot, Collins called for a voice vote on McCormack's motion. To most observers, the "Ayes" and "Nos" seemed equally loud. For a moment, Collins hesitated, while Sam Rayburn, Johnson's confidante and campaign manager, scowled fiercely at the wavering chairman. Then Collins plunged ahead, and, disregarding the two-thirds requirement, banged his gavel above the din.

"The motion is adopted," he said, "and Senator Lyndon B. Johnson of Texas has been nominated for the Vice-Presidency of the United States by acclamation."

If selection of the earthy Johnson offended many of Kennedy's supporters, the Texan's acceptance of the second spot puzzled even more people. The Johnson personality and manner, often and deliberately crude and graceless, clashed with Kennedy's urbane sophistication. On political grounds alone, Kennedy had to overlook Johnson's defects. But why did the powerful majority leader of the Senate finally trade a vote for a gavel? Why was he willing to play a secondary role that would keep him eclipsed by the man he had contemptuously referred to as "Sonny Boy"?

There were at least three reasons, all of them valid. The 1958 Congress had many new, young, liberal senators who now threatened revolt against Johnson's archaic one-man rule in the upper house. Senator Russell Long of Louisiana revealed the core of Johnson's problem:

"Lyndon was living on borrowed time as a strong majority leader. Those guys would have pinned his hide to the wall."

Then there was Johnson's wife, Lady Bird, who was concerned about another kind of borrowed time. In July of 1955, Johnson had suffered a massive heart attack that would have killed anyone else. He followed his doctors' urgent pleas by cutting his workday down from eighteen to fourteen hours. The vice-presidency, Lady Bird was certain, would be far less taxing to her impatient, never resting husband. (Even the presidency itself, she thought, would have been easier than the majority leadership of the Senate.)

Lastly, there was the lure of the White House, a prize that had temporarily escaped Lyndon Johnson. In the past, the vice-presidency had proven to be a one-way ticket to nowhere. But Nixon's phenomenal success demonstrated that a vice-president can make it all the way, at least to the nomination for the number one spot. No need any longer for the second man to sit around waiting for the chief to pass away. From now on, the vice-president could use his backup chair as the stepping stone it once had been for John Adams, Thomas Jefferson and Martin Van Buren. For Johnson, a regional, southwestern senator, the vice-presidency could provide the national image he had to have if he hoped to achieve the presidency by 1968, and so he voluntarily stepped into the Kennedy shadow.

One old friend on the other side of the Senate chamber did not approve. Conservative Republican Senator Barry Goldwater of Arizona expressed his contempt in a note he sent to Johnson. "I'm nauseated," he wrote.

It was indeed a strange ticket the Democrats presented to the country in opposition to the Republicans, who selected, to no one's surprise, Richard M. Nixon of California and Henry Cabot Lodge of Massachusetts.

Johnson traveled into forty-three states during the campaign, but he concentrated on the South, where his homey manner went over big with the local folks. The *LBJ Victory Special* pulled into whistlestop, hamlet, and village, blaring out "The Yellow Rose of Texas," while Johnson urged his countrymen to come closer for the "speakin'."

"Yuh-all make us feel so wonderful to come out here," he would say, "and look us in the eye and give us a chance to press the flesh." And then, as the *Special* rolled away, he would call out, "God bless yuh, Culpeper, vote Democratic."

Culpeper, as it happened, preferred Nixon, but enough Southern towns voted Democratic to give one of the closest elections on record to Kennedy and Johnson. Out of almost 69,000,000 votes, Kennedy and Johnson had a bare plurality of 119,450. In the electoral total, they had 303 to 219 for the Republicans. Johnson's principal contribution was recapturing Texas and Louisiana, which had gone to the Republicans in 1956, and retaining shaky states, such as the two Carolinas. If all of these had voted Republican, Nixon and Lodge would have won.

Lyndon Baines Johnson was born into politics. His grandfather on his mother's side and his father were both members of the Texas state legislature. His father, who had the highest of hopes for Lyndon, would shake him awake early every morning. "Get up, son! Every boy in town has a two-hour start on you." Lyndon always cherished another of the elder Johnson's homespun mottos: "When you're talkin', you ain't learnin' nothin'."

The Johnson prominence in Texas politics brought glory to the family but no riches. For Lyndon's father, failure seemed to be a way of life. The arid, desolate land where they lived in southwest Texas when Lyndon was a small child was too dry and choked with mesquite to support much life. As LBJ later described it, farming in that section of the state was not "worth a cotton-pickin' damn."

But Johnson struggled through high school and college by supporting himself at many jobs, janitoring, housepainting, and acting as secretary to the president of San Marcos Southwest Texas State Teachers College. He graduated from Southwest Texas in 1930, when he was twenty-two. After teaching for a year, he went to Washington as legislative assistant to newly-elected Congressman Richard M. Kleberg, Sr., a friend of Lyndon's father and an owner of the mammoth King Ranch.

Washington was exactly what Johnson wanted. He soon had the sponsorship of fellow Texan Sam Rayburn, an established congressional power, and the admiring friendship of FDR himself. President Roosevelt, to quote Johnson, "was like a Daddy to me." In 1935, when Johnson was not quite twenty-seven, FDR appointed him Texas state director of the National Youth Administration. Two years later, LBJ defeated ten other candidates to fill out the term of a congressman who had died. This was the beginning of twelve years continuous service in the House of Representatives.

In 1948, Johnson entered the Texas Democratic primary to compete for a vacated United States Senate seat. Of eleven candidates, not one received the required majority; a runoff election between the two men with the highest votes, former Governor Coke Stevenson and Representative Lyndon Johnson, was held at the end of August.

With "Calculating Coke" ahead by more than 70,000 in the first primary, Johnson's prospects in the runoff were none too bright. But he conducted a typically Johnsonian campaign by charging all over Texas in a helicopter, the *Johnson City Windmill*. Wherever he saw people, whether in a town or on a farm, he would hover above them and boom down through a specially equipped public address system: "Hello down there . . . this is your friend Lyndon Johnson." Many a voter gaped up at him in open-mouthed astonishment.

The results of the second primary were startling—out of more than 900,000 votes, Johnson won by 87. There were anguished howls of ballot-box stuffing, votes by dead or nonexistent voters, fraud, etc. Charges and countercharges flew from both sides. After suits and decisions that went all the way up to the Supreme Court, Johnson was declared the winner. In a book called "My Brother Lyndon," Sam Houston Johnson blithely dismissed accusations of vote tampering:

"If you're going to steal an election," he wrote, "you sure don't fool around with a piddling margin of 87 votes."

However the results were achieved, this was Johnson's most important victory, for he easily defeated his Republican opponent that fall to take a seat as the junior senator from Texas. When he arrived in the upper house, his new colleagues wryly applauded "Landslide Lyndon."

Within a few years Lyndon Johnson, the perpetual motion machine, propelled himself to the Democratic leadership in the Senate. Blessed with an uncanny ability to project the chances for passage of given legislation, Johnson knew how to count noses and where to get the votes he needed. He did not hesitate to shout, to cajole, to bluster, to sweet-talk, to twist arms or threaten or promise, to bring a weaker senator around to his point of view. He was a master at the art of controlling and/or compromising.

Prior to the 1958 off year elections, Johnson's power in the Senate was absolute, but the senatorial results that year, when a new breed of young liberals came into the upper house, signaled a change ahead. He therefore started to look to 1960, and the choice of a new president. Not too long before, he had minimized his chances for the presidency.

"I'm conscious of my limitations," he told reporters. "I think it's fair to say nobody but my Mama ever thought I'd get as far as I am."

Now he agreed with his mother, for he decided that both he and the country were ready for President Lyndon Johnson.

When the Democratic convention rebuffed him in July of 1960, his unhappiness was evident. Even though he willingly took second spot to John F. Kennedy, it was reported that at one point he was close to tears.

Some of Johnson's friends feared that he would be lost in the vice-presidency, but he brushed their apprehensions aside. "Power is where power goes," he insisted.

Lyndon Johnson did not subscribe to the theory that events create the man. In his world of manipulative politics, the man dominated events, so that it was perfectly logical for him to believe that the immense influence he had wielded as the Senate's majority leader would be carried over to the vice-presidency.

Under a recently enacted Texas law, Johnson had been permitted to run for both the Senate and the vice-presidency. He won another six-year Senate term with an overwhelming majority, even while he was being voted into the vice-presidency. On the morning of his inauguration, therefore, he first had to be sworn in for his third term as senator, and then he promptly resigned.

He did not intend to relinquish his influence along with his senatorial seat. Number one, he refused to give up, as was customary, the plush offices he had occupied as majority leader. Traditionally, the incoming majority leader, in this case Mike Mansfield of Montana, would move in, but Johnson had transformed an ordinary suite into a luxurious "Taj Mahal" (at the government's expense) and he meant to stay. Rather than create a fuss over what was, in his view, a minor matter, Mansfield accepted smaller space elsewhere, even though Johnson was given three other offices.

Secondly, Johnson requested that he be allowed to preside over Senate Democratic caucuses. No longer a senator, he nevertheless expected unanimous approval from his former senatorial colleagues; much to his astonishment, his request was granted only by a vote of 46 to 17. There was considerable animosity toward him in the caucus, even from those who had voted for him, because, as a member of the executive, he had no right to intrude on the legislative branch. Johnson presided for exactly one session. He was greeted so coldly that he handed over the gavel to Mansfield and never returned.

To President Kennedy, his Vice-President had to be an integral part of the team. Prior to the beginning of their term, he had said about LBJ:

"It is my belief that Senator Johnson's great talents and experience equip him to be the most effective Vice-President in our history."

At Kennedy's suggestion, the Space Act of 1958, which Johnson had coauthored, was revised to permit the vice-president to be chairman of the Space Council, rather than the president. For awhile Johnson raced around from one space installation to another and reaped for himself a harvest of newspaper coverage. But he tired of this chore, and convened the Space Council only on infrequent occasions.

Kennedy also invited his Vice-President to sit in on cabinet meetings. Johnson contributed little to these sessions; he usually sat morose and uncommunicative, and offered suggestions only when a direct question was put to him.

Although President Kennedy went out of his way to accommodate his Vice-President, he soon learned that the tall Texan with the blunt and homespun personality did not fit. Only nine years older than the President, Lyndon Johnson, at fifty-two, had no place in the grand Kennedy design of government by the young. Nor did he endear himself with the inner circle.

Kennedy's "Irish Mafia," the Harvard intellectuals, the Wall Street executives, the foundation directors, secretly derided Johnson as "Uncle Cornpone." The bright young men of the New Frontier dismissed him as a backward relic of the Old Frontier. For his part, Johnson's mistrust of the "red hots" and the "lib-lab boys" was indicative of the widening gulf between the two chief executives.

During their first year in office, Kennedy relied upon Johnson for help on Capitol Hill, and Johnson did manage some of his old legislative magic, with the aid and assistance of his dear friend Sam Rayburn. But the elderly Rayburn died of cancer in November of 1961, and Johnson lost another "Daddy." Even more, he also lost whatever incentive he may have had for pushing Kennedy legislation. After that, Kennedy no longer looked to Johnson, and the Vice-President slowly fell deeper and deeper into the Kennedy shadow. The thousand days they served together were described by Johnson's brother as "three miserable years."

But Johnson was not permitted to lie fallow; there was too much richness in his broad Texas ways, his drawl, his friendly earthiness. Kennedy sent him on a series of trips abroad as a goodwill ambassador extraordinary. All told, Johnson traveled through the cities, towns, villages, and mudholes of thirty-three countries, and covered 120,000 miles.

One of Vice-President Johnson's most celebrated journeys took him, in May of 1961, on a twenty thousand mile swing throughout Asia. In India, he dashed into the poorest slums to give away campaign pencils that read: "Compliments of your Senator, Lyndon B. Johnson—the greatest good for the greatest number." In Pakistan he unwittingly managed to extend an invitation to a camel driver to come visit him in the United States.

Bashir Ahmad, who could neither read nor write, did come, much to the delight of Johnson antagonists, who figured the Texan would be embarrassed both socially and politically by the camel driver's unexpected arrival. But Johnson sternly ordered that the Pakistani was to be treated with deference and respect, and he gave the camel driver the VIP treatment. Newspapers all over the country were charmed and delighted by the beaming Bashir Ahmad and his equally beaming host. It was a publicity bonanza for LBJ.

There would be few such triumphs for Vice-President Johnson. President Kennedy's Attorney General, his younger brother Bobby, became the number two man in the administration. Johnson was shut out of major decisions; even the press seemed to be aware of the Vice-President's waning influence. In its reporting of important Kennedy meetings, Johnson's name was either omitted altogether, or simply listed as "among those present."

By the fall of 1963, there was persistent talk that Johnson would be dumped from the 1964 ticket. Kennedy tried to dispel these rumors by insisting that Johnson would be renominated for the vice-presidency. But the Bobby Baker affair in October of 1963 hurt the Vice-President. Baker, a Johnson protégé and friend, and Senate employee, had used his congressional ties to build up a tremendous personal fortune. Disclosure of the Baker maneuvers brought no comfort to the Vice-President, for Baker had always been thought of as Johnson's "boy."

The political situation back home in Texas was equally disheartening for LBJ. The Democrats were badly split between the conservative wing headed by Governor John Connally and Senator Ralph Yarborough's liberals. The intramural squabbling and Johnson's consistent opposition to Yarborough did not help his carefully nurtured image of national leader.

For the Democratic Party, which had barely won Texas in 1960, the rift in that state meant bad news in 1964. President Kennedy decided to make a fence-mending trip to Texas in November of 1963 and bring the warring factions back together. His party arrived in Dallas on November 22. At a little past 12:30 P.M., the Kennedy motorcade passed the Texas School Book Depository Building. Three rifle shots came from the sixth floor of the building. Governor Connally, riding in the Kennedy car, was seriously wounded; President Kennedy was struck by two bullets and died shortly after.

When the death of President Franklin D. Roosevelt was announced in Washington on the afternoon of April 12, 1945, one of Lyndon Johnson's secretaries came into his office weeping into a handkerchief. "I feel so lost," she sobbed. "Who will take care of us now?" The congressman from Texas put his arm around her.

"Why, honey," he said, "there's Mr. Truman."

Similarly, on the afternoon of November 22, 1963, a nation reeling from the shock of President Kennedy's assassination suddenly became aware of Lyndon Baines Johnson.

"My God," the country seemed to say, "now *he's* the President."

But Johnson's first words to the people of the United States as its new chief executive had a simple and warming reassurance about them. At 6:15 that evening, he stepped before the TV cameras and read a statement of exactly 58 words:

"This is a sad time for all people. We have suffered a loss that cannot be weighed. For me, it is a deep personal tragedy. I know that the world shares the sorrow that Mrs. Kennedy and her family bear. I will do my best. That is all I can do. I ask for your help—and God's."

38th Vice-President Hubert H. Humphrey—Democrat, Minnesota, 1965–1969 (President Lyndon Baines Johnson). Born: May 27, 1911, Wallace, S. D.

Madmen and Geniuses

Hubert H. Humphrey

Skeptics and scoffers intended to ridicule the new President; instead, they grudgingly gave him their respect and praise for the way he grasped the reins of government firmly and without nonsense.

Partly because of President Johnson's own persuasive methods, and partly because of the emotional aftermath of John F. Kennedy's senseless assassination, much of Kennedy's social program, which had been stalled by an obstinate Congress, was enacted into law. Continuing the ideals of the New Deal and the New Frontier, Johnson embarked on his "Great Society," which began with a "War on Poverty," and the sweeping Civil Rights Act of 1964.

For many people, it was difficult to accept this new image of the man from Texas as he stood before a joint session of Congress to declare, in a nationally televised address, that "We shall overcome." But he was obviously sincere; whether his motives were political or practical or personal, he achieved with the Civil Rights Act what no other president before him had ever managed to accomplish. Even those who did not like LBJ, as a senator, a president, or just as a human being, now were forced to agree that his achievements in the first half of 1964 had about them an element of greatness.

Here was a clear case of the office making the man, for in the presidency Lyndon Johnson was a far different figure than he had been either in the vice-presidency or in Congress. He had traveled, ideologically, a tremendous distance from his early senatorial days when he had sneered at "all those bleeding heart liberals, those red-hots, red-eyes, and pinkos."

Whatever Johnson may have been in the past was now forgotten, for he rode a crest of immense popularity. No Democrat could possibly hope to take the presidential nomination away from him. Not even race riots in the summer of 1964 or the unfortunate and questionable Tonkin Gulf incident, which occurred prior to the Democratic convention of August, diminished the confidence that the people of the United States demonstrated for the thirty-sixth president. That Tonkin Gulf, within a short time, would involve us in the longest, costliest, and dirtiest war in our history was not yet apparent to the country at large. For the moment, President Johnson was unquestionably the man of the year.

For his choice of a vice-presidential running mate, Johnson played a drawn-out, cliffhanging game that one nationally syndicated columnist called "The Splendid Tease." There was no question that Johnson would name the man to run with him. Too long had the prerogative been given to the presidential candidate; with the immense power of the presidency in his hands, Johnson was not about to abdicate his right to make his own personal selection of the number two man.

There were a number of possible contenders for the vice-presidency. One of them, Attorney General Robert F. Kennedy, was eliminated by Johnson because he did not like JFK's younger brother. Even though Johnson had asked Robert Kennedy to remain in his cabinet, he always thought of him as a "young squirt." And, too, the memory of the Kennedy steamroller that had flattened Johnson's hopes for the presidency in 1960 still rankled. Kennedy, as vice-presidential candidate, might well have assured more votes for the Democratic ticket, but LBJ was too confident of victory to worry about a few votes here and there. He did not need a Kennedy on his ticket to help him win.

The next serious contender to go was Senator Eugene McCarthy of Minnesota. McCarthy voluntarily withdrew from the running because he would not accept the conditions Johnson imposed upon his vice-president-to-be. In an interview published both in the Washington *Star* and the Washington *Post*, President Johnson had made it clear that his vice-president would have no independent positions; he must agree with every decision taken by the President; he could not dispute, for publication, anything said by LBJ; he could do no lobbying for special interests; and he must, above all, *be a Johnson man*, first, last, and always. In short, LBJ's vice-president would be, as a disgusted senator later put it, a "trained seal."

With Kennedy and McCarthy now definitely ruled out, the last one left, with any real hopes for the position, was the senior senator from Minnesota, Hubert Horatio Humphrey. Although Johnson appeared to be considering others, he had decided on Humphrey long before the Democratic convention, which was to meet in Atlantic City, August 24 to 27. To add suspense and interest to what threatened to be a lackluster gathering, Johnson skillfully dangled the vice-presidency before Humphrey and others, and the public as well. LBJ made the rules and played the game as he wanted.

Johnson finally summoned Humphrey to the White House on the afternoon of Wednesday, August 26. As the two men sat in LBJ's office, the President once more insisted upon a vow of absolute fidelity from Humphrey and again made it "crystal clear" that he and he alone was to be the boss, all the way.

"I've done a lot of research on Vice-Presidents," said Johnson, "and not a single President ever got along with his Vice-President. . . But," he went on, "we will be different, because no two men ever got along better than we do."

Humphrey agreed. He assured Johnson of his loyalty, and so it was settled.

A short time later they flew to Atlantic City, where Johnson appeared in person before the convention to disclose his vice-presidential choice. Although the official nominating speech was made by Humphrey's Minnesota colleague, Eugene McCarthy, Johnson's unique appearance was the first and only time a presidential candidate personally placed his running mate in nomination. Both Johnson and Humphrey were named by acclamation.

Six weeks earlier, the conservative wing of the Republican Party had taken over the GOP convention and had succeeded in winning both halves of the Republican ticket, with Senator Barry Goldwater of Arizona for president and Representative William Miller of New York for vice-president. They made a sorry opposition to the Democrats.

Much of the Democratic campaigning was left to Humphrey, who crisscrossed the country enthusiastically and euphorically, proclaiming "the joy of politics." Lyndon B. Johnson was "the greatest president in the history of the United States," and the campaign itself was "not a chore, but a happy, joyful effort."

It was indeed a happy effort, and a source of unbounded joy to the Democrats, for Johnson and Humphrey swamped Goldwater and Miller with one of the most lopsided election victories ever recorded. The Democrats piled up a plurality of close to 16,000,000, receiving 42,825,000 votes to 27,175,000 for the Republicans.

Quite a difference from the 87 vote margin "Landslide Lyndon" had been given in 1948.

If there is one word to describe Hubert Humphrey's political career, that word is "accommodation." In a July, 1964, interview he said: "Nobody has to woo me. I'm old reliable, available Hubert." In 1943, when he made his first try for public office, he ran for mayor with the support of the Democratic and Farmer Labor Parties in Minneapolis; at the same time, because he was virtually unknown to the voters of that city, he used campaign posters of himself reading Wendell Willkie's popular book One World—"a pitch to the little Republicans," explained one of his associates.

He gladly accepted the help of the Minnesota CIO, when he needed that labor group; later, he had no compunction about denounc-

ing Communist infiltration of the CIO when the political climate demanded such denunciation. He took a strong public position against the
McCarran Act of 1950, which required the Communist Party to register,
and then, four years later, introduced his own legislation to outlaw the
Communist Party altogether. His bill, constitutionally doubtful, was
never enforced, and he admitted, with the passage of time, that it was
"not one of the things I'm proudest of."

As for the Humphrey personality, that can best be characterized
as eager and joyfully optimistic. At the age of twenty-four, he made his
first trip to Washington, D.C. with a Boy Scout troop visiting the national capital. The city fired his imagination, as he wrote to his fiancee:

"I intend to set my aim at Congress. Don't laugh at me, Muriel. . .
Oh Gosh, I hope my dreams come true. . . ."

Humphrey was always a young man in a hurry. At high school,
in Doland, South Dakota, he was the senior class valedictorian, captain
of the debating team, a letterman in football, basketball, and track, lead
in the senior class play, featured baritone in an operetta, and a member
of the school band. When his father needed him to help in the family
drug store in Huron, South Dakota, Humphrey completed a two-year
pharmaceutical course in six months. And shortly after his marriage,
when he was twenty-six, Humphrey entered the University of Minnesota
and graduated two years later, *magna cum laude*, with a degree in political science.

Humphrey's political career began in Minneapolis in 1943. With
no experience whatsoever and not enough money for a proper campaign,
he ran for mayor, and lost to the incumbent by only 4900 votes. The
following year, with Humphrey as one of the architects of the merger,
the Democrats and Farmer Laborites of Minnesota joined together as
the Democratic Farmer Labor Party. Humphrey, who had been teaching
political science at St. Paul's Macalester College, gave up his teaching
job to make a second try for the mayoralty of Minneapolis with the full-
fledged support of the merged Democrats-Farmer Laborites. This time
he beat the same incumbent by 31,000.

At the age of thirty-four, Humphrey became the youngest mayor
in the history of Minneapolis.

The performance of Hubert Humphrey as mayor brought a mixed
bag of deprecation and praise from the Minneapolis *Times*.

". . . He talks too much. . . he often jumps to superficial judgements
and conclusions which he afterwards regrets . . . he is sometimes guilty
of political double-talk which distresses even his most ardent admirers.

"But when the evidence is impartially weighed, the scales tip far
toward Humphrey as an honest, progressive and efficient mayor."

This appraisal typified the Humphrey activity as a politician. He did
indeed talk too much, as he himself conceded; he did sometimes look at
issues superficially; and like so many of his peers, he could indulge in
meaningless gobbledygook when the occasion demanded. Yet with all
of that, he emerged as a liberal with a decent regard for civil liberties

and the rights of minorities. (Years later, Lyndon Johnson learned to deplore Humphrey's volubility; when the Minnesotan was his vice-president, LBJ said of him: "If I could just breed him to Calvin Coolidge. . .")

Humphrey's first major performance, one that brought him national attention, took place at the Democratic convention of 1948, where he served as a member of the Minnesota delegation. During the debate on the platform, he made a stirring and eloquent speech on behalf of a strong civil rights plank. Before then, the resolutions committee had recommended a watered down statement in deference to the Southerners. But Humphrey's inspired pleas and demands aroused the convention; his final words brought the cheering delegates to their feet.

"The time has arrived for the Democratic Party to get out of the shadow of states' rights and walk forthrightly into the bright sunshine of human rights!"

The resolutions committee was overruled by a vote of 651½ to 582½. The resulting firm declaration for civil rights brought an angry walkout by many Southerners, led by Strom Thurmond of South Carolina.

In the election that fall, Hubert Humphrey realized the ambition he had boyishly voiced to his fiancée thirteen years before. He made it to Washington, as a United States senator. He easily defeated the incumbent Republican senator of Minnesota by a convincing 244,000 votes, to join another freshman senator in the upper chamber, Lyndon B. Johnson of Texas.

Although Humphrey's spectacular feat of reaching the United States Senate only five years after his first try for public office was admittedly impressive, he was not overwhelmed with plaudits. One political writer described him as "too cocky, too slick, too shallow, too ambitious, a brain-picker rather than a scholar"; Time magazine, however, liked his style, for it spoke of Humphrey as a "hard-working, fast-talking fireball. . . (a) glib, jaunty spellbinder."

It was Humphrey's intent to battle the senatorial establishment, but he soon learned that was no way for a freshman senator to get along. A maverick might make waves, but he generally ended up all wet, unless he knew how to adapt. Humphrey's willingness to accommodate was one of the keys to his rapid congressional rise.

"You have to know the system," he said, "which I learned, and may I say that I think I'm one of the few liberals who learned how to use the system."

He learned well enough to think seriously of the presidency in 1952, and he even received 26 votes as Minnesota's favorite son at the Democratic convention of that year. Two years later, when he and Lyndon Johnson were reelected to the Senate, he supported the Texan for majority leader. The grateful Johnson made good use of Humphrey's reputation as a liberal and a champion of civil rights, for he considered the Minnesotan his "link with the bomb throwers."

As he had mastered the art of accommodating the senatorial establishment, Humphrey learned how to scale his ambition down to a realizable level. When it became apparent, in 1956, that Adlai E. Stevenson II was certain to receive the Democrats' presidential nomination once again, Humphrey aimed for the vice-presidency. But his party and America were not yet ready for him. The Democrats' 1956 vice-presidential nomination went to Estes Kefauver of Tennessee.

The ebullient Humphrey was not one to be dismayed. If he could not be the vice-president in 1956, he would try for the presidency in 1960; he needed only to convince his party that the country wanted him, so he entered a number of primaries against John F. Kennedy.

But Humphrey had one terrible disadvantage; unlike the young Massachusetts senator, he was not a millionaire. He was far from it in fact, while Kennedy had $10 million in his own right and his father's $250 million to draw upon. The Kennedys poured a fortune into the various primaries and slaughtered Humphrey at every turn, for Humphrey had only "a shoestring cut in half" to meet the onslaught of the Kennedy millions.

The final blow came in West Virginia. Humphrey's campaign, already $17,000 in debt, ran out of funds and out of steam. He needed $750 for a last desperate TV appearance. When his staff could not raise the money, he wrote out a check from his own meager resources. To no avail. Once again, Kennedy overwhelmed him.

The West Virginia defeat was the end of Humphrey's presidential dream for 1960. Papa Kennedy's "little black bag" had shattered his chances. Normally genial, Humphrey was embittered by the Kennedy tactics and riches. "Anybody who gets in the way of papa's pet is going to be destroyed," he said.

Triumph, however, did come to Humphrey in 1961. Beginning his third term as senator, he was chosen to be the assistant majority leader in the upper chamber. The Happy Warrior now turned his thoughts away from the White House, for he thoroughly enjoyed his new prestige as the Democratic whip. If the situation required it, he was willing to bargain and to settle for half a loaf. He did not want to "glory in defeat," as he accused the "professional liberals" of doing.

President Johnson's Civil Rights Act of 1964 was engineered to its successful culmination by Senator Humphrey, who worked patiently and endlessly over a three and a half month period to shepherd the legislation through the Senate. Two months after the Senate's historic approval of the Act, a grateful President Johnson asked Senator Humphrey to be his vice-presidential candidate on the Democrats' 1964 ticket.

The smashing election victory, three months later, of the Johnson-Humphrey team gave President Johnson what he considered to be a mandate. Within three weeks after their inauguration, which took place on a bright and chilly January 20, LBJ decided to commit the United States unequivocally to a war in Vietnam when he ordered the start of "Operation Rolling Thunder"—massive bombing raids against selected North Vietnamese military targets.

United States involvement in Vietnam had been building slowly. Johnson himself had always been in favor of intervention in Southeast Asia, for he firmly believed that the spread of Communism on that continent had to be stopped. He gave his views in a confidential memo to President John F. Kennedy, written on May 23, 1961, after Johnson's widely publicized trip through Southeast Asia, India, and Pakistan.

"The battle against Communism must be joined in Southeast Asia with strength and determination to achieve success there," wrote Johnson, then completing his fourth month as vice-president, "—or the United States, inevitably, must surrender the Pacific and take up our defenses on our own shores."

Johnson advocated political and economic aid, and if necessary, military, including the actual use of American men and equipment. In the spring of 1965, Johnson did at last commit his country to military intervention in Southeast Asia. Hubert Humphrey, his vice-president, questioned the timing of the bombing raids ordered by Johnson, and he openly expressed his doubts at a meeting of the National Security Council on February 10. The Vice-President's early breach of his agreement with LBJ never to disagree publicly with his President (and that meant in front of others of the Johnson team) did not sit well with President Johnson. LBJ particularly took exception to a follow-up memorandum Humphrey wrote a short time later.

"We don't need all those memos, Hubert," the President told him. After that, for almost a year, Vice-President Humphrey was excluded from important meetings, especially those dealing with foreign affairs.

Humphrey's consignment to a Johnsonian Coventry was strange irony, for the Minnesotan was just as committed as LBJ to intervention in Southeast Asia. In August, 1964, while he was still in the Senate, Humphrey declared:

"We ought to make it clear to the world that we do not intend to sit at the conference table with a Communist gun at our heads."

A year and a half later, during an Asian tour Humphrey undertook at Johnson's request, the Vice-President echoed LBJ's sentiments of 1961, when he spoke about the Chinese Communists. "If we don't stop 'em in South Vietnam," said Humphrey, "they'll be in Honolulu and San Francisco."

Although Vice-President Humphrey was left out of foreign affairs for some eleven months, he worked valiantly on Johnson's domestic program. When he was restored to the President's good graces in early 1966, he gladly accepted the role of super salesman for the Johnson policies both at home and abroad. That meant selling the Vietnam War to the United States, and it meant trying to overcome a growing hostility from disenchanted youth, from his former liberal colleagues, from a divided country that could find no true justification for our military participation in Southeast Asia.

Despite the mushrooming criticism and the anguish of his fellow liberals, Humphrey doggedly clung to his loyal support of his President and unwavering defense of the Vietnamese war. Regarding "basic administration policies," Humphrey insisted: "I am supporting them out of clear intellectual commitment."

There were many who found such loyalty to LBJ reason enough to turn away from Humphrey. As one of his Senate colleagues phrased it: "Poor Hubert. . . . He has no enemies, but more ex-friends than any man I know."

The many remarkable accomplishments of the Johnson administration were submerged by the Vietnam War, which had become the most poisonous issue of the decade. By March of 1968, President Johnson decided he could no longer face the country's anger over the war, and he therefore announced he would not seek reelection. The way was cleared at last for Hubert Humphrey to realize his dream of reaching the White House on his own. (Humphrey's only real rival, Robert Kennedy, was assassinated in Los Angeles two months after Johnson's withdrawal from the presidential race.)

Humphrey's subsequent first ballot nomination for the presidency at the Democrats' Chicago convention in August of 1968 was doubly jeopardized: his continuing loyalty to LBJ and his refusal to denounce Johnson's bombing of North Vietnam alienated many people who might otherwise have supported him. And just three hours before the Democrats' presidential balloting was to begin, every television network suddenly deserted the convention floor to focus their cameras on the streets, where violence erupted between thousands of young, antiwar demonstrators and hundreds of helmeted, masked Chicago police wielding nightsticks and throwing tear gas. Millions of viewers were horrified at the ugliness being revealed on camera before their very eyes. That the demonstrations were aimed against the Vietnam War did Humphrey no good at all.

But the Happy Warrior brushed off the demonstrators as "kooks and rioters" and, the following day, delivered a forty-minute acceptance speech to his fellow Democrats. Toward the end, he said this:

"I say to America: put aside recrimination and dissension. Turn away from violence and hatred."

Unfortunately, his own willingness to accept the violence of the Vietnam War disenchanted hundreds of thousands of the electorate all across the country. Even his last minute turnabout, when he finally announced in late September that, if elected president, he would halt the bombing of North Vietnam under certain specified conditions, was not enough to overcome the onus of his loyalty to Johnson.

Twenty-three years after his first upset victory for the mayoralty of Minneapolis, he lost the most important election of his life, and for him, the "joy of politics" turned to the agony of defeat.

39th Vice-President   Spiro T. Agnew—Republican, Maryland, 1969–
1973 (President Richard M. Nixon). Born: November 9, 1918, Baltimore, Md.

Madmen and Geniuses

Spiro T. Agnew

On the evening of Thursday, August 8, 1968, Richard M. Nixon stood before thousands of cheering Republicans with his arms raised in a happy V. He had been nominated for the presidency that afternoon, and three months later he would achieve even greater honors. But this moment in the convention hall at Miami, Florida, represented a high point of his career, for it marked his return to power and triumph after an exile of six years.

To many people, the comeback of Richard Nixon seemed like a political miracle, almost as if it had happened spontaneously. But Nixon's rejuvenation did not occur suddenly or overnight. It was carefully planned and organized, for it was the product of a well-oiled machine, primed with money and influence, carried out over a long period of time.

Not quite six years earlier, on Wednesday, November 7, 1962, Nixon was convinced his life as a politician had ended. He had suffered a stinging defeat at the hands of incumbent Governor Pat Brown in Californa's gubernatorial election the day before, and he now faced a startled press corps in the lobby of the Los Angeles Beverly Hilton Hotel to announce that he was finished with politics.

Bitterness and rancor showed in every word, as he revealed the depth of his anger and frustration over his loss to an unexciting, middle-drawer governor:

"You won't have Nixon to kick around anymore," he said, "because, gentlemen, this is my last press conference. . . ."

Perhaps he wondered at the uncertainty and perversity of politics.

In 1960, he had actually won California while losing the presidency to John F. Kennedy by the closest of margins, a heartbreaking 49.7% of the popular national vote to 49.6%.

Why then did the same Californians turn away from him as overwhelmingly in 1962, to rebuke his bid for their governorship by an astounding 300,000 votes? There was no one single reason, as Nixon well knew. Sadly, his illustrious reputation as a national and international figure had done him no good at all.

Nixon did retire from politics—for a year or so. By 1964 he was once again in the thick of his party's affairs, and slowly the old Nixon magic reasserted itself, to rise to a peak in the first hours of August 8, 1968.

In Miami, the Republicans placed twelve names in nomination for the presidency, and consumed nine hours for nominating and seconding speeches. When they at last got around to voting, they took exactly one ballot to choose Richard M. Nixon to be their new standard bearer.

Candidate Nixon did not announce his vice-presidential running mate until the following afternoon, even though he had known for some time who it would be. Weeks before the convention, he had canvassed Republican leaders for their suggestions. The total spectrum of GOP ideologies was covered by the names put forward, including young liberals like New York City Mayor John V. Lindsay and conservatives like California Governor Ronald Reagan.

But Nixon wanted neither a liberal nor a conservative. Each would alienate sizable wings of the GOP. What was needed was a "centrist," a political neuter who would meet minimum requirements without arousing factional antagonism or sectional protest. Beyond that, he could not be a superstar, for Nixon wanted no one who might threaten to take the spotlight away from him.

Shortly after 12:30 P.M. on Thursday, Nixon met with the press to make his announcement. The representatives of the news media were not prepared for the name he gave them; earlier speculation in many newspapers had centered around men like Lindsay and Governor Nelson Rockefeller of New York. When Nixon told the press that his man was Spiro T. Agnew, governor of Maryland, disbelief and bewilderment exploded in a question that quickly became a national joke: "Spiro who?"

It was a good question. No one, but no one, had ever heard of Agnew. Actually, this wasn't entirely true, for the country had read of him during the course of a harrowing racial riot in Baltimore's ghetto a few months before. And he had made the nominating speech on behalf of Nixon on Wednesday evening. But who pays attention to nominating speeches, with all their profound clichés and rhetorical emptiness, or to the ones who deliver them?

Nixon blandly waited for the confusion and the shock to die down. He knew what he was doing. He wanted a "political eunuch," a nonluminary, someone the South and the uncertain border states would tolerate.

Besides, said Nixon, Agnew was "an old-fashioned patriot." And, as the GOP's southern strong man, Strom Thurmond, put it, Spiro Agnew "was the least worst of the candidates that were proposed by Mr. Nixon."

What of the vice-presidential candidate himself? How did he feel about this sudden propulsion to national fame? It was, he told the press, "like a bolt out of the blue." Later, in his acceptance speech, he confessed to the Republican convention:

"I stand here with a deep sense of the improbability of this moment."

The *New York Times* editorially agreed when it said about him a few weeks later:

". . . He is not fit to stand one step away from the Presidency."

Agnew demonstrated, during the hectic weeks of the election campaign, that his assessment and that of the *Times* were both fundamentally correct. He made one gaffe after another, blunders that were intolerable coming from a potential president.

In September, Agnew accused the Democratic presidential candidate, Hubert Humphrey, of being "squishy soft on Communism." Even for the agonized Republicans this was too much, for they wanted the world to forget that their own Richard Nixon had pushed his way to the top by using the same line. And "soft on communism" had been discredited along with Joseph McCarthy. For Agnew to revive this charge was naive and unforgivable.

The loose-tongued Agnew was to say much more. In Chicago, which he thought was in "Illi-noise," he referred to a Negro, an Italian, a Greek, and a *Polack*. On the way to Hawaii, he saw a plumpish reporter sleeping on the campaign plane, and he said: "What's the matter with the fat *Jap?*"

When he was asked, at another point, why he avoided campaigning in ghettos, his answer was: "If you've seen one city slum, you've seen them all."

All this time, Richard Nixon made no attempt to muzzle his running mate. Toward the crucial final weeks of the campaign, Agnew concentrated on the South, where his brand of "liberal" right-wing rhetoric went over big with the voters who had to be wooed away from George Wallace, the governor of Alabama and formidable third party candidate.

How well did Agnew perform for the Republicans? His presence on the ticket undoubtedly helped the Republicans win three uncertain border states, Tennessee and North and South Carolina, for in each of them George Wallace came in second, decisively beating Humphrey.

With a national total of 302 electoral votes, Nixon still would have won without the three states Agnew helped to carry. But if the Republicans had lost these three states, which had a total of 32 electoral votes, it would have meant another heartstopper for Nixon, for he would have ended with 270, exactly the number needed to win; one electoral vote less and the election would have gone to the House of Representatives.

Shortly after the Republican convention, Nixon had said of his running mate:

"This guy's got it. If he doesn't, Nixon has made a bum choice."

On the morning of Wednesday, November 5, 1968, when Hubert Humphrey finally conceded, Nixon could say he had not made a bum choice after all. George Wallace, who won only the Solid South with 45 electoral votes, had been effectively stopped by Agnew where it counted. Richard Nixon had reason enough to be grateful to Spiro Agnew, even though the new Vice-President failed to carry his own state of Maryland.

Spiro Theodore Agnew had much to brag about. He could rightfully claim an astonishing rise out of obscurity, and he could boast the only Greek parentage of any vice-president, or president for that matter. In a country whose chief elective officers were overwhelmingly of English, Scotch, or Irish extraction, a vice-president of Greek origin was indeed unique.

Spiro's father, Theofrastos Spiro Anagnostopoulos, was born in 1878, in a house at the corner of Socrates and Aristotle Streets in the Greek village of Gargalianoi. When he came to the United States as a young penniless man, his name went through two changes, to Anagnost and finally Agnew. He became a successful restaurateur in Baltimore, Maryland, and married an American widow from Virginia. Their only child, Spiro Theodore, was born in November, 1918. Mr. Agnew agreed that his son would be raised as an Episcopalian.

Although young Spiro was aware that he was different in some way, as would any member of an ethnic minority at that time, he assimilated quickly and easily into Middle America. (Spiro Agnew never thought of himself as a practicing Greek until he had been nominated for the vice-presidency in 1968. He never learned his father's native tongue, and throughout most of his life preferred that people call him by the anglicized "Ted.")

Spiro Ted Agnew was only an average student. He entered Johns Hopkins University in Baltimore to study chemistry, gave that up when he found he couldn't concentrate on his studies, and went to work for an insurance company, where he was an "assistant underwriter in the sprinkler leakage and water damage division." He married, served in World War II and later in Korea, studied law at night, had various jobs, none of them prestigious or well-paying, and finally went into practice as a lawyer at the age of thirty-five.

From that point on, his career slowly and yet inexorably led to the top in a series of fantastically fortuitous circumstances. He did nothing spectacular or outstanding, but somehow destiny pushed him forward, from licking stamps and stuffing envelopes in 1957, to the Baltimore County Board of Appeals the following year, to County Executive in 1962, and to the governorship of Maryland in 1966.

Throughout Agnew's service as an elective official in Maryland, he established himself as a moderate on key issues such as civil rights and inflation. By the time he graduated to the national political arena, however, he managed to tarnish the "moderate" image of his reputation.

The assassination of Martin Luther King, Jr., in April of 1968 led to a tragic riot in Baltimore's ghetto, as it did in much of the country. But the Baltimore disturbances, which ended with six people dead, seven hundred injured, and five thousand arrested, crystallized Agnew's attitudes, and showed that he had always been a conservative hard-liner rather than a moderate. He took a tough, immovable position with Baltimore's black leaders, and infuriated most of them with his failure to understand the root causes of ghetto discontent. Much more than public pronouncements on law and order and a get-tough policy were needed to combat the violence and the extremists. Agnew did not understand it then, or later, for most of his white constituents applauded his position, and he could point with pride to praise from the news media for his overall performance.

There were those who kept insisting he was a liberal, while others blasted him as a bigot. With Agnew, there could be no middle ground. Yet, in Richard Nixon's eyes, Agnew was the perfect centrist, and the ideal man to balance Nixon's presidency. The two men, who had met briefly in 1964, and then two or three more times in early 1968, liked and admired one another, although Agnew did not have as high a regard for Nixon. "He'd make a great Secretary of State," Agnew told a friend.

After his surprise selection for the vice-presidency, Spiro Agnew admitted that his name was not a household word, but he hoped to make it one. He succeeded even beyond his own expectations.

President Nixon made it clear that Vice-President Agnew would be given a "full plate" of assignments, and so he was. Nixon created one council upon another, committees and liaison groups, and put Agnew at their head or on them. He sent the Vice-President to the minor functions he himself did not want to attend. Agnew was indeed kept busy. He even attended many more Senate sessions than vice-presidents normally do; as the first vice-president since Henry Wallace to have no congressional experience, Agnew felt it was his duty to learn all he could about senatorial and parliamentary procedure.

For awhile, it seemed as if Agnew were the working vice-president that Nixon had promised to the country. But it soon became evident to Agnew that his functions were, at best, ceremonial. He was being left out of all the important discussions, and major administration decisions were being made without his participation and advice. Within six months of his inauguration, he had what one aide characterized as "the vice-presidential blues."

But Spiro T. Agnew was not one to be daunted by presidential neglect. With the last years of the delirious '60s climbing to a peak of permissiveness, with college campus disorders and demonstrations against the Vietnam War breaking out with increasing frequency, Agnew took it upon himself to demolish President Nixon's critics, particularly the anti-war snipers. Whether Nixon and Agnew liked it or not, the war in Vietnam was still the most divisive issue in the country and the hundreds of thousands who demanded that it be brought to an end were becoming more and more vocal.

The Vice-President's first venture against the administration's enemies found him sticking a tentative toe into the muddied waters, but it was enough to inspire him to go on. In June of 1969, he said to an audience at Ohio State University:

"A society which comes to fear its children is effete. A sniveling, hand-wringing power structure deserves the violent rebellion it encourages."

Agnew had rediscovered words. Always a lover of language, he now embarked on a new crusade, the politics of polysyllables. He blasted away at the intellectuals, and after them, at the long-haired hippies, the campus demonstrators, all the "rotten apples" in the barrel. He was prepared to sweep "that kind of garbage out of our society."

Protests against a dirty, undeclared war were not to be tolerated. "The time has come," said the Vice-President, "to call a halt to this spiritual Theatre of the Absurd, to examine the motivation of the authors of the absurdity, and challenge the star players in the cast."

A week after that one, he spoke in New Orleans, and came up with an attack against "an effete corps of impudent snobs who characterize themselves as intellectuals."

Middle America went wild. Here was one of their own, speaking to them in a calm, relaxed, friendly manner, never raising his voice, as smooth and unruffled as the meticulously groomed clothes he wore, never a hair or an expression out of place. He was talking as no politician before ever had. (Adlai E. Stevenson II and Senator Eugene McCarthy had used the same kind of language, but they were genuine intellectuals and therefore not to be trusted. Agnew did not pretend to anything so lofty. He was part of the vast "Silent Majority," only now he was their spokesman, and a most articulate one.)

Spiro Agnew was at last off and running. The press and the TV newscasts gave his utterances featured billing; almost overnight he became the superstar Richard Nixon had not wanted. Between June and October of 1969, the Vice-President emerged from the cocoon of anonymity to become the most famous political personality of the year. Speaking engagements poured in upon him at the rate of fifty a day.

He did not disappoint his constituents. In November of 1969, with full coverage from all three television networks, Agnew turned his guns on the news media—the television newscasters and the unseen producers behind them. Calling them a "tiny and closed fraternity of privileged men" who indulged in "instant analysis" and "querulous criticism," he accused the entire news media of bias against the Nixon administration, simply because television news, watched by millions all over the country, did not always offer immediate and fulsome praise to Nixon's efforts, especially in the Vietnam War. This was the most blatant government interference with the traditional freedom of the press, and an obvious attempt at censorship.

The harsh accusations at least temporarily muzzled extreme journalistic criticism. There was of course a pained outcry from the press. *Newsweek* said that Agnew's speech had about it an "odor of sanctity. . . mingled with the burning tar of demagoguery." Liberal columnist Max Lerner of the New York *Post* labeled the Vice-President "a one-man ground-to-air-missile, a multiple reentry vehicle guaranteed to shoot off in every direction."

But Middle America once again cheered. Encouraged by outspoken plaudits from his countrymen, Agnew returned to the attack, his vigor renewed and his resolve strengthened.

From polysyllables, he moved to alliteration, and gave the nation "supercilious sophisticates," "pusillanimous pussyfooting," "vicars of vacillation," "nattering nabobs of negativism," "hopeless, hysterical hypochondriacs of history," and "Pablum for the permissivists." He had embarked on an all-out holy crusade he himself called "positive polarization."

By the middle of 1970, Vice-President Spiro Agnew was the Republicans' main attraction. He was cheered and applauded as lustily as he was despised. An Agnew appearance at a fund raising dinner guaranteed overflowing coffers.

Not everyone in the GOP approved of his conduct, but little was done within his party to oppose him. Because of his fantastic success as a speaker, it was decided to repeat in the 1970 off year election campaigns the tactics of 1954, when then Vice-President Richard Nixon had been sent out to scuttle the opposition with harsh accusations and distorted half-truths. It apparently did not occur to the GOP chieftains that Nixon's low road, in 1954, had led to failure.

Agnew went out after the Democrats with gusto. The major role had been assigned to him, for President Nixon had decided to remain aloof and detached; the President would of course watch carefully from the sidelines, but the principal task of destruction would be left to Agnew.

Once again the Vice-President brought delight to his constituency. Appealing to the "workingmen of this country," he assaulted "the pampered prodigies of the radical liberals in the United States Senate," while praising a "progressive President carrying out his mandate for reform." He blamed the Democrats for all the ills besetting the nation—pornography, rising crime, inflation, drugs.

The opposition fought back. Democratic Senator Albert Gore of Tennessee angrily called Agnew "our greatest disaster next to Vietnam." Disappointingly for the Republicans, Agnew's inflammatory elocution did not do the trick, and President Nixon himself had to make a last minute desperation swing through many doubtful states. But neither member of the executive team proved effective, and the Democrats retained control of both Houses.

Agnew had failed; once again the low road for the vice-president ended in the middle of nowhere. As had happened with Nixon in 1954, Agnew became an embarrassing liability for the Republicans after 1970.

Talk of dumping the Vice-President from the GOP ticket in 1972 began early, and continued through 1971 almost to convention eve. Nixon refused to make a commitment either for or against Agnew, but, notably, the Vice-President no longer was used as the administration's all-purpose blunderbuss or "cutting edge." His rhetoric had been completely toned down and his image revamped, so that he was made to appear a benign, thoughtful statesman rather than a caustic polarizer. The new image fooled no one, for it was all too apparent that Agnew was no more than a ritualistic figurehead in the Nixon game plan.

A month before the Republican convention, which was to meet once again in Miami the latter part of August, 1972, Nixon finally announced that he was retaining Spiro Theodore Agnew as his vice-president. Nixon did not want to break up a winning team.

Thus alerted by their chieftain, the GOP delegates awarded an historic renomination to Agnew. When the Republican convention chose him by acclamation to run for a second term with Nixon, it marked only the fifth time that an incumbent vice-president received his party's nomination. His subsequent overwhelming reelection along with Nixon two and a half months later marked another milestone, for it was the first time in American history that two former vice-presidents won election as the country's executive team.

But the triumph of Spiro T. Agnew was, at best, transitory. His had been a most unlikely and improbable career. Any man who accomplished what he did with minimal ability could not be lightly dismissed. He had had at least two things going for him—extraordinary luck and a simplistic confidence, both of which were suddenly shattered in August of 1973 when he told the nation that he had been under investigation for some time in a matter involving bribery, extortion, and kickbacks in Maryland.

It was a shocking disclosure, but surely not to the administration, for Agnew himself had known of the investigation for a number of months and Nixon must have known as well.

Agnew now found himself fighting for his political life. He called a press conference, carried over nationwide television, to label reports and rumors that he might be involved in criminal violations as "false, scurrilous, and malicious." He was, he said, "denying them outright." He said, too, that he "had nothing to hide." This was a phrase he was to use time and again over the coming weeks.

One report he may have been alluding to charged that he had received $1,000 a week in kickbacks from Maryland contractors while he was governor of that state, and that one payment of $50,000 had been made to him while he was vice-president.

There were other matters to trouble him, for it was reported that White House aide Melvin R. Laird had warned an influential congressman not "to go out on a limb for Agnew." It had suddenly become painfully apparent that the Nixon administration meant to desert its vice-president.

Burdened with new revelations that seemed to be divulged by the hour, Agnew had reason to be concerned. He angrily accused the Justice Department of deliberately leaking these stories to the press. He said he was being unfairly tried in the newspapers, and was already judged to be guilty even though no formal charges had ever been brought against him.

At the end of September, Agnew went to California to address the National Federation of Republican Women, meeting in Los Angeles. After the close of his prepared speech, he spoke extemporaneously and proclaimed, in a defiant refrain:

"I will not resign if indicted! I will not resign if indicted!"

Thirteen-hundred adoring and screaming women jumped to their feet, hysterically waving their "Spiro Is Our Hero" banners, while those in front mobbed the beaming Vice-President. Said one feminine admirer:

"He'll look you in the eye, and Nixon won't."

Not quite two weeks later, Agnew did resign, and he fell sickeningly to the lowest point any vice-president had ever occupied when he pleaded "nolo contendere" to a charge of tax evasion. His resignation from the vice-presidency and his confession that he had committed at least one felony set off a shock wave that traveled from one corner of the world to the other.

One of Agnew's coconspirators in the bribery campaign perhaps best summed up the numbed attitude of the nation. Lester Matz, a close friend and associate of Agnew's, told how he had once met with the Vice-President in the latter's Washington office and had given him approximately $10,000 in cash in an envelope as money owing from previous extortions. Matz said that he had been "shaken by his own actions because he had just made a payoff to the Vice-President of the United States."

In a sense, Agnew had the prestige of his high office to thank for the relative lightness of the penalties imposed upon him. When Judge Hoffman passed sentence, he said that he preferred to send the former Vice-President to prison, but because of the personal intercession of Attorney General Elliot Richardson, who argued that "leniency is justified," Judge Hoffman fined Agnew $10,000 and placed him on three years' unsupervised probation.

Spiro Agnew made one last appearance on national TV to explain why he had resigned and why he had agreed to a plea of no contest. Beyond a few brief flashes of the old Agnew style, his farewell speech was a dull and labored plea for sympathy that almost no one was willing to give him. He did, however, have a few words of wisdom for his viewers. He told of how James Garfield had calmed a panicky audience after they had learned of the assassination of Abraham Lincoln:

"Fellow citizens," Garfield said, "God reigns, and the Government in Washington still lives."

True. Washington would survive, and so would the nation—fortunately without Spiro Agnew to guide it.

40th Vice-President   Gerald R. Ford—Republican, Michigan, 1973–
(President Richard M. Nixon). Born: July 14, 1913, Omaha, Nebr.

Madmen and Geniuses

Gerald R. Ford

The break-in at the Democratic National Committee headquarters in the early morning hours of Saturday, June 17, 1972, was denounced by Ron Ziegler, President Nixon's press secretary, as "a third-rate burglary." It was that, of course, for the five burglars, seized within the DNC offices by three members of Washington, D.C.'s Second District Casual Clothes Squad, had operated as though they had come out of the pages of a spy thriller, but without the expertise and savoir faire of fictional espionage agents. It was a bungled, stupid burglary, conducted on the sixth floor of Washington's Watergate Hotel, a complex of expensive business offices and luxurious private apartments.

Beyond its patent stupidity, however, the Watergate break-in ultimately proved to be the most colossal political blunder of the century. As one anguished Republican later said about Watergate, it was "only the tip of the iceberg." One after another, trusted Nixon associates and members of his administration were accussed of illegal procedures and, in a number of cases, indicted for criminal activity. The President, through his official spokesmen, protested his own innocence, but too much of the country refused to believe him. The Watergate revelations had exposed a rotten vein that unsupported denials from the White House could not camouflage; once it was revealed that Nixon aides had actively been involved in the planning and subsequent cover-up of the Watergate break-in, many more embarrassing disclosures came to light.

When all the implications of Watergate began to be made public in the spring of 1973 (both by special prosecutor Archibald Cox and by a select seven-man Senate committee headed by septuagenarian Senator Sam Ervin of North Carolina), President Nixon found himself defending one charge after another, not only Watergate but other accusations involving deals with giant corporations; a possible payoff to the milk industry by way of accelerating price increases; illegal assaults against civil liberties in the name of "national security"; questionable tax write-offs on his income tax returns, and huge expenditures paid from public funds to improve his personal properties at San Clemente, California, and Key Biscayne, Florida. More and more of the iceberg came into view, and none of it helped either the image of the President or his popularity. For the first time in a hundred years, there were insistent and widespread demands for the impeachment of the President or his resignation.

By the summer of 1973, the presidency as an office was threatened by a complete breakdown of respect and confidence. Much of the country believed that the President was a liar, if not worse, and said so. As a reflection of the nation's disenchantment with its chief executive, the office of the presidency was now viewed by the common man with suspicion and mistrust; the President's obvious reluctance to produce proof that he was innocent of all the charges being leveled against him only convinced the country that the proof was not available. The office, as well as the man, was in danger.

That the investigation of Spiro Agnew should suddenly have been announced in the midst of all these monumental problems plaguing the President seems too coincidental and providential. Surely the President must have known, along with Agnew himself, that the Justice Department (always under the president's jurisdiction) was conducting such an investigation. Surely the timing of the announcement of this investigation could not have been an accident, for once the Agnew affair was made public, the heat was off the President, at least for a brief period.

Whether by plan or providence, the Agnew matter did bring a temporary reprieve to President Nixon. He had time to prepare a counter-offensive against his critics. Agnew's subsequent resignation gave Nixon a further opportunity to regain some measure of the public's confidence, which he had lost to an alarming degree.

Under the specifications of the Twenty-fifth Amendment, ratified into law in February of 1967, President Nixon was now empowered to select a new vice-president to replace Agnew. His choice would be confirmed only by consent of both Houses of Congress. The sponsors of the Twenty-fifth Amendment, who had worked for years to make it into law, believed that it had sufficient safeguards to guarantee that the replacement vice-president would be democratically chosen, for Congress reserved unto itself the final right of approval or disapproval of the president's choice.

On paper, all of this sounded fine, as the Amendment's sponsors claimed, for there would be a check and balance between the executive and legislative branches of our government, and this was exactly what the original framers of the Constitution had intended. Our government had successfully operated, since 1789, under such a system of checks and balances; the Twenty-fifth Amendment continued the system.

But the sponsors of the Amendment, when it was being discussed during the early 1960s, could not have foreseen Watergate or the insistent demands in 1973 that the President resign or be impeached. They could not possibly have imagined that a vice-president of the United States would become a convicted felon.

How could anyone in 1964 or '65 or '66 have known that 1973 would produce the most traumatic political events in our history? How could anyone have known then that most members of Congress would literally jump with relief and joy to have, as the fortieth vice-president of the United States, an uninspiring, conservative congressman who, by his own admission, had been "only a B student," and was, in the eyes of many of his colleagues and peers, "not real bright"?

But this was the man Congress was willing to accept as a replacement for Spiro Agnew, despite the claimed safeguards of the Twenty-fifth Amendment. Under other circumstances, he would have had no chance for nomination, but now, after Watergate and Agnew, Congress was all too ready to accept him as the possible next president of the country. Members of both Houses candidly admitted he might well succeed to the presidency, for they envisioned either the resignation or impeachment of Richard Nixon.

If the selection of this candidate, timidly approved by a nervous Congress, presented a study in paradox, then President Nixon's announcement of his choice can only be classified as even more bizarre.

In a glittering scene that would have warmed the monarchical heart of John Adams, hundreds of assorted congressmen, Nixon cabinet members, and other Republican faithfuls gathered on the evening of Friday, October 12, 1973, in the East Room of the White House. Here, under the brilliant glare of gleaming chandeliers, President Nixon was to announce to his assembled guests and to the country via television and radio, at precisely 9:00 P.M., his vice-president designate.

When the time came for the President to make his triumphal entry into the East Room, the TV cameras turned toward the door where he was to enter and the murmuring of the guests muted to a hushed expectancy. A military orchestra swung into the heroic strains of "Hail to the Chief" as a smiling President Nixon, accompanied by his wife and followed by members of his cabinet, confidently strode into the festive East Room, to be greeted by the fervent applause of his guests and admirers. It was a moment for the President to savor, even though it had about it the elements of carefully contrived staging.

In his opening remarks, which he began shortly after nine that evening, Nixon sounded as if he were making an inaugural address, rather than a speech in the fifth year of his administration.

"This is a time for a new beginning for America," he said, "a new beginning in which we all dedicate ourselves to the tasks of meeting the challenges we face, seizing the opportunities for greatness and meeting the dangers wherever they are at home or abroad."

He then went on to outline the three criteria that he had in mind for the new vice-president:

First, he had to be qualified to be president;

Second, he had to share Nixon's views on "the critical issues of foreign policy and national defense";

And third, he had to be someone who could work with both parties in Congress so that he could help to gain congressional approval of Nixon-sponsored legislation.

Sustaining the suspense for all it was worth, Nixon said he did have such a man, a man who had "served for twenty-five years in the House of Representatives with great distinction."

With that, the assembled guests burst into wild applause and shouts of approval, for they knew now what they had only been guessing at for the past two days. They knew, even before Nixon smilingly confirmed the guess, that the Nixon choice for the fortieth vice-president was Congressman Gerald R. Ford of Michigan.

Significantly, during the brief ceremony, stretched out to take advantage of the prime TV coverage, not one word was said about the former Vice-President, Spiro Agnew, who had resigned in disgrace and humiliation only two days before. Not once was his name mentioned either by the President or by the Vice-President Designate Gerald Ford. As far as the new Nixon team was concerned, the thirty-ninth vice-president of the United States had never existed.

The enthusiastic huzzahs that greeted Representative Ford in the East Room were not universally echoed in the rest of the country. But influential congressmen from both Houses and both parties fell all over themselves in their eagerness to endorse the President's choice. The fact that Ford had already been passed over for the vice-presidency four times by his own party (beginning in 1960, when he lost out to Henry Cabot Lodge of Massachusetts), seemed not to matter at this decisive moment on October 12, 1973. Now he was "perfectly acceptable," "a choice I can support without reservation," and "a first-rate politician." Ford's selection, said one senator, "solves all kinds of problems." Other senators foresaw a quick confirmation by Congress.

Upon more sober reflection, however, Congress decided to take its time about bestowing confirmation upon President Nixon's nominee. It would not be as simple as either Nixon may have thought, or Ford may have hoped. For Congress realized it would have to tread carefully, and make a thorough investigation of Ford's background. Another Agnew would have been disastrous.

One fact about Ford immediately became apparent. He was no superstar who might steal the limelight from the President, and he was no original thinker. He adhered ploddingly to Nixonian principles. He would deviate very little from the Nixon program or game plan. In short,

Congressman Gerald Ford was exactly the kind of conservative disciple Nixon needed in the second chair; he would make no waves and take no independent position on the issues that mattered to the President. He may not have been the best possible choice for the country, but most certainly he was right for Nixon.

The fortieth vice-president was born in Omaha, Nebraska, in July of 1913 and named Leslie King, Jr. When he was still a baby, his parents divorced and his mother married a Grand Rapids, Michigan, business-man named Gerald Rudolph Ford. The elder Ford adopted the boy and gave him his name.

Jerry's childhood and adolescence were placid and uneventful, as befitted the son of a successful Middle American paint manufacturer. Jerry learned at an early age the virtues of hard work, for he waited on tables during high school at a salary of $2.00 per week, and in the summer worked in his father's paint factory. In the meantime, football became a consuming passion and he starred on his high school team, winning all-city and all-state honors. He was, one admiring aide later said about him, "a mixture of Horatio Alger, Tom Swift, and Jack Armstrong, the All-American boy."

The passion for football carried over into college. He was the center for Ann Arbor's University of Michigan team, helping to bring championships to the Wolverines. In 1934, his senior year, he was chosen the team's most valuable player. (Political opponents, including Lyndon B. Johnson, scathingly referred to Ford's football days by claiming he had "played too long without a helmet.")

Professional football, in the form of offers from the Green Bay Packers and Detroit Lions, beckoned Ford upon graduation, but pro football in those perilous Depression days was more black and blue than golden. Ford's adequate marks were enough to get him into the Yale Law School, where he helped to pay his way by working as an assistant football coach and boxing instructor.

He received his law degree in 1941, just in time to fight in World War II. He joined the Navy and served until 1946, when he left with the rank of lieutenant commander and nine battle stars.

Upon his return to Grand Rapids, he joined a law firm and offered his services to "every committee in town," so that he could make himself well known. To Ford, the future lay in politics.

In 1948, with the help of his stepfather, chairman of the Kent County Republicans, and with the backing of Michigan's distinguished Senator Arthur H. Vandenberg, Gerald Ford defeated the incumbent congressman in his district, an ultra-isolationist. Although boasting liberal views on international affairs, Representative Ford hewed much more closely to the conservative line, and that suited his constituency for his voters returned him to Congress eleven consecutive times.

To Representative Ford, the key to success in the lower House lay in party loyalty and hard work. He plodded through one term after another, making himself more and more useful to the Republican leadership. An early appointment to the Appropriations Committee, responsible for the Pentagon budget, did him no harm.

The smashing defeat of the Republican Party in the Johnson landslide of 1964 provided Ford's big opportunity. Younger Republicans chafed at the Neanderthal policies of the older, entrenched leaders of the GOP, who had helped to bring about their crushing losses.

Boosted by Charles Goodell of New York, Robert Griffin of Michigan, and Melvin Laird of Wisconsin, Gerald Ford challenged the much older Charles Halleck of Indiana for the post of House Minority Leader, and easily defeated the crusty, autocratic Halleck, who had held the position for many years, but now had to give way to a new and younger element. It was a triumph not only for the rank and file, but for the persevering purity of Gerald Ford, as one of his backers explained it: "He had the All-American image and nobody was mad at him."

If liberal Republicans expected Ford to push their kind of legislation, they were doomed to bitter disappointment, but they should not have been surprised. A review of his voting record in the House showed a consistently conservative position, for he voted against many social and reform measures, including Medicare, minimum wage bills, food stamps, hospital construction and aid to education. That he actively opposed President Lyndon Johnson's "Great Society" programs should also have come as no surprise. He did, however, agree with Johnson on the Vietnam War, which Ford militantly supported, even to the point of attacking Johnson for "shocking mismanagement" of the Vietnamese hostilities. Ford would have preferred more diligence in pursuing the war, even though President Johnson's handling of the matter was *too* diligent for many Americans.

Ford's one major ambition, during his career as a congressman, was to become Speaker of the House. Unfortunately, when he was in a position finally to achieve that goal, it was the Democrats rather than the Republicans who had the majority. But Ford did his best to see to it that his fellow Republicans were reelected to the House; he went campaigning across the country year after year, piling up impressive mileages. One year he traveled by air for a total of 138,436 miles, or five and a half times around the world.

When Richard Nixon assumed the presidency in 1969, his old friend Gerald Ford did everything within his power to see to it that Congress gave its blessing to the Nixon policies and programs. Unquestionably, Ford turned out to be Nixon's strong right arm in the House; in nine of President Nixon's controversial vetoes, Ford helped the President to sustain eight of them.

But Ford stubbed his congressional toe in 1970 when he labored to put across two of President Nixon's most unpopular nominations— Clement Haynsworth and G. Harrold Carswell for the Supreme Court. They were obviously unsuited for the nation's highest court even to loyal Nixonites. Both nominations were rejected, in spite of Ford's efforts.

In anger at his failure, Gerald Ford then began one of his less noteworthy projects—he set out to have liberal Supreme Court Justice William O. Douglas impeached.

Justice Douglas's offense, as it turned out, consisted of an article he wrote for the magazine *Evergreen Review*. The article, titled "Redress and Revolution," was an excerpt from Douglas's most recent book, *Points of Rebellion*. Congressman Ford and his cosponsors of the impeachment resolution objected to the appearance of the article in a magazine that also had a collection of erotic photographs as well as advertisements for sex books. Ford said he considered the *Evergreen Review* "shocking." One of his cosponsors went a bit further, and voiced his abhorrence of the subject matter in Douglas's writings, which he claimed advocated violence. In his opinion, the Douglas philosophy constituted "judicial misbehavior."

To others, Ford's impeachment proposal was purely political, perhaps an attempt to remove from the Supreme Court a liberal justice and thereby make room for a Nixon appointment cut more along conservative lines. But Ford saw it differently. He had a perfect right to institute his impeachment proceeding against Douglas for whatever reason he thought to be proper, as he explained on the floor of the House:

"What then is an impeachable offense?

"The only honest answer is that an impeachable offense is whatever a majority of the House of Representatives considers it to be at a given moment in history. . ."

One man who took a contrary position was Ford's former professor of law, Fred Rodell of the Yale Law School. In a letter to the *New York Times*, Professor Rodell scolded Ford for what he called an "obviously vengeful and basically absurd effort to impeach Justice Douglas. . ." In his final paragraph, Professor Rodell used much harsher terminology when he spoke of "the blatant and patent intellectual dishonesty of my old student and one-time friend Representative Gerald Ford."

The House Judiciary Committee, under the chairmanship of New York's Emanuel Celler, sidetracked the Douglas impeachment proposal and allowed it to die. After that, Ford gave up.

Gerald Ford's overwhelming confirmation by both Houses of Congress to be the fortieth vice-president of the United States had a curious quality about it. There were many congressmen and senators who felt he did not measure up to the office, yet he received a commanding vote, far more than the simple majority he needed. As a Democratic fellow congressman from Michigan phrased it, Ford for vice-president was "both the worst and the best" choice Nixon had ever made.

A number of Ford's more outspoken critics condemned him for lacking vision and scope, yet even some of them admitted that he was, above all, honest, and they guessed that he would make a competent president, if he ever succeeded to the executive chair itself. He was "a viable and attractive alternative to Mr. Nixon," and for this alone he received grudging approval from his detractors.

Unlike Nixon, it was further reasoned, Ford would work closely with Congress, since he had spent so many years there, and he had made lasting congressional relationships that could only help him in the future. As a further plus, he knew how to go "to the heart of a problem," said his supporters. This ability, they claimed, made him the kind of leader the country needed, despite his lack of charisma and flamboyance. A Ford administration might not be too exciting, but it would be stable.

Perhaps, at this particular "point in time," stability would not be such a bad idea.

Ford's confirmation was made official in the late afternoon of Thursday, December 6, 1973, when the House of Representatives voted 387 to 35 in his favor. Two weeks earlier, the Senate had given its approval by an even more lopsided margin, 92 to 3. Thus, for the first time in the history of the republic, a vice-president was chosen by a method other than a national electoral vote.

An hour after his confirmation, Gerald Ford appeared before a joint session of the Congress to be sworn in as the fortieth vice-president. The swearing in ceremony, witnessed on countrywide television by millions of people, took place in the House chamber, where Ford had spent twenty-five years as a representative from Michigan.

It was a simple ceremony, without the frills and fuss that normally accompany an inauguration of the executive team. In his address following the oath of office, administered by Chief Justice Warren E. Burger, Vice-President Ford sounded what might well have been the keynote to his own presidential administration, when he said, "I'm a Ford not a Lincoln."

No one could deny the warm appeal of his modesty. His direct simplicity seemed comforting, at a time when the American people needed a soothing voice it could trust.

But it was his opening line that perhaps told the story of Gerald Ford.

"Together," he said to the joint session and to the nation, "we have made history here today."

Madmen and Geniuses

The Eagleton Affair

In the summer of 1972, before Watergate and Maryland numbed the nation with their endless round of shocking disclosures, there was a growing movement to invest the vice-presidency with the real importance it was meant to have. More and more people, experts and common man alike, asserted that the second executive chair had moved out of the glare of ridicule to the softer light of respect. The office that humorist Finley Peter Dunne once referred to as "not exactly a crime" had finally become the nation's second highest honor.

Or had it?

John Nance Garner, widely credited with eradicating the bumbling Throttlebottom image of the vice-presidency, viewed the office with a contradictory lack of reverence. One day a circus clown met Garner in the Senate Office Building, and said to the thirty-second vice-president:

"I am head clown in the circus."

"And I am Vice-President of the United States," Garner replied. "You'd better stick around here awhile—you might pick up some new ideas."

Seven vice-presidents later, top members of President Nixon's staff often referred to Spiro Agnew as "the clown."

"Send out the clown to put on a show for the right wingers."

This at a time when Nixon himself solemnly proclaimed that the vice-presidency, under Agnew, had at last achieved the stature it deserved.

Nor did the Democratic party, the ever faithful opposition, treat the office any better. At their 1972 convention in Miami, the Democrats did everything they could to persuade the nation that the vice-presidency had no value at all; they went through the motions of selecting a second man only because they had to.

Once the presidential nomination of liberal Senator George McGovern of South Dakota had been settled, McGovern and his advisers met at 9:00 A.M. of the convention's closing day to choose his vice-presidential running mate. Fifty-five names were proposed, including the Rev. Theodore Hesburgh, president of the University of Notre Dame, and Walter Cronkite, CBS newscaster.

A Catholic educator or a TV journalist as a potential president of the United States? Why not? In the light of what later happened, choice of either one of them would have made as much sense as the one the Democrats finally accepted.

After wholesale trimming and rejecting, the list came down, by midafternoon, to Thomas Francis Eagleton, forty-two-year-old senator from Missouri. Announcement of McGovern's choice of Eagleton precipitated the same kind of stunned surprise that had greeted Agnew's name in 1968, only now the joke was: "Tom who?"

Far from being McGovern's primary choice (the South Dakotan really wanted Senator Edward Kennedy of Massachusetts because he needed the electoral magic of the Kennedy name to bolster his none too promising candidacy), Eagleton did not elicit convention enthusiasm. Many delegates revolted and spread their votes among some eighty other names (two of the eighty were the television bigot Archie Bunker and the irrepressible Martha Mitchell, wife of GOP leader John Mitchell). When the charade ended hours later, Eagleton had somehow survived the nonsense to emerge as the Democrats' vice-presidential nominee on the first ballot.

For McGovern, the relatively unknown Eagleton seemed to be an excellent choice, for the young senator was a bright and witty man, a popular liberal in a conservative state. Geographically, the two men did not balance one another, for they both came from the middle section of the country. But in this enlightened moment of representative politics, when previously disenfranchised blacks, women, youth, and the poor, had been given their vote by the Democratic convention, traditional needs no longer mattered. Still, some kind of balance was necessary, so it was proper for the Protestant McGovern to choose Roman Catholic Eagleton; nor did it hurt that Eagleton was well-liked by labor, which had already threatened to desert the progressive McGovern in droves (and eventually did).

So the Democrats gave their official approval to McGovern's choice, and the party machinery set out to transform Eagleton into a top-rung personality. Exactly eleven days later, disaster struck.

On Tuesday, July 25th, Senator Eagleton held his first press conference as the Democratic vice-presidential nominee. Visibly ill at ease, Eagleton admitted that he had been hospitalized three times between 1960 and 1966 for nervous exhaustion and fatigue; further, he had been

under psychiatric treatment during that period, and had twice undergone electric shock therapy for depression. But, he added, he had taken
a complete medical checkup only a few days before, and he was fine,
except that he was two pounds overweight.

Whatever Eagleton expected from his revelations, they did accomplish at least one thing, as he himself wryly noted—overnight he
went "from anonymity to notoriety in a shockingly brilliant way."

Presidential candidate McGovern admitted that he had not known
of Eagleton's medical history when he had chosen the Missourian as
his running mate. But, he insisted, "there is no one sounder in body,
mind and spirit than Tom Eagleton." As to whether he would ask Eagleton to remove himself from the Democratic ticket, McGovern categorically said he would not. He had no intention whatever of dropping
Eagleton, for he was behind the Missouri senator, "1,000 percent."

It was an ill-considered statement for McGovern to make; when reaction from the Democratic Party and from the normally pro-Democratic
newspapers ran against Eagleton, sometimes violently, McGovern began
to back away from his "1,000 percent". Within a few days, he was saying
that the decision to remain on the ticket was largely up to Eagleton. For
McGovern to vacillate so quickly did him incalculable harm. Many undecided voters, never too happy with the South Dakotan's radically
progressive proposals on welfare and civil rights, now saw in his desertion of his announced "1,000 percent" support for Eagleton an indication that here was a man who could not really make up his mind. Indecision was unforgivable in a candidate for the world's most demanding
position.

Most people agreed that Eagleton's prior history of mental difficulties should not preclude his standing for any high office. But what did
matter was his failure to tell McGovern of his previous medical problems. Here, too, was an indication of untrustworthiness.

Why had it happened? How had the McGovern forces allowed this
catastrophe to kill their campaign before it had started?

When it was decided, shortly before 3:30 on the afternoon of July
14, that Eagleton was to be McGovern's running mate, members of
McGovern's staff routinely asked Eagleton whether he had "any skeletons in the closet." He answered "No," and that was the end of it. The
McGovern men did no digging and no checking, nor did Eagleton offer
any information. McGovern and his staff took the Missourian at his
word.

Contrast this careless investigation of Eagleton's past with Lyndon
B. Johnson's exhaustive probing into Hubert Humphrey's background
in 1964. Before Johnson had settled on Humphrey as his running mate,
he instructed a Washington attorney and old friend, James Rowe, that
Humphrey was to be "horseshedded." Long ago, a lawyer would take
his client "out behind the horse shed" and grill him backwards and forwards until they were both certain exactly what the truth was, and only
then would they be ready to go to court.

Rowe prepared four pages of questions for Humphrey, and spent two irritating hours putting these questions to the prospective vice-president. Rowe did not miss a trick. He covered every possibility—Humphrey's finances, his physical and mental health, scandals, women, parties, gambling, and Humphrey's relatives. When Humphrey protested the scope of the interrogation, Rowe answered:

"If you become the vice-presidential candidate, a lot of other people are going to be going over your record just like I am."

Humphrey survived the annoyance of Rowe's grilling. Four years later, when *he* was running for the presidency, Humphrey summoned James Rowe to meet with the man who was eventually chosen to run with him, Senator Edmund Muskie of Maine. When the three of them were together, Humphrey said to Rowe:

"Ask him those tough questions you asked me."

Why the McGovern staff did not investigate Eagleton as thoroughly remains unexplained. Senator McGovern later insisted that he still would have chosen Eagleton even had he been told the truth. But it became too painfully obvious that Eagleton's original lack of candor had made it impossible for him to continue on the Democratic ticket, and he withdrew on July 31, six days after his ill-fated press conference.

So, for the first time in the history of American presidential elections, a vice-presidential candidate resigned from the ticket, and the public was treated to the unprecedented spectacle of a second nominating convention, this time composed of members of the Democratic National Committee.

With every major prospect, from Hubert Humphrey through Edward Kennedy and Edmund Muskie, turning thumbs down on what was now looked upon as a "suicide mission," a Kennedy brother-in-law, Sargent Shriver of Maryland, was chosen in the end as the Democrats' new vice-presidential candidate. His selection didn't really matter, for McGovern's chances of winning the presidency, never too bright to begin with, were irrevocably doomed by the Eagleton affair. Too many disillusioned voters said they could never cast their ballots for anyone as guilty as McGovern had been of misjudgment, miscalculation, and indecision.

Sargent Shriver, however, plunged into the campaign as if he believed he had been the unanimous *first choice* of the Democrats for the vice-presidency instead of a despairing last minute selection. He crisscrossed the country with zest and unabashed cheerfulness, trying to convince his listeners that he and Senator McGovern could and would win the election in November.

The voters were not impressed. The electorate gave vent to its displeasure with the Democrats by awarding Nixon and Agnew a victory of landslide proportions, a triumph that rated with the lopsided wins of Harding and Coolidge in 1920, Roosevelt and Garner in 1936, and Johnson and Humphrey in 1964.

For McGovern and Shriver it was a crushing defeat made even more painful by the statistics. Nixon and Agnew won 60.83 percent of the popular vote, second only to the record 61.09 percent rolled up by Johnson and Humphrey in 1964. Of the electoral votes, McGovern and Shriver received a bare 17 (14 from Massachusetts, the only state they won, and 3 from the District of Columbia), while Nixon and Agnew amassed 521, just 2 less than the humiliating 523 to 8 total piled up by Franklin Roosevelt and John Nance Garner in 1936.

Madmen and Geniuses

Epilogue

The enormous loss suffered by McGovern and Shriver in the November, 1972 election could be traced in part to their party convention four months earlier. While the Miami Beach debacle could not be entirely blamed for the Democratic defeat, it did contribute to voter disaffection, and it graphically illustrated the weakness of the selection process of the vice-presidential candidate. Beyond that, it pointed up the still prevailing lack of respect for the second office.

The Republicans, meeting at the same Miami hall a month later, were almost as guilty. They once again meekly accepted Spiro Agnew as their next potential president, despite the fact that he had not as yet established any claim whatever to the executive chair, and proved, fourteen months later, how tragically unsuited he was for the presidency. Nor did the process that went into the choice of Congressman Gerald Ford to be our fortieth vice-president, after Agnew's resignation in October of 1973, give any hint that either party, or the country, had heeded the past or learned its lessons.

The vice-presidency can no longer be treated cavalierly, nor can we afford to be casual about it. But the problem of the vice-presidency still resolves itself to two basic points, as it has practically from the inception of our republic: (1) how to choose the man to fill the office, and (2) what to do with him once he has become the vice-president.

The first point depends upon the second, for we have seen throughout our history that men of caliber consistently refuse the second office because of its built-in unimportance. That such men can become president in an accidental instant can hardly influence their thinking, even though so far we have seen eight vice-presidents, or one-fifth of the total, succeed to the executive chair upon the death of the president. No one, as President Truman once remarked, wants to wake up every morning inquiring after the health of his chief.

Ever since Richard Nixon and Hubert Humphrey won their parties' nominations for the presidency, it is fashionable to believe that the vice-presidency has at last become a true stepping-stone to the presidency itself. The truth is, Nixon's nominations in 1960 and 1968 and Humphrey's nomination in 1968 were due only in part to the growing strength of the second office; the composition and needs of each major party had just as much to do with it. Under Spiro Agnew, the stature of the second office was as tangible as his rectitude. As for Gerald Ford, his emergence as a national figure resulted not from his occupancy of the vice-presidency, but rather from Richard Nixon's Watergate vulnerability.

The essential question still remains: how do we improve the vice-presidency? Once we find the answer to that, we will find candidates for the office who deserve to be there.

Over the years, a number of proposals have been made either for the elimination or improvement of the second office. While some of the suggestions are admittedly provocative, no one as yet has found the solution. In December of 1955, former President Herbert Hoover recommended to a Senate committee that we have *two* vice-presidents, the constitutional vice-president elected by the people and an administrative vice-president appointed by the president. The appointee would work closely with the president and would do much of the day-to-day chores, the incidentals, the details. If the president were dissatisfied with his appointee, he could simply fire him (as he could not do with the constitutional vice-president, who is an elected official).

Of the 62 agencies then reporting directly to the president (there are many more now), Hoover suggested that 28 would continue to report to the president, while the other 34 would report to the administrative vice-president. That seemed like an impressive load for the second vice-president, but a closer examination of Hoover's list reveals that many of the 34, such as the American Battle Monuments Commission or the Smithsonian Institution or the Arlington Memorial Amphitheater Commission, would have taken little of his time.

Nevertheless, Hoover's notion had merit, for it would have relieved a very busy president of routine tasks that almost anyone else could have handled. But Hoover's plan overlooked a basic problem. The potential president, the constitutional vice-president, still would have had nothing to do and would still be unequipped and unprepared to assume the presidency.

Seventeen years after Hoover's testimony, former Senator Eugene McCarthy, who had been both a presidential and vice-presidential hopeful, wrote an article in which he attempted to clarify the role of the vice-president. It was McCarthy's thesis that "a Vice-President in office should be treated much as a crown prince is treated in a monarchy." He should be trained, said McCarthy, "in the arts of government."

Senator McCarthy was at least on the right track; the vice-president *should* be skilled "in the arts of government," but the American people would probably balk at the idea of treating him like a crown prince.

It was McCarthy's thinking that the vice-president should rise above partisan identification, and should not be required "to do the President's dirty jobs."

"The holder of (the Vice-Presidency)," McCarthy wrote, "should use it so as to make the office more honorable and to make himself respected by the people and more ready for the Presidency."

This of course has always been the heart of the matter. As the office now stands, however, there is very little chance for this kind of thing to happen. Under the conditions set forth by the Constitution, the vice-president is woefully handicapped and assumes importance only at the discretion of the president. Unfortunately, almost without exception, every president has been sparing, if not·churlish, in his use of the vice-president.

The way to solve it, then, is to change the Constitution. Make it mandatory for the vice-president to be delegated more authority and responsibility. When the Constitution was formulated and the composition of the government established, our founding fathers could not possibly have imagined the immense complexities that would literally engulf the presidency. It is now an office of awesome power and scope, reaching far beyond the boundaries of our country to every corner of the world and even millions of miles into space. The president has become responsible for almost everything that affects our lives and the lives of hundreds of millions of others; he must be knowledgeable and perceptive in both domestic and foreign affairs. He supervises and administers a vast organization, with branches and employees covering the globe. He is on duty seven days a week for fifty-two weeks of every year.

No one man can be expected to handle so many responsibilities and do the job the people expect of him. Why not take Hoover's suggestion a step further and assign some of these responsibilities to the constitutional vice-president, who is, after all, the man who is supposed to step into the presidency at a moment's notice? For example, the vice-president could be given responsibility for some of the domestic matters Hoover left to the president, such as housing, education, and welfare, transportation and labor. Let him develop necessary legislation and administer that legislation once it has been adopted. The president would still have the final authority and the power to veto, but the preparation and the bulk of the work will have been entrusted to the vice-president.

Traditionalists may object that taking any of these concerns away from the president will lessen his prestige. But the office has become too big and powerful to be measurably affected by a relatively minor diminution of its responsibilities. Rather, the effect would be to heighten the prestige of the vice-president instead of weakening the president's. No less an authority than Harry Truman agreed with this in principle, for he once recommended that a vice-president should be voted into office as "a spare chief executive."

There will also be those who will say that we need not be so drastic as to amend the Constitution; we will simply require the president to work more closely with his vice-president by having him sit in on major conferences and participate in administration matters. The problem here is that many presidents promised to do exactly that, and then turned around and shut the vice-president out of practically everything.

Or perhaps, with its unfortunate track record, the time has come to abolish the vice-presidency. This may seem like an irreverent proposal to those who regard the Constitution with religious awe. To anyone who insists that we cannot, and must not, tamper with the Constitution, it should be pointed out that the vice-presidency was probably the most poorly conceived feature of the Philadelphia Constitutional Convention of 1787.

By the time delegates to the convention got around to the vice-presidency, they were exhausted and anxious to get home. They had spent many months wrangling and debating and nitpicking; they had suffered through a hot and humid summer in a hall that gave little ventilation and less comfort. They were in no mood to devote additional demanding days inspecting every comma and every syllable of the section on the vice-presidency. The office and its duties were decided upon toward the close of the convention, and passed over quickly, without the intense deliberation that had been given to everything else.

Ever since then, we have lived with an executive office that is neither fish nor fowl, neither bird nor beast. We have learned to accept it simply because that's what we have always had, and Americans, like their English cousins, don't like to fiddle with tradition.

But the vice-presidency, as it is presently set up, is a mistake. Let's finally admit that our founding fathers were human after all, and in their fallibility, made a botch of the second executive office. We have already made changes in the original document that must have many of its framers spinning violently in their graves—women's suffrage, to mention one.

Why not, then, abolish the vice-presidency?

We don't need a backup president, as history has amply proven. Two-fifths of the total time served by all of our presidents were served without a vice-president, and the country survived. (As for the only constitutional duty required of a vice-president, presiding over the Senate, this too is in danger of becoming obsolete. In the first half of 1973 Spiro Agnew presided only for two hours and twenty-six minutes out of the 667 hours the Senate was in session.)

If the presidency should suddenly become vacant, either through death or removal from office, a special election could be held within a matter of weeks to choose a new president. We don't need long conventions and months of campaigning, capped by the expenditure of untold millions. One major TV appearance for each candidate would do the job. And the country, in those few weeks necessary to choose the candidates and finally to elect the president, would not collapse. Aren't we too strong for that? We'd have the Speaker of the House, an elected official, to be our caretaker president in the meantime.

Is this too radical a suggestion? Then at least let's change our method of choosing our vice-presidential candidates. Let's not give such power to one man, as we now do for each party's presidential candidate, and as we allow the president under the terms of the Twenty-fifth Amendment. As one possible and workable alternative, let's have open conventions, as the Democrats did in 1956. Adlai E. Stevenson II refused, after his nomination for the presidency that year, to make the choice of a running mate. He insisted that it was the duty of the convention to choose the second man. After an exciting battle, Senator Estes Kefauver of Tennessee finally beat out another senator, a much younger man, John F. Kennedy of Massachusetts.

In a departure from custom, Kennedy had sought the vice-presidency only. Perhaps we should encourage that approach, since Kennedy proved, four years later, that he had deserved the highest office itself. In 1972, another Massachusetts man, former Governor Endicott Peabody, tried to duplicate the Kennedy strategy by making an active try for the vice-presidency in that year. He didn't get very far, for almost no one in the Democratic Party took him seriously. It was difficult for Democratic leaders to believe that anyone actually wanted just the vice-presidency.

What the Democrats should have realized, and the Republicans as well, is that on-the-job training for the presidency may not be such a bad idea. There is no reason why qualified men should not run only for the vice-presidency, particularly if they are young enough to sit in the second chair for at least four years and possibly eight, while the president serves his one or two terms, and, in the meantime, prepare themselves to take over.

A possible objection does suggest itself. If a man believes he is qualified only for the vice-presidency and runs for that office alone, what happens if his president suddenly dies and he succeeds to an office he didn't think he was capable of handling?

The answer to that is to make the vice-presidency attractive enough so that men truly qualified for the number one spot will *want* to try for the number two position instead of turning away from it as they now do.

Our first vice-president, John Adams, had some telling comments on the second office.

"Gentlemen, I do not know whether the framers of the Constitution had in view the two kings of Sparta or the two consuls of Rome when they formed it; one to have all the power while he held it, and the other to be nothing. . .

"I feel great difficulty how to act. I am possessed of two separate powers; the one in esse and the other in posse. I am Vice-President. In this I am nothing, but I may be everything. . ."

About a hundred years later, Woodrow Wilson wrote a doctoral thesis on Congressional government, and he too had something to say about the vice-president:

". . . The chief embarrassment in discussing his office is, that in explaining how little there is to be said about it one has evidently said all there is to say."

Thomas Riley Marshall, who served two terms as Wilson's vice-president, offered his own view of the office he occupied for eight years:

"Once upon a time there was a farmer who had two sons. One of them ran off to sea. The other was elected Vice-President of the United States. Nothing was ever heard of either of them again."

With such a low opinion of the vice-presidency prevailing right from the start and continuing into the present, it is little wonder that men who belong there shy away. Among others, *The New York Times* applauded Endicott Peabody's "gallant effort to force more serious discussion of the Vice Presidency."

But it was the closing lines of the *Times* editorial that summed it all up:

"For the second man on the ticket as for the first, excellence has to be the prevailing standard."

Madmen and Geniuses

Bibliography

General Sources

Abels, Jules. *The Degeneration of Our Presidential Election.* New York: The Macmillan Co., 1968.

Appletons' Cyclopaedia of American Biography. 6 vols. New York: D. Appleton & Co., 1888–1889.

Armbruster, Maxim E. *The Presidents of the United States.* New York: Horizon Press, 1966.

Barnes, Thurlow Weed. *The Life of Thurlow Weed.* 2 vols. New York: Houghton Mifflin Co., 1884.

Barzman, Sol. *The First Ladies.* New York: Cowles Book Co., 1970.

Bendiner, Robert. *Just Around the Corner.* New York: Harper & Row, 1967.

Binkley, Wilfred E. *American Political Parties.* New York: Alfred E. Knopf, 1943/1962.

Brigham, Clarence S. *History and Bibliography of American Newspapers, 1690–1820.* Worchester, Mass.: American Antiquarian Society, 1947.

Butterfield, Roger. *The American Past.* New York: Simon & Schuster, 1966.

Cole, Arthur Charles, Ph.D. *The Whig Party in the South.* Gloucester, Mass., Peter Smith, 1962.

Dictionary of American Biography. 10 vols. New York: Charles Scribner's Sons, 1927–1936.

DiSalle, Michael V., with Lawrence G. Blochman. *Second Choice.* New York: Hawthorn Books, 1966.

Donovan, Robert J. *The Assassins.* New York: Harper & Brothers, 1955.

Dorman, Michael, *The Second Man.* New York: Delacorte Press, 1968.

Dumond, Dwight Lowell. *America in Our Time 1896–1946.* New York: Henry Holt & Co., 1947.

Dunne, Finley Peter. *Mr. Dooley on Ivrything and Ivrybody.* New York: Dover Publications, 1963.

Faulkner, Harold U. *Politics, Reform and Expansion 1890–1900.* New York: Harper & Brothers, 1959.

Franklin, John Hope. *Reconstruction.* Chicago: University of Chicago Press, 1961.

Gregory, Winifred, ed. *American Newspapers, 1821–1936.* New York: H. W. Wilson Company, 1937.

Hamilton, Alexander; Madison, James; and Jay, John. *The Federalist Papers.* New York: The New American Library, 1961.

Hudson, William C. *Random Recollections of an Old Political Reporter.* New York: Cupples & Leon Company, 1911.

Kane, Joseph Nathan. *Facts about the Presidents.* New York: H. W. Wilson Co., 1968.

Kaufman, George S. and Ryskind, Morrie. *Of Thee I Sing.* New York: Alfred A. Knopf, 1932.

Kohlsaat, H. H. *From McKinley to Harding.* New York: Charles Scribner's Sons, 1923.

Krock, Arthur. *Memoirs.* New York: Funk & Wagnalls, 1968.

Lorant, Stefan. *The Glorious Burden.* New York: Harper & Row, 1968.

Lord, Walter, *The Good Years.* New York: Harper & Brothers, 1960.

Marx, Rudolph, M.D. *The Health of the Presidents.* New York: G. P. Putnam's Sons, 1960.

Miller, John C. *The Federalist Era, 1789–1801.* New York: Harper & Row, 1960.

Mitchell, Broadus and Mitchell, Louise. *A Biography of the Constitution of the United States.* New York: Oxford University Press, 1964.

Morison, Samuel Eliot. *The Oxford History of the American People.* New York: Oxford University Press, 1965.

Nevins, Allan, ed. *The Diary of John Quincy Adams, 1794–1845.* New York: Charles Scribner's Sons, 1951.

Poore, Benjamin Perley. *Reminiscences of Sixty Years in the National Metropolis.* Philadelphia: Hubbard Brothers, 1886.

Roseboom, Eugene H. *A History of Presidential Elections.* New York: The Macmillan Co., 1957.

Runyon, John H.; Verdini, Jennefer; and Runyon, Sally S., compilers and editors. *Source Book of American Presidential Campaign & Election Statistics, 1948–1968.* New York: Frederick Ungar Publishing Co., 1971.

Schachner, Nathan. *The Founding Fathers.* New York: A. S. Barnes & Co., 1970.

Schnapper, M. B. *Grand Old Party, The First Hundred Years of The Republican Party.* Washington, D.C.: Public Affairs Press, 1955.

Sheehan, Neil; Smith, Hedrick; Kenworthy, E. W.; and Butterfield, Fox. *The Pentagon Papers—The Complete and Unabridged Series as Published by The New York Times.* New York: Bantam Books, 1971.

Stanwood, Edward. *American Tariff Controversies in the Nineteenth Century.* 2 vols. New York: Russell & Russell, 1967.

Waugh, Edgar Wiggins. *Second Consul.* Indianapolis: The Bobbs-Merrill Co., 1956.

Young, Donald. *American Roulette.* New York: Holt Rinehart & Winston, 1972.

Specific Sources

Adams, Jefferson, and Burr

Adams, James Truslow. *The Adams Family.* New York: Blue Ribbon Books, 1933.

Bowen, Catherine Drinker. *John Adams and the American Revolution.* Boston: Little Brown & Co., 1954.

Bowers, Claude, G. *Jefferson.* 3 vols. Boston: Houghton Mifflin & Co., 1945–1964.

Butterfield, L. H. ed. *Diary and Autobiography of John Adams.* Vol. 3. Cambridge, Mass: The Belknap Press of Harvard University, 1962.

Chinard, Gilbert. *Honest John Adams.* Boston: Little Brown & Co., 1933.

Daniels, Jonathan. *Ordeal of Ambition.* Garden City, N.Y.: Doubleday & Co., 1970.

Dos Passos, John. *The Shackles of Power.* Garden City N.Y.: Doubleday & Co., 1966.

Freeman, Douglas Southall. *George Washington.* Vol. 6. New York: Charles Scribner's Sons, 1954.

_____ with Carrol, Alexander and Ashworth, Mary Wells. *George Washington.* Vol. 7. New York: Charles Scribner's Sons, 1957.

Malone, Dumas. *Jefferson.* 3 vols. Boston: Little Brown & Co., 1948–1962.

Mitchell, Broadus. *Alexander Hamilton: The National Adventure, 1788–1804.* New York: The Macmillan Co., 1962.

Mitchell, Steward, ed. *New Letters of Abigail Adams, 1786–1801.* Boston: Houghton Mifflin Co., 1947.

Padover, Saul K. *A Jefferson Profile.* New York: The John Day Co., 1956.

Parmet, Herbert S. and Hecht, Marie B. *Aaron Burr.* New York: The Macmillan Co., 1967.

Parton, James. *The Life and Times of Aaron Burr.* Boston: Houghton Mifflin Co., 1881.

Peterson, Merrill D. *Thomas Jefferson and the New Nation.* New York: Oxford University Press, 1970.

Smith, Page, *John Adams.* 2 vols. Garden City, N.Y.: Doubleday & Co., 1962.

Wandell, Samuel H. and Minnigerode, Meade. *Aaron Burr.* New York: G. P. Putnam's Sons, 1927.

Clinton, Gerry, and Tompkins

Alexander, De Alva Stanwood. *A Political History of the State of New York.* Vol. 1. Port Washington, N.Y.: Ira J. Friedman, 1909–1969.

Ammon, Harry. *James Monroe, The Quest for National Identity.* New York: McGraw Hill Book Co., 1971.

Austin, James Trecothick. *The Life of Elbridge Gerry.* Boston: Wells & Lilly, 1828–1829.

Bowen, Catherine Drinker. *Miracle at Philadelphia.* Boston: Little Brown & Co., 1966.

Brant, Irving. *James Madison.* 4 vols. Indianapolis: The Bobbs-Merrill Company, 1950–1961.

Ernst, Robert, *Rufus King, American Federalist.* Chapel Hill, N.C.: University of North Carolina Press, 1968.

Fiske, John. *The Critical Period of American History 1783–1789.* Boston: Houghton Mifflin Co., 1897.

Gardiner, C. Harvey, ed. *A Study in Dissent, The Warren-Gerry Correspondence.* Carbondale and Edwardsville, Ill.: Southern Illinois University Press, 1968.

Gerry, Elbridge. *Observations on the New Constitution.* Philadelphia: Independent Gazeteer, 1788.

Jenkins, John S. *Lives of the Governors of the State of New York.* Auburn, N.Y.: Derby & Miller, 1851.

Monroe, James. *Autobiography.* Stuart Gerry Brown, ed. Syracuse: N.Y., Syracuse University Press, 1959.

Spaulding, E. Wilder. *His Excellency George Clinton.* Port Washington, N.Y.: Ira J. Friedman, 1964.

Styron, Arthur. *The Last of the Cocked Hats.* Norman, Okla.: University of Oklahoma Press, 1955.

Vanpelt, Peter J. *An Oration, Containing Sketches of the Life of Daniel D. Tompkins, Governor of New York.* New York: C. C. & E. Childs, Jr., 1843.

Zahniser, Marvin R. *Charles Cotesworth Pinckney.* Chapel Hill, N.C.: University of North Carolina Press, 1967.

Calhoun, Van Buren, R. M. Johnson, and Tyler

Alexander, Holmes. *The American Talleyrand.* New York: Russell & Russell, 1968.

Chambers, William Nisbet. *Old Bullion Benton, Senator from the New West.* Boston: Little Brown & Co., 1956.

Chitwood, Oliver Perry. *John Tyler, Champion of the Old South.* New York: Russell & Russell, 1964.

Cleaves, Freeman. *Old Tippecanoe, William Henry Harrison and His Time.* New York: Charles Scribner's Sons, 1939.

Coit, Margaret L. *John C. Calhoun.* Boston: Houghton Mifflin Co., 1950.

Gunderson, Robert Gray. *The Log-Cabin Campaign.* Lexington, Ky: University of Kentucky Press, 1957.

James, Marquis. *The Life of Andrew Jackson.* Indianapolis: Bobbs- Merril Company, 1938.

Meyer, Leland Winfield. *The Life and Times of Colonel Richard M. Johnson Of Kentucky.* New York: AMS Press, 1967.

Nathans, Sidney. *Daniel Webster and Jacksonian Democracy.* Baltimore: John Hopkins University Press, 1973.

Schlesinger, Arthur M., Jr. *The Age of Jackson.* Boston: Little Brown & Co., 1945.

Seager, Robert, II. *And Tyler Too.* New York: McGraw-Hill Book Co., 1963.

Van Deusen, Glyndon G. *The Life of Henry Clay.* Boston: Little Brown & Co., 1937.

Wiltse, Charles M. *John C. Calhoun.* New York: Russell & Russell, 1968.

Dallas, Fillmore, and King

Bancroft, Frederic. *The Life of William Seward.* Vol. 1. Gloucester, Mass.: Peter Smith, 1967.

Bemis, Samuel Flagg. ed. *The American Secretaries of State and Their Diplomacy.* Vols. 5 and 6. New York: Cooper Square Publishers, 1963.

Chambers, William Nisbet. *Old Bullion Benton, Senator from the New West.* Boston: Little Brown & Co., 1956.

Curtis, George Ticknor. *Life of Daniel Webster.* Vol. 2. New York: D. Appleton & Co., 1870.

————. *Life of James Buchanan.* Vol. 1. New York: Harper & Brothers, 1883.

Hamilton, Holman. *Zachary Taylor, Soldier in the White House.* Indianapolis: Bobbs-Merrill Company, 1951.

Jenkins, John S. *The Life of Silas Wright.* Auburn, N.Y.: Alden & Markham, 1847.

Merk, Frederick, with Lois Bannister Merk. *Manifest Destiny and Mission in American History.* New York: Alfred A. Knopf, 1963.

Morrison, Chaplain W. *Democratic Politics and Sectionalism, The Wilmot Proviso Controversy.* Chapel Hill, N. C.: University of North Carolina Press, 1967.

Nichols, Roy Franklin. *Franklin Pierce.* Philadelphia: University of Pennnsylvania Press, 1969.

Rayback, Robert J. *Millard Fillmore.* Published for the Buffalo Historical Society. East Aurora, N.Y.: Henry Stewart, Inc., 1959.

Sellers, Charles. *James K. Polk.* Vol. 2. Princeton, N. J.: Princeton University Press, 1966.

Smith, Elbert B. *Magnificent Missourian, The Life of Thomas Hart Benton.* Philadelphia: J. B. Lippincott Co., 1958.

Stoddard, Henry Luther. *Horace Greeley.* New York: G. P. Putnam's Sons, 1946.

Van Deusen, Glyndon G. *Horace Greeley.* Philadelphia: University of Pennsylvania Press, 1953.

Woodford, Frank B. *Lewis Cass, The Last Jeffersonian.* New Brunswick, N. J.: Rutgers University Press, 1950.

Breckenridge, Hamlin, and A. Johnson

Bowers, Claude G. *The Tragic Era.* Boston: Houghton Mifflin Co., 1920.

Burger, Nash K. and Bettersworth, John K. *South of Appomattox.* New York: Harcourt Brace & Co., 1959.

Curtis, George Ticknor. *Life of James Buchanan.* Vol. 2. New York: Harper & Brothers, 1883.

Dorris, Jonathan Truman. *Pardon and Amnesty under Lincoln and Johnson.* Chapel Hill, N. C.: University of North Carolina Press, 1953.

Hamlin, Charles Eugene. *The Life and Times of Hannibal Hamlin.* Published by subscription. Cambridge, Mass.: Riverside Press, 1899.

Hunt, H. Draper. *Hannibal Hamlin of Maine.* Syracuse, N.Y.: Syracuse University Press, 1969.

Klein, Philip Shriver. *President James Buchanan.* University Park, Pa.: Pennsylvania State University Press, 1962.

Leech, Margaret. *Reveille in Washington, 1860–1865.* New York: Grosset & Dunlap, 1941.

Lomask, Milton. *Andrew Johnson, President on Trial.* New York: Farrar Straus & Giroux, 1960.

McKitrick, Eric. L., ed. *Andrew Johnson, A Profile.* New York: Hill & Wang, 1969.

Nichols, Roy Franklin. *The Disruption of American Democracy.* New York: The Macmillan Co., 1948.

Sandburg, Carl. *Abraham Lincoln, The Prairie Years and the War Years.*
New York: Harcourt Brace & Co., 1954.
Seitz, Don C. *Lincoln the Politician.* New York: Coward-McCann, 1931.
Seward, Frederick W. *Seward at Washington.* New York: Derby &
Miller, 1891.
Strode, Hudson. *Jefferson Davis.* 3 vols. New York, Harcourt, Brace &
Co., 1955–1964.
Thomas, Lately. *The First President Johnson.* New York: William Mor-
row & Co., 1968.
Van Deusen, Glyndon G. *William Henry Seward.* New York: Oxford
University Press, 1967.
Winston, Robert W. *Andrew Johnson, Plebeian and Patriot.* New York:
Barnes & Noble, 1969.

Colfax, H. Wilson, and Wheeler

Ames, Charles Edgar. *Pioneering the Union Pacific.* New York: Apple-
ton-Century-Crofts, 1969.
Ekenrode, H. J. *Rutherford B. Hayes, Statesman of Reunion.* New York:
Dodd Mead & Co., 1930.
Griswold, Wesley S. *A Work of Giants.* New York: McGraw-Hill Book
Co., 1962.
Haworth, Paul Leland. *The Hayes-Tilden Disputed Presidential Elec-
tion of 1876.* New York: Russell & Russell, 1966.
Hesseltine, William B. *Ulysses S. Grant, Politician.* New York: Dodd
Mead & Co., 1935.
Hoar, George F. *Autobiography of Seventy Years.* New York: Charles
Scribner's Sons, 1903.
Loth, David. *Public Plunder, A History of Graft in America.* New York:
Carrick & Evans, 1938.
Mann, Jonathan B. *The Life of Henry Wilson.* Boston: James R. Osgood
& Co., 1872.
Nevins, Allan. *Hamilton Fish.* Vol. 2. New York: Frederick Ungar Pub-
lishing Co., 1957.
Rhodes, James Ford. *History of the United States 1872–1887.* Vol. 7.
New York: The Macmillan Co., 1916.
Williams, Charles Richard. *The Life of Rutherford Birchard Hayes.* 2
vols. Boston: Houghton Mifflin Co., 1914.

Arthur, Hendricks, Morton, and Stevenson

Balch, William Ralston. *The Life of James Abram Garfield.* Philadelphia: Hubbard Bros., 1881.

Bowers, Claude G. *Beveridge and the Progressive Era.* Boston: Houghton Mifflin Co., 1932.

Braeman, John. *Albert J. Beveridge,* Chicago: University of Chicago Press, 1971.

Caldwell, Robert G. *James A. Garfield.* New York: Dodd Mead & Co., 1931.

Chidsey. Donald Barr. *The Gentleman from New York, A Life of Roscoe Conkling.* New Haven: Yale University Press, 1935.

Davis, Kenneth S. *The Politics of Honor, A Biography of Adlai E. Stevenson.* New York: G. P. Putnam's Sons, 1957.

Flick, Alexander Clarence. *Samuel Tilden.* Port Washington, N. Y.: Kennikat Press, 1939.

Howe, George F. *Chester A. Arthur.* New York, Dodd Mead & Co., 1934.

Jordan, David M. *Roscoe Conkling of New York.* Ithaca, N. Y.: Cornell University Press, 1971.

McElroy, Robert. *Levi Parsons Morton.* New York: G. P. Putnam's Sons, 1930.

Nevins, Allan. *Grover Cleveland, A Study in Courage.* New York: Dodd Mead & Co., 1934.

Russell, Charles Edward. *Blaine of Maine.* New York: Cosmopolitan Book Corp., 1931.

Sievers, Harry J., S.J. *Benjamin Harrison, Hoosier President.* Indianapolis: Bobbs-Merrill Co., 1968.

Tugwell, Rexford G. *Grover Cleveland.* New York: The Macmillan Co., 1968.

Hobart, T. Roosevelt, and Fairbanks

Croly, Herbert. *Marcus Alonzo Hanna.* New York: The Macmillan Co., 1912.

Gosnell, Harold F. *Boss Platt and His New York Machine.* Chicago: University of Chicago Press, 1924.

Hagedorn, Hermann. *The Roosevelt Family of Sagamore Hill.* New York: The Macmillan Co., 1954.

Koenig, Louis W. *Bryan, A Political Biography of William Jennings Bryan.* New York: G. P. Putnam's Sons, 1971.

Lang, Louis J., compiler and editor. *The Autobiography of Thomas Collier Platt.* New York: B. W. Dodge & Co., 1919.

Leech, Margaret. *In the Days of McKinley.* New York: Harper & Brothers, 1959.

Morgan, H. Wayne. *William McKinley and His America.* Syracuse, N.Y.: Syracuse University Press, 1963.

Mowry, George E. *The Era of Theodore Roosevelt, 1900–1912.* New York: Harper & Brothers, 1958.

Oberholtzer, Ellis P. *A History of the United States Since the Civil War.* Vol. 5. New York: The Macmillan Co., 1937.

Pringle, Henry F. *Theodore Roosevelt, A Biography.* New York: Harcourt Brace & Co., 1931.

Pusey, Merlo J. *Charles Evans Hughes.* Vol. 1. New York: The Macmillan Co., 1951.

Roosevelt, Theodore and Lodge, Henry Cabot. *Selections from the Correspondence of.* Vol. 1. New York: Charles Scribner's Sons, 1925.

Roosevelt, Theodore. *Letters of.* Vols. 2 through 6. Cambridge, Mass.: Harvard University Press, 1951–1952.

Schriftgiesser, Karl. *The Gentleman from Massachusetts, Henry Cabot Lodge.* Boston: Little Brown and Co., 1944.

Sherman and Marshall

Baker, Ray Stannard. *Woodrow Wilson, Life and Letters.* Vols. 4 through 8. New York: Doubleday Doran & Co., 1931–1939.

Butler, Nicholas Murray. *Across the Busy Years.* New York: Charles Scribner's Sons, 1939.

Butt, Archie. *Taft and Roosevelt, Vol. 2, The Intimate Letters of Archie Butt.* New York: Doubleday Doran & Co., 1930.

Duffy, Herbert S. *William Howard Taft.* New York: Minton Balch & Co., 1930.

Grayson, Cary T. *Woodrow Wilson, An Intimate Memoir.* New York: Holt Rinehart & Winston, 1960.

Marshall, Thomas R. *Recollections of Thomas R. Marshall, A Hoosier Salad.* Indianapolis: Bobbs-Merrill Co., 1925.

Pringle, Henry F. *Life and Times of William Howard Taft.* New York: Farrar & Rinehart, 1939.

Smith, Gene. *When the Cheering Stopped.* New York: William Morrow & Co., 1964.

Sullivan, Mark. *Our Times: Over Here, 1914–1918.* New York: Charles Scribner's Sons, 1933.

Taft, Mrs. William Howard. *Recollections of Full Years.* New York: Dodd Mead & Co., 1914.

Thomas, Charles M. *Thomas Riley Marshall, Hoosier Statesman.* Oxford, Ohio: Mississippi Valley Press, 1939.

Walworth, Arthur. *Woodrow Wilson.* New York: Longmans Green & Co., 1958.

Wilson, Edith Bolling. *My Memoir.* Indianapolis: Bobbs-Merrill Co., 1938.

Coolidge, Dawes, and Curtis

Coolidge, Calvin. *The Autobiography of Calvin Coolidge.* New York: Cosmopolitan Book Corp., 1929.

Dawes, Charles G. *Notes as Vice President, 1928–1929.* Boston: Little Brown & Co., 1935.

Gann, Dolly. *Dolly Gann's Book.* New York: Doubleday Doran & Co., 1933.

Hoover, Herbert. *Memoirs, Vol. 2, The Cabinet and the Presidency.* New York: The Macmillan Co., 1952.

Lathem, Connery, ed. *Meet Calvin Coolidge.* Brattleboro, Vt.: Stephen Greene Press, 1960.

Longworth, Alice Roosevelt. *Crowded Hours.* New York: Charles Scribner's Sons, 1933.

Lyons, Eugene. *Herbert Hoover.* Garden City, N.Y.: Doubleday & Co., 1964.

Ross, Ishbel. *Grace Coolidge and Her Era.* New York: Dodd Mead & Co., 1962.

Russell, Francis. *The Shadow of Blooming Grove.* New York: McGraw-Hill Book Co., 1968.

Seitz, Don C. *From Kaw Teepee to Capitol, The Story of Charles Curtis.* New York: Frederick A. Stokes Co., 1928.

Smith, Gene. *The Shattered Dream.* New York: William Morrow & Co., 1970.

Sullivan, Mark. *Our Times: The Twenties.* New York: Charles Scribner's Sons, 1935.

Timmons, Bascom N. *Portrait of An American, Charles G. Dawes.* New York: Henry Holt & Co., 1953.

White, William Allen. *A Puritan in Babylon.* New York: The Macmillan Co., 1958.

Garner, Wallace,Truman, and Barkley

Barkley, Alben W. *That Reminds Me.* Garden City, N.Y.: Doubleday & Co., 1954.

Barkley, Jane R. (as told to Frances Spatz Leighton). *I Married The Veep.* New York: Vanguard Press, 1958.

Blum, John Morton. *From the Morgenthau Diaries, Years of Crisis, 1928–1938.* Boston: Houghton Mifflin Co., 1959.

————. *Roosevelt & Morgenthau.* Boston: Houghton Mifflin Co., 1970.

Burns, James MacGregor. *Roosevelt, The Lion and the Fox.* New York: Harcourt Brace & Co., 1956.

————. *Roosevelt, The Soldier of Freedom.* New York: Harcourt Brace Jovanovich, 1970.

Byrnes, James F. *All in One Lifetime*. New York: Harper & Brothers, 1958.

Coit, Margaret L. *Mr. Baruch*. Boston: Houghton Mifflin Co., 1957.

Daniels, Jonathan. *The Man of Independence*. Philadelphia: J. P. Lippincott Co., 1950.

Dayton, Eldorous L. *Give 'em Hell Harry*. New York: Devin-Adair Co., 1956.

Dorough, C. Dwight. *Mr. Sam*. New York: Random House, 1962.

Farley, James A. *Behind the Ballots*. New York: Harcourt Brace & Co., 1938.

Flynn, Edward J. *You're the Boss*. New York: Viking Press, 1947.

Gunther, John. *Roosevelt in Retrospect*. New York: Harper & Brothers, 1950.

Ickes, Harold L. *Secret Diary of Harold L. Ickes*. 3 vols. New York: Simon & Schuster, 1953–1954.

James, Marquis. *Mr. Garner of Texas*. Indianapolis: Bobbs-Merrill Co., 1939.

Kingdon, Frank. *Henry Wallace and 60 Million Jobs*. New York: Readers Press, 1945.

Lash, Joseph P. *Eleanor and Franklin*. New York: W. W. Norton & Co., 1971.

Lord, Russell. *The Wallaces of Iowa*. Boston: Houghton Mifflin Co., 1947.

O'Connor, Richard. *The First Hurrah, A Biography of Alfred E. Smith*. New York: G. P. Putnam's Sons, 1970.

Redding, Jack. *Inside the Democratic Party*. Indianapolis: Bobbs-Merrill Co., 1958.

Schapsmeier, Edward L. and Frederick H. *Henry A. Wallace of Iowa, The Agrarian Years*. Ames, Ia.: Iowa State University Press, 1968.

————. *Prophet in Politics, Henry A. Wallace and the War Years*. Ames, Ia.: Iowa State University Press, 1970.

Schmidt, Karl M. *Henry A. Wallace, Quixotic Crusade 1948*. Syracuse, N. Y.: Syracuse University Press, 1960.

Sherwood, Robert E. *Roosevelt and Hopkins, An Intimate History*. New York: Harper & Brothers, 1948.

Steinberg, Alfred. *The Man from Missouri, The Life and Times of Harry S. Truman*. New York: G. P. Putnam's Sons, 1962.

Swanberg, W. A. *Citizen Hearst*. New York: Charles Scribner's Sons, 1961.

Truman, Harry S. *Mr. Citizen*. New York: Bernard Geis Associates, 1953.

Truman, Margaret. *Harry S. Truman*. New York: William Morrow & Co., 1973.

Tugwell, Rexford G. *The Democratic Roosevelt*. Garden City, N.Y.: Doubleday & Co., 1957.

Wallace, Henry A. *The Century of the Common Man*. New York: Reynal & Hitchcock, 1943.

Nixon, L. B. Johnson, and Humphrey

Amrine, Michael. *This is Humphrey*. Garden City, N.Y.: Doubleday & Co., 1960.

Baker, Leonard. *The Johnson Eclipse*. New York: The Macmillan Co., 1966.

Bishop, Jim. *A Day in the Life of President Johnson*. New York: Random House, 1967.

Burns, James MacGregor. *John Kennedy, A Political Profile*. New York: Harcourt Brace & Co., 1960.

Costello, William. *The Facts About Nixon*. New York: Viking Press, 1960.

de Toledano, Ralph. *One Man Alone, Richard Nixon*. New York: Funk & Wagnalls, 1969.

Donovan, Robert J. *Eisenhower: The Inside Story*. New York: Harper & Brothers, 1956.

Douglas, Paul H. *In the Fullness of Time, The Memoirs of Paul H. Douglas*. New York: Harcourt Brace Jovanovich, 1971.

Eisele, Albert. *Almost to the Presidency*. Blue Earth, Minn.: Piper Company, 1972.

Eisenhower, Dwight D. *The White House Years 1953–1956, Mandate for Change*. Garden City, N.Y.: Doubleday & Co., 1963.

————. *The White House Years 1956–1961, Waging Peace*. Garden City, N.Y.: Doubleday & Co., 1965.

Goldman, Eric F. *The Tragedy of Lyndon Johnson*. New York: Alfred A. Knopf, 1969.

Griffith, Winthrop. *Humphrey, A Candid Biography*. New York: William Morrow & Co., 1965.

Halberstam, David. *The Best and the Brightest*. New York: Random House, 1972.

Hughes, Emmet John. *The Ordeal of Power*. New York: Atheneum Publishers, 1963.

Johnson, Lady Bird. *Lady Bird Johnson, A White House Diary*. New York: Holt Rinehart & Winston, 1970.

Johnson, Lyndon Baines. *The Vantage Point*. New York: Holt Rinehart & Winston, 1971.

Johnson, Sam Houston. *My Brother Lyndon*. New York: Cowles Book Co., 1969.

Keogh, James. *This is Nixon*. New York: G. P. Putnam's Sons, 1956.

Lasky, Victor. *Robert F. Kennedy: The Myth and the Man*. New York: Trident Press, 1968.

Lincoln, Evelyn. *Kennedy & Johnson*. New York: Holt Rinehart and Winston, 1968.

Lurie, Leonard. *The King Makers*. New York: Coward McCann & Geoghegan, 1971.

Mazo, Earl and Hess, Stephen. *Nixon, A Political Portrait*. New York: Harper & Row, 1968.

Mooney, Booth. *The Lyndon Johnson Story*. New York: Farrar Straus & Co., 1956.

Muller, Herbert J. *Adlai Stevenson, A Study in Values*. New York: Harper & Row, 1967.

Newfield, Jack. *Robert Kennedy, A Memoir*. New York: E. P. Dutton & Co., 1969.

Ryskind, Allan H. *Hubert*. New York: Arlington House, 1968.

Salinger, Pierre. *With Kennedy*. Garden City, N.Y.: Doubleday & Co., 1966.

Schlesinger, Arthur M., Jr. *A Thousand Days, John F. Kennedy in the White House*. Boston: Houghton Mifflin Co., 1965.

Sherrill, Robert. *The Accidental President*. New York: Grossman Publishers, 1967.

_____ and Ernst, Harry W. *Drugstore Liberal*. New York: Grossman Publishers, 1968.

Sidey, Hugh. *John F. Kennedy, President*. New York: Atheneum Publishers, 1963.

Sorenson, Theodore. *Kennedy*. New York: Harper & Row, 1965.

Steinberg, Alfred. *Sam Johnson's Boy*. New York: The Macmillan Co., 1968.

Voorhis, Jerry. *The Strange Case of Richard Milhous Nixon*. New York: Paul S. Eriksson, 1972.

White, Theodore H. *The Making of the President 1960*. New York: Atheneum Publishers, 1961.

_____. *The Making of the President 1964*. New York: Atheneum Publishers, 1965.

White, William S. *The Professional: Lyndon B. Johnson*. Boston: Houghton Mifflin Co., 1964.

Wicker, Tom. *JFK and LBJ*. New York: William Morrow & Co., Inc., 1968.

Witcover, Jules. *The Resurrection of Richard Nixon*. New York: G. P. Putnam's Sons, 1970.

Agnew and Ford

Albright, Joseph. *What Makes Spiro Run*. New York: Dodd Mead & Co., 1972.

Evans, Rowland, Jr. and Novak, Robert D. *Nixon in the White House*. New York: Random House, 1971.

Lippman, Theo, Jr. *Spiro Agnew's America*. New York: W. W. Norton & Co., 1972.

Lukas, J. Anthony. "The Story So Far." New York: *The New York Times Magazine*, July 22, 1973.

————. "The Story Continued." New York: *The New York Times Magazine*, January 13, 1974.

Lurie, Leonard. *The Running of Richard Nixon*. New York: Coward McCann & Geoghegan, 1972.

Marsh, Robert. *Agnew, The Unexamined Man*. New York: M. Evans & Co., 1971.

Mazlish, Bruce. *In Search of Nixon*. New York: Basic Books, 1972.

Newsweek Magazine, 1973 and 1974.

New York Post, 1973 and 1974.

Osborne, John. *The Nixon Watch*. New York: Liveright Publishing, 1970.

The New York Times, 1973 and 1974.

Time Magazine, 1973 and 1974.

White, Theodore H. *The Making of the President 1968*. New York: Atheneum Publishers, 1969.

————. *The Making of the President 1972*. New York: Atheneum Publishers, 1973.

Wills, Garry. *Nixon Agonistes, The Crisis of the Self-Made Man*. Boston: Houghton Mifflin Co., 1969.

Witcover, Jules. *White Knight, The Rise of Spiro Agnew*. New York: Random House, 1972.

Madmen and Geniuses

Index

A

Adams, Abigail, 19, 24
Adams, Charles Francis, 86
Adams, John, 8, 14–19, 21–22, 23, 24, 27–28, 30, 35, 42, 92, 167, 178–179, 192, 265, 295, 311–312
Adams, John Quincy, 7, 8, 37–38, 53, 54, 55, 56, 63, 75, 76, 93, 192
Adams, Samuel, 17, 42
Adams, Sherman, 259
Agnew, Spiro T., 3–5, 31, 55–56, 58, 282, 284–292, 294–296, 301, 304–306, 307–308, 310
Ahmad, Bashir, 269
Albany, Regency, 62
Alien and Sedition Acts, 24–25
American Communist Party. *See* Communist Party
American Federation of Labor, 200

American Revolution, 17, 18, 29, 30, 36
Ames, Oakes, 119, 123
Anagostopoulos, Theofrastos Spiro, 286
Anderson, Marion, 226
Anderson, Sherwood, 233
Appomattox, 100
Arthur, Chester A., 8, 9, 134, 136–139, 141, 167
Astor, David, 260
Atlanta, fall of, 110

B

Baker, Bobby, 270
Bank of the United States, The, 65, 74
Barkley, Alben W., 229, 235, 237, 244, 246–250
Barkley, Mrs. Jane Hadley, 249–250
Bayard, James, 28–29
Bell, John, 100
Benton, Thomas Hart, 64, 82–83

Beveridge, Albert J., 178, 179, 184
Biddle, Charles J., 82–83
Blackstone Hotel, 198
Blaine, James G., 129, 136, 141, 148
"Bleeding Kansas", 98
Board of Economic Warfare, 234
Bonus Marchers, 217–218
Booth, John Wilkes, 112
Borah, William E., 194, 206, 216, 241
Boston Massacre, 16–17
Boyd, Linn, 99
Breckenridge, John Cabell, 96, 98–101, 116
Bricker, John W., 235, 242
Browder, Earl, 235
Brown, Aaron, 93
Brown, Governor Pat, 283
Bryan, William Jennings, 159–160, 161, 171, 184, 185, 190
Byrnes, James, 237, 238
Buchanan, James, 9, 81, 83, 91, 92, 93–94, 98, 99
Bunker, Archie, 302
Burger, Chief Justice Warren E., 300
Burke, Edmund, 185
Burr, Aaron, 15, 22, 26–32, 35, 37, 99, 100, 116, 166, 167
Burr, Reverend Aaron (Father), 29
Butler, Benjamin F., 106
Butler, William O., 85

C

Calhoun, John C., 52–59, 61, 64, 68, 87, 91, 92, 143, 167, 178, 192
Calhoun, Floride, 56–57
California, Territory of, 87–88
Cannon, "Uncle Joe", 185–186, 224
Carnegie, Andrew, 207
Carswell, C. Harrold, 298
Cass, Lewis, 85, 86, 92
Celler, Emanuel, 299

Central Pacific Railroad, 117
Chamberlain, Sir Austen, 208
Chambers, Whittaker, 256
"Checkers Speech", 258
Chicago *Tribune*, 234, 248
Chinn, Julia, 68
Chotiner, Murray, 255–256, 258
Civil Rights Act of 1964, 273, 278
Civil Service Commission, 139
Civil War, 59, 98, 100, 109, 110, 143, 195
Clay, Cassius M., 104
Clay, Henry, 53, 54, 68, 74, 79, 80, 86, 87, 99
Cleveland, Grover, 8, 142–143, 147–148, 153–157, 191
Clinton, DeWitt, 37, 41, 47, 48, 49, 63
Clinton, George, 30, 34–39, 41, 47, 53, 178
Clinton, Sir Henry, 36
Colbath, Jeremiah Jones. *See* Wilson, Henry
Colfax, Schuyler, 114, 116–120, 126
Collins, Leroy, 264–265
Committee of One Hundred, 255
Committees of correspondence, 17
Communism, 254–255, 256, 257, 258, 259, 279, 285
Communist Party, 235, 276
Compromise of 1850, 87–88, 92, 97, 195
Confederacy, 77, 100
Conkling, Roscoe, 129, 130, 135–136, 137, 138, 139, 148, 149
Connally, John, 270
Constitution, Article II, Section 1.75; Article II, Section 1.3, 12, 21, 28, 32; Twelfth Amendment, 32, 35; Twentieth Amendment, 226; Twenty-fifth Amendment, 76, 294–295, 311

Constitutional Convention, 42,
43, 312
Constitutional Union Party, 100
Continental Congress, 17, 22, 23,
42
Coolidge, Calvin, 8, 9, 196–202,
205, 206–207, 209–210,
214, 216, 233, 277, 304
Cooper Institute, 103
Cooper, John Sherman, 250
Cortelyou, George B., 178, 179
Cox, Archibald, 293
Cox, James M., 199
Crane, Winthrop Murray, 200
Crawford, William, 54
Credit Mobilier, 118–119, 123–
124, 126, 127, 249
Cronkite, Walter, 302
"Cross of Gold", 160
Cummins, Albert B., 184
Curtis, Charles, 9, 212–218, 221
Curtis, Helen, 214–215
Curtis, Leona, 216

D

Dallas, George Mifflin, 78, 80–
83, 117, 206
Daughters of the American
Revolution, 226
Davis, Henry Gassaway, 176,
179
Davis, Jefferson, 100
Davis, John W., 206
Dawes, Charles G., 204, 206–210
"Dawes Plan", 208
Debs, Eugene, 190
Declaration of Independence,
18, 23, 42
Democratic Party, 56, 64, 65, 69,
73, 79, 82, 85–86, 91, 92–
93, 94, 98, 99, 100, 105,
110, 130–131, 141–143,
148, 150, 153–154, 155–
156, 157, 159–160, 171,
176, 179–180, 184–185,
189–191, 197, 199, 206–
207, 214, 217, 221–223,
225, 227, 229–232, 235,

237–239, 242, 246–248,
249–250, 264–266, 275,
277, 280, 289, 301–305,
311
Democratic-Republicans, 27–28,
31, 35, 37, 38, 41, 43, 44,
47, 48, 49, 53
Depew, Chauncey, 178–179
Dercum, Dr. Francis X., 194
de Toledano, Ralph, 256
Dewey, Commodore George,
168
Dewey, Thomas E., 242, 246,
248, 253–254, 257
Dixiecrat Party, 247
Dolliver, Jonathan P., 184
Douglas, Helen Gahagan, 256–
257, 260
Douglas, Stephen A., 92, 98, 100,
103, 155
Douglas, William O., 237, 238,
246, 299
Dunne, Finley Peter, ix, 301

E

Eagleton, Thomas Francis, 302–
304
Eaton, John, 56, 63–64
Eaton, Peggy, 56–57, 61, 63
Edwards, Jonathan, 29
Eisenhower, Dwight D., 9, 246,
250, 253–254, 257–260
English, William Hayden, 138
Ervin, Sam, 294

F

Fairbanks, Charles Warren, 9,
174, 176–180, 184, 193
Farley, James, 230
Farmer Labor Party, 275, 276
Federalists, 15, 18, 21–22, 24–
25, 27–29, 31, 36, 44–45,
53
Fessenden, William P., 113
Fillmore, Millard, 8, 9, 84, 86–
89, 94, 98, 167, 195
Fish, Hamilton, 124
Fish, Hamilton, Jr., 216

Flynn, Ed, 237
Ford, Gerald R., 5, 292, 295-300, 307–308
Ford, Gerald Rudolph (step-father), 297
Franklin, Benjamin, 23, 132
Free Soil Party, 86, 125
Frelinghuysen, Theodore, 79
Frémont, John Charles, 98, 99
Frick, Henry, 207
Fugitive Slave Act, 88, 97

G

Gallatin, Albert, 80
Gallup Poll, 235, 238, 245
Gann, Dolly, 215–217
Gardiner, Julia, 76
Garfield, James, 8, 10, 124, 136, 137, 138–139, 149–150, 291
Garner, John Nance, 11, 217, 218, 220, 222–227, 229, 241, 264, 301, 304–305
Geography, as political expedient, 9–10, 27, 74, 79, 85, 92, 98, 104, 184, 190, 223, 232
George III, King of England, 23, 36
Gerrymander, 44–45
Gerry, Elbridge, 40–45, 47, 53
Gettysburg Address, 109
Godkin, E. L., 137
Gold standard, 154, 156, 159–161
Goldwater, Barry, 265–266, 275
Gompers, Samuel, 200–201
Goodell, Charles, 298
Gore, Albert, 289
Grant, Ulysses S., 9, 106, 116, 117, 118, 124, 126, 129, 136, 137, 249
Gray, Isaac P., 156
"Great Society", 273, 298
Greeley, Horace, 85, 103, 116
Green, Duff, 68–69
Gresham, Walter Q., 177

Griffin, Robert, 298
Guiteau, Charles J., 138–139
Gulf of Tonkin, 274

H

Half-Breeds, 136
Halleck, Charles, 298
Hamilton, Alexander, 18, 21–22, 24, 27–29, 30, 31
Hamlin, Charles Eugene, 106
Hamlin, Hannibal, 102, 104–107, 112, 113, 115
Hancock, Winfield Scott, 138
Hanna, Mark, 11, 159, 160, 161, 167, 170, 171, 172, 175–176
Hannegan, Bob, 237, 238, 239, 243
Harding, Warren G., 9, 197–199, 201–202, 205, 213, 214, 233, 304
Harrison, Benjamin, 9, 10, 148, 150, 151, 153, 154, 177
Harrison, William Henry, 7, 8, 67, 69, 70, 74, 75, 88, 95, 194
Hayden, Carl, 241
Hayes, Rutherford B., 8–9, 106, 129, 130, 131, 132, 136, 137
Haynsworth, Clement, 298
Hearst, William Randolph, 222–223
Hendricks, Thomas Andrews, 130, 131, 140–144, 147–148, 156
Hesburgh, Rev. Theodore, 302
Hiss, Alger, 256
Hoar, George F., 123, 125
Hobart, Garret Augustus, 10–11, 158, 160–163, 165, 170, 171
Hoffman, Judge Walter B., 4
Hoover, Herbert, 9, 213–218, 221, 225, 308, 309
Hoover, Lou Henry, 217
House Un-American Activities Committee, 256

Hughes, Charles Evans, 179–
180, 193
Humphrey, Hubert H., 263, 272,
274–281, 285–286, 303–
305, 308

I

Ickes, Harold, 225, 226
Impeachment of Andrew
Johnson, 112–113

J

Jackson, Andrew, 8, 54, 56, 57–
58, 61, 63–65, 67, 68, 69,
74, 75, 79, 93, 183, 192
Jackson, Samuel D., 239
Jacobson, Eddie, 240
Jay, John, 36
Jefferson, Thomas, 8, 15, 18, 20,
22–25, 27–29, 30, 31, 33,
35, 37, 57, 92, 166, 167,
178–179, 183, 265
Jeffersonian Republicans. See
Democratic-Republicans
Jeffersonians. See Democratic-
Republicans
Johnson, Andrew, 8, 9, 101, 106,
108–113, 115, 116, 167,
243
Johnson, Hiram W., 190, 194,
197, 206
Johnson, Lady Bird, 265
Johnson, Lyndon B., 8, 262–270,
273–275, 277–280, 297,
298, 303–305
Johnson, Richard Mentor, 9, 66–
71, 74, 91, 93
Johnson, Sam Houston, 267, 269
Jones, Jesse, 234

K

Kansas-Nebraska Act, 97–98,
144
Kaufman, George S., ix
Kefauver, Estes, 278, 311
Kelly, Ed, 237, 239
Kennedy, Edward, 302, 304

Kennedy, John F., 8, 263–266,
268–270, 278, 279, 284,
311
Kennedy, Robert F., 264, 269–
270, 274, 280
Kentucky Resolutions, 24–25
Khruschev, Nikita, 260
Kilgore, Harley, 245
King, Leslie, Jr. See Ford, Gerald
R.
King, Martin Luther, Jr., 287
King, Rufus, 37
King, William Rufus De Vane, 9,
90, 92–95, 99, 115
Kissinger, Henry, 4
Kleberg, Richard M., Sr., 266
"Knights of the Golden Circle",
143
"Know-Nothings", 89, 98, 125
Knox, Frank, 225
Korean War, 243, 286
Kreisler, Fritz, 207

L

LaFollette, Robert, 206, 207
Laird, Melvin B., 290, 298
Landon, Alfred M., 225
Lane, Harriet, 93
Langdon, John, 41
League of Nations, 193–195
Lee, Robert E., 100
Lenroot, Irvine, 198–199
Lerner, Max, 289
Lewis, John L., 226
Lewis, Morgan, 31
Lincoln, Abraham, 8, 99, 100,
103–105, 106, 109, 110,
111, 112, 115, 117, 189,
291, 300
Lindsay, John V., 284
Locke, John, 17
Lodge, Henry Cabot, 165–167,
168, 169, 186, 194, 198–
199, 201
Lodge, Henry Cabot
(grandson), 266, 296
Long, John Davis, 168

Long, Russell, 265
Longworth, Alice Roosevelt.
    198, 201, 217
Longworth, Nicholas, 217, 224
Lowden, Frank, 197, 205, 206
Loyalists, 36
Luce, Clare Booth, 246

M

MacArthur, General Douglas,
    218
MacDonald, Ramsey, 217
Madison, James, 8, 25, 33, 35,
    38, 41, 43–44, 47, 183
Maine, Battleship, 168
Mansfield, Mike, 268
Marcantonio, Vito, 257
Marcy, William L., 62, 83, 92
Marshall, John, 42, 43
Marshall Plan, 243
Marshall, Thomas Riley, 179–
    180, 188, 190–195, 199,
    312
Matz, Lester, 291
McCamant, Wallace, 198–199
McCarran Act of 1950, 276
McCarthy, Eugene, 274, 275,
    288, 308–309
McCarthy, Joseph, 257, 285
McClellan, George B., 110
McCormack, John, 264–265
McGovern, George, 302–305,
    307
McKinley, Ida, 163
McKinley, William, 9, 10–11,
    160–161, 162, 165, 168,
    170–172, 175–176, 177,
    179, 207
McNary, Charles, 232, 241
Mencken, H. L., 215
Mexican War, 82–83, 86, 89
Miller, William, 275
Milligan, Lambdin P., 143–144
"Minute Men of the
    Constitution", 208
Missouri Compromise, 98, 144
Mitchell, Martha, 302

Monroe, James, 9, 33, 35, 47, 48,
    54, 55, 192
Moore, Gabriel, 64
Morgan, J. Pierpont, 149, 207
Morgan, Junius Spencer, 149
Morrow, Dwight, 200
Morse, Samuel F. B., 79–80
Morton, Levi Parsons, 9, 136,
    137, 146, 148–151, 170,
    207
Muskie, Edmund, 304

N

Nast, Thomas, 138
National Security Council, 249,
    279
National Union Party, 109
NATO, 243, 257
New Deal, 225, 226, 234, 273
New Frontier, 269, 273
New York *Post*, 257–258
New York *Sun*, 118, 126, 139
New York *Tribune*, 85, 103, 116,
    119, 151
New York *World*, 110, 112, 115,
    155
Nixon, Mrs. Pat, 255, 258, 259,
    260
Nixon, Richard M., 3, 4, 252,
    254–260, 265, 266, 283–
    286, 287–291, 293–300,
    301, 304–305, 308
Nixon, Tricia, 258
Nom-pa-wa-rah, 214
Nullification, 57–58, 64–65

O

Of Thee I Sing, ix, 9, 221
"Ohio Gang", 201–202
O'Neale, Peggy, *See* Eaton,
    Peggy
"Operation Rolling Thunder",
    278

P

Panic of 1837, 65, 73
Pappan, Julie, 214–215

Parker, Alton Brooks, 176
Pauley, Edwin, 237, 239
Peabody, Endicott, 311–312
Pendergast, Jim, 240, 241
Pendergast, Mike, 240
Pendergast, Tom, 239–241
Pendleton, George Hunt, 110
People's Party. *See* Populists
Pershing, General John J., 207
Philippine Islands, 162
Pierce, Franklin, 9, 92, 94, 95,
    97–98
Pinckney, Charles Cotesworth,
    27–28, 37, 42–43
Pinckney, Thomas, 21–22
Platt, Thomas C., 138, 148, 167,
    169–170, 185
Plumer, William, 38
Political Action Committee, 255
Polk, James K., 8, 79, 80, 81–82,
    83, 93
Populists, 153–154, 157
Preston, Captain Thomas, 17
Progressive Party, of 1912, 190;
    of 1924, 206, 207; of 1948,
    246, 247
Pruitt, Stephen, 249
Pulitzer, Joseph, 155

Q

Quackenbos, G. P., 70
Quay, Matthew, 167, 170

R

Radical Republicans, 112–113
Randolph, John, 54
Rayburn, Sam, 223, 235, 264,
    265, 266, 269
Reagan, Ronald, 284
Reconstruction, 112–113
Reconstruction Finance
    Corporation, 210, 234
Reed, Thomas B., 185, 215
Reid, Whitelaw, 151, 154
Republican Party, 98, 99, 103–
    105, 106, 109, 111, 117,
    118, 126, 129–131, 135–
    138, 141, 142, 143, 148,

150–151, 153–154, 155–
    156, 159–161, 167, 171,
    176, 178, 179, 183–185,
    187, 189–191, 197–199,
    201, 205–207, 208, 209–
    210, 213–214, 216, 217,
    221, 242, 246, 247–248,
    253–254, 257–259, 260,
    266, 275, 283–286, 289–
    290
Richardson, Elliot, 291
Rip Rap contract, 55–56
Robinson, Joseph T., 214
Rockefeller, John D., 207
Rockefeller, Nelson, 284
Rodell, Professor Fred, 299
Roosevelt, Eleanor, 226, 231,
    238, 246
Roosevelt, Franklin D., 8, 10, 11,
    199, 217, 218, 221–223,
    225–227, 229–235, 237–
    239, 242–243, 245, 246,
    249, 253, 266, 267, 270,
    304, 305
Roosevelt, Theodore, 8, 9, 10–
    11, 164, 167–172, 175–179,
    183, 184, 186–187, 189–
    191
Root, Elihu, 183
Rough Riders, 169
Rowe, James, 303–304
Rule XXII, 209
Rush, Richard, 56
Ryskind, Morrie, ix

S

San Juan Hill, 169
Schlesinger, Arthur M. Sr., 8
Schuyler, Philip, 36
Scott, General Winfield, 82, 89,
    93
Serurier, Louis, 43–44
Sewall, Arthur, 160
Seward, William H., 87, 104
Seymour, Horatio, 117
Sherman, James Schoolcraft,
    182, 184–187, 192

Sherman, John, 136, 137
Shriver, Sargent, 304–305, 307
Silver, coinage of, 153–154,
    156–157, 159–160
Silver Republicans, 157, 159
Smith, Alfred E., 214, 222–223
Smithsonian Institute, 192
Socialist Party, 190
Space Act of 1958, 268
Spanish-American War, 162,
    165, 168–169
Sparkman, John, 258
Spencer, Ambrose, 48
Stalwarts, 136, 138
Stamp Act, 16
Stanford, Leland, 117
Stearns, Frank, 200
Stevens, Thaddeus, 113
Stevenson, Adlai E. II, 154, 258,
    278, 288, 311
Stevenson, Adlai Ewing, 152,
    154–157, 171
Stevenson, Coke, 267
Stowe, Harriet Beecher, 97
Sumner, Charles, 109
Symington, Stuart, 263

T

Taft, Robert, 254, 257
Taft, William Howard, 9, 179,
    183–187, 189–191, 192
Talleyrand, Maurice, 42–43
Tammany Hall, 62, 154, 156
Tariff, Act of 1846, 81–82;
    protective, 58, 81
Tarleton, Lieutenant Colonel
    Banastre, 23
Taylor, Zachary, 9, 10, 82, 86,
    87–88, 89, 94, 195
Tecumseh, 67, 70
Telegraph, electromagnetic, 79–
    80
Teller, Henry Moore, 159
Thames, Battle of, 70
Throttlebottom, Alexander, ix, x,
    9, 221
Thurmond, Strom, 247, 277, 285

Thurman, Allen Granberry, 148
Tilden, Samuel Jones, 130, 131,
    141–142, 144
Timberlake, Mrs. John B. See
    Eaton, Peggy
Tippecanoe and Tyler Too, 69,
    70, 75
Tompkins, Daniel D., 46–51, 53,
    62, 192
Tonkin Gulf. See Gulf of Tonkin
Triple A, 233–234
"Truman Committee", 242
Truman Doctrine, 243
Truman, Harry S, 8, 9, 11, 235,
    236, 238–243, 245–248,
    249, 253, 254, 256, 259,
    270, 308, 310
Tugwell, Rexford G., 225
Tuttle, Socrates, 161
Twelfth Amendment. See
    Constitution
Twentieth Amendment. See
    Constitution
Twenty-fifth Amendment. See
    Constitution
Tyler, John, 7–8, 9, 58, 68, 69,
    70, 72, 74–77, 79, 88, 93,
    167, 194

U

Uncle Tom's Cabin, 97
Underwood, Oscar W., 190
Union Pacific Railway, 117, 118,
    123, 124

V

Vail, Alfred, 80
Van Buren, Martin, 9, 49, 60–65,
    67, 68, 69, 70, 73, 74, 79,
    86, 92, 167, 177, 178, 183,
    265
Vandenberg, Arthur H., 297
Vietnam, 274, 278–280, 287–
    289, 298
Virginia Resolutions, 25
Voorhis, Jerry, 255–256

W

Wade, Benjamin, 116
Wages-Hours Act, 226
Walker, Frank, 237
Walker, Robert James, 83
Wallace, George, 285–286
Wallace, Henry A., 11, 228,
    230–235, 237–239, 242–
    243, 246, 247, 287
Wanamaker, John, 148
War Hawks, 54, 68
War of 1812, 48, 49, 67, 68, 83
Warren, Charles Beecher, 209–
    210
Warren, Earl, 253, 254
Washington, George, 8, 15, 16,
    18, 19, 21, 24, 30, 83
Washington Monument, 88
Watergate, 3, 4, 293–295, 301,
    308
Webster, Daniel, 87, 91
Weed, Thurlow, 87
Wheeler, William Almon, 128,
    130–132
Whig Party, 65, 67, 69, 73–74,
    75, 76, 79, 80, 83, 85, 86,
    89, 92–93, 98, 99, 117, 125

White, William Allen, 198
Wilkie, Wendell, 232, 235, 275
Wilson, Henry, 9, 116, 118, 119,
    122–127, 129
Wilson, Mrs. Woodrow, 193–194
Wilson, Woodrow, 8, 179–180,
    190–195, 199, 201, 259,
    312
Windom, William, 150
Woodford, Stewart L., 130
Woodruff, Timothy, 170
Wood, General Leonard, 197
World War I, 193, 207, 208, 240
World War II, 229, 234, 242,
    255, 286
Wright, Silas, 79–80, 206

X

XYZ Affair, 42–43, 44

Y

Yarborough, Ralph, 270

Z

Ziegler, Ron, 293